THE *Menuchah* PRINCIPLE

In Marriage

THE *Menuchah* PRINCIPLE

In Marriage

The Pathway to Shalom Bayis

*Based on the teachings of
Rav Chaim Friedlander, zt"l,
and the wisdom of Chazal*

Shaya Ostrov L.C.S.W.

AUTHOR OF *THE INNER CIRCLE: SEVEN GATES TO MARRIAGE*

The *Menuchah* Principle In Marriage
© 2010 Shaya Ostrov

ISBN: 978-1-60763-039-5

Editor: Nina Ackerman Indig
Proofreader: R' Moshe Ibsen, Hadassa Goldsmith
Designer: Justine Elliott

Distributed by:

THE JUDAICA PRESS, INC.
123 Ditmas Avenue / Brooklyn, NY 11218
718-972-6200 / 800-972-6201
info@judaicapress.com
www.judaicapress.com

Manufactured in the United States of America

Rabbi Yechiel I. Perr
Rosh HaYeshiva

Rabbi Aaron M. Brafman
Menahel

Rabbi Eli Goldgrab
General Studies Principal

Rabbi Shayeh Kohn
Executive Director

In his <u>The Menuchah Principle in Marriage</u>, Reb Shaya Ostrov shares his own heart and soul with us. A lifetime of experience and a lifetime of wisdom are to be found between the covers of this book. It should surprise us that one only in midlife, as is the author, has distilled much of life's wisdom onto the leaves of this work. But we have already been assured by the ancient Rabi Meir (Avos 4:27) "there are indeed new casks filled with old wine." Reading or rather studying this work, is indeed and educational and maturing experience.

One of the special graces of this work are the many stories and parables with which the author illustrates his teachings. These are culled from our sacred sources and from other places, as well as from the experiences of life. It is sad that our generation suffers a shortage of role models of authentic Torah living. However, properly understood stories of our Torah greats continue to provide us with inspiration and direction even when living examples are absent.

Although this work is primarily directed toward shalom bayis, every person has much to gain from its teachings. The author is to be congratulated for increasing the peace and the welfare of our people.

בתקוה רבה חוין לבב שלום פר

16th of Tammuz 5770

"Deep water is counsel in the heart of man, and the man of understanding will draw it forth" (*Mishlei* 20:5). This is comparable to a deep well of cold, refreshing water that was inaccessible until someone came and fashioned a rope to draw it forth. Then all were able to draw its waters and slake their thirst (*Bereishis Rabbah*).

The S'fas Emes explains that within every one of us there is counsel. To access this counsel, we must turn to the man of understanding, who by means of the Torah can draw it forth.

My dear and wise friend, Reb Shaya Ostrov, נ"י, has devoted many years to guiding and advising others, particularly in family matters. Reb Shaya's previous *sefarim* have been well accepted and now he adds another link to this chain, with his current work, *The Menuchah Principle In Marriage*. Completely based on the teachings of *Chazal* and our teachers, the giants of Mussar and Torah thought, this book enables the reader to attain calmness of spirit and to avoid confusion.

Reb Shaya is a cherished presence in our *beis medrash*. He spends hours each day toiling in Torah, so it is fitting for him to delve into these matters.

I am certain that one who earnestly studies his books with intent to implement the ideas contained within will fulfill the words of Eliyahu *HaNavi*: "If a person has Torah and suffering comes upon him, his heart remains settled, but the heart of a person devoid of Torah will be embittered" (*Tana D'vei Eliyahu*, Ch. 27).

We owe Reb Shaya a debt of gratitude for his insights and advice on how to live a life focused on eternity — a life of Torah and fear of Hashem. Through them, the heart becomes settled, and one merits true happiness.

I humbly bless him that his wellsprings should flow outwards to give ... "to the hungry, bread (there is no bread but Torah), and bring to your home the downtrodden poor (there is no poverty but that of understanding) ... Then your light will break forth like the dawn and your healing will quickly sprout. Your righteousness will precede you, and the glory of Hashem will gather you in" (*Yeshayah* 59:7-8).

In recognition and gratitude for all he does.

With deep endearment,

Naftali HaLevi Jaeger

שער ישוב
SH'OR YOSHUV
INSTITUTE

ONE CEDARLAWN AVENUE • LAWRENCE, NEW YORK 11559 • (516) 239-9002 • FAX: (516) 239-9003

PHONE NO. 516-239-2444 EXT. 103
E-MAIL: RABBI@SHAARAY-TEFILAH.ORG

FAX NO. 516-239-2199

CONGREGATION SHAARAY TEFILA
CENTRAL AND LORD AVENUES
LAWRENCE, N.Y. 11559

DAVID WEINBERGER
RABBI

בס"ד

I read with great pleasure the most recent work of my dear friend, Rabbi Shaya Ostrov "The Menuchah Principle in Marriage." As in his previous works Rabbi Ostrov has based his ideas and concepts on Chazal in addition to effectively using the chochma b'goyim for practical tips.

We are living in an unprecedented difficult time in preparing our children for marriage and ultimately their sustaining a life l'shalom bayis. Many books have been written and many seminars held to deal with the new complexities of our challenging society. Shaya Ostrov is making a difference in the lives of the many that he counsels but will be most effective to the broader Jewish community through the very practical and usable work that he has presently authored.

We are all frazzled and living under a myriad of stresses and tensions that undoubtedly affects our Sholom Bayis. Learning how to have menuchas hanefesh during these trying times will have a major impact in improving ourselves and our families.

I wish him continuous hatzlacha in all of his endeavors in helping to create healthy marriages and homes in Klal Yisroel.

Sincerely

Rabbi Dovid Weinberger

YESHIVA OF FAR ROCKAWAY ⬥ DERECH AYSON RABBINICAL SEMINARY
802 HICKSVILLE ROAD ⬥ FAR ROCKAWAY, NEW YORK 11691 ⬥ 718.327.7600 ⬥ FAX: 718.327.1430

בס"ד

Rabbi Yechiel I. Perr
Rosh HaYeshiva

Rabbi Aaron M. Brafman
Menahel

Rabbi Eli Goldgrab
General Studies Principal

Rabbi Shayeh Kohn
Executive Director

The name Kelm – or the Alter of Kelm evokes an image of one of the main mussar Yeshivas founded by R' Yisroel Salanter's greatest talmid. Kelm cultivated menuchas hanefesh – calmness of spirit – as the most prized and most necessary quality to achieve spiritual greatness.

This gives the individual the ability to be organized, to concentrate, not to be easily distracted and remain free of anger. Some of the greatest Gedolim and baalei mussar were a product of Kelm: the Alter of Slabodka, R' Yechezkel Levenstein, R' Elya Lopian, Rav Elchonon Wasserman, Rav Yeruchem Levovitz, Rav Eliyahu Dessler, Rav Nossan Wachtfogel, among others.

If one wants to get an idea of what it was and try to achieve this prized state – this is the book for you. It is not easy reading, as are many of the self help Jewish books on the market. It is very deep and makes a very profound analysis of the human nature and the connection of mind, soul and body. But it does not stop at the theoretical, but rather walks you through the difficult work of attaining the goal as one would if he were part of a mussar vaad at Kelm or Slabodka or the Mir.

If one could take these lessons to heart it would go a long way to solve so many problem areas of life. In the world of frenzied, out of control living today, menuchas hanefesh would be a true blessing for all of us.

with Sincere wishes
for success in helping
others
Aaron M. Brafman

*W*ith deep gratitude to Hashem,
I dedicate this work to my beloved wife

Vivian

Thank you for devoting yourself to filling our
marriage and family with love, wisdom and
kindness for the past forty-four years.

This book is a testimony to how we have
learned to share our lives.

*A*nd to our children

R' Mordy and Esti
R' Dovid and Miriam
R' Nosson and Racheli

You and your wonderful families fill our
hearts with pride and gratitude. May you
all continue to build your lives with the
love and chessed of Torah.

*D*edicated to the loving memory of our mother

Sorah Tchernah bas Dovid Reuven, ע״ה

We are forever grateful for her legendary chessed, her incomparable love of Torah and a smile that illuminated all our spirits, even at life's most difficult moments.

In the end, it was she who triumphed over all adversity.

Contents

INTRODUCING THE
Menuchah Principle

◇

Marriage and *shalom bayis* are at the heart of Jewish life. Yet at no time in our long history have the stability and well-being of our families been challenged as they are today in contemporary Western society. The culture we live in has had a powerful influence on our most precious and valued sanctuaries of marriage and family life. As we witness the increasing casualties within our Torah community — as evidenced by failed marriages, broken engagements, the rising number of singles, the proliferation of adolescents at risk and an increase in criminally punishable behavior — we realize that so many members of our community are ill-equipped to lead a healthy and fulfilling Torah life within the greater society and culture that surrounds us.

There is a single concept crucial to the well-being and stability of the Jewish individual, family, culture and institution of marriage. It is *menuchas hanefesh*. As individuals and families learn to integrate *menuchas hanefesh* into their daily lives, they are empowered to lead healthier, more fulfilling, stable lives. The *Menuchah* Principle as a concept for living brings centuries of *Chazal's* wisdom into teaching singles, married couples, parents, children, professionals and businesspeople ways to acquire the transforming and life-enhancing gift of *menuchas hanefesh*. Acquiring this gift has the power to bring our lives harmoniously together, while deepening our commitment to Hashem and Torah life.

This book, *The Menuchah Principle in Marriage*, is the first in a series dedicated to the goal of enlightening our *kehillah* about the precious gift of *menuchas hanefesh*.

◇

The Inner Road to *Shalom Bayis*

My Fateful Meeting with Rav Simcha Wasserman, *zt"l*, and His *Rebbetzin*

On rare occasions in our lives, we find ourselves in the presence of a married couple whose very being enables us to sense that they have cultivated a life of marital love and closeness. It is not that we are taken in by the superficial trappings of their lives — whether financial prosperity, a high lifestyle or even their attempts to demonstrate their love and affection for each other. Rather, the signs are more subtle and gentle — almost imperceptible. One such couple that I encountered, albeit briefly, was Rav Simcha Wasserman, *zt"l*, and his *rebbetzin, a"h*.

It was in 1989, when my family and I were living in Israel. At that time, we were faced with a serious family dilemma that required a decision as to whether to return to the United States for treatment or remain in Israel and obtain care there. Seeking guidance from *da'as* Torah, I approached no less than six *gedolim*, including Rav Shlomo Zalman Auerbach, *zt"l*, and Dayan Fischer, *zt"l*. One of the last individuals I approached was Rav Simcha Wasserman. At that time, he lived on Rechov Panim Me'iros in the Mattersdorf section of Yerushalayim. I was introduced by a close friend and *chavrusa*, a *talmid* of Rav

Simcha, who assured me that Rav Simcha was an individual from whom I could receive clear guidance.

> We entered the small apartment and stood in front of Rav Simcha, his wife and a few young men, all in their late twenties. Rav Simcha appeared to be in his mid-seventies at the time; in fact, he was older.
>
> As I explained the nature of the medical issue, Rav Simcha listened intently to each word. After a few moments of thoughtful silence, he responded that when he was a young boy living in Baranovich, he had a severe oral infection and required the services of a dentist. It was *erev* Shabbos, and he needed to know: Should he leave for Warsaw immediately or wait until *motza'ei* Shabbos? He approached his father, the *Gaon* Rav Elchanan Wasserman, *zt"l*, one of the leaders of European Torah Jewry, for help in reaching a decision. His father informed him that since it was a health issue, he should set out for Warsaw immediately, not withstanding the proximity to Shabbos.
>
> Rav Simcha then looked at me—sensing my ambivalence about leaving Israel—and very unequivocally said, "I tell you the same thing that my father told me: Leave for Warsaw (the United States) immediately." His response was very direct and proved to be correct in many ways.

The reason I am relating this story is not for the purpose of repeating the advice that Rav Simcha gave, but rather to portray another dimension of his life that I witnessed as he offered this advice.

> As Rav Simcha spoke, his wife was listening intently to every word. She was not simply listening; she was literally living within his words, moving her lips as she silently repeated every syllable her husband uttered.
>
> At first I was puzzled by her behavior. Then I looked at her eyes and expression and I realized that her lip

movements were an almost unconscious sign of the adoration, respect and deep affection she felt for her husband. I understood that to her, the thoughts her husband was sharing with me seemed like an incredibly wise and beautiful poem. She was repeating the words because for her, after all the years of their marriage, they still evoked a sense of wonder.

For me, it took the experiences of the next few months, and even years, to understand just how wise his words were. Yet the *rebbetzin* believed in their wisdom because of everything she understood about her husband, based on their relationship that must have begun more than fifty years earlier.

As we left, I turned to my friend and thanked him. My decision to leave for America was now clear. But I also remarked about what I had just seen. I told him, "Chaim, I have been working with couples for many years and have come to know many marital relationships, both personally and professionally, but I don't believe I have ever seen a marriage so filled with respect and adoration as the one I just witnessed."

"Yes," he responded. "It's known that Rav Simcha and the *rebbetzin* are very close."

"And who were the young men? Were they their children?"

"No," Chaim replied. "They never had children."

At first I was taken aback. I understood that Rav Simcha had been one of the premier Jewish educators in the United States before leaving for Israel. And even when he arrived in Israel after retiring from his yeshivah, he went on to build yet another great Torah institution in Yerushalayim. I realized that perhaps thousands of young students had passed through the lives of Rav Simcha and his *rebbetzin* and gone on to build families of their own. But the couple I just saw never had their own child. In a moment, I understood how difficult it must have been for them to care for the children of others and never be blessed with their own.

Then I also realized that all the years of expectation, hope, disappointment and pain must have been a critical factor in bringing the lives of these two individuals even closer together. I had never before seen a couple so caring and loving in their own quiet and gentle manner. There was an aura of inner peace between them, strengthened by all they had been through. I was seeing and witnessing the effects of this trial that had lasted for many years. For the first time in my personal life and career, I understood the meaning of how a husband and wife could, within themselves, be so peaceful and create a bond of profound depth and meaning.

A few years after our meeting, when I was already living in the United States, I sadly learned that Reb Simcha had died. I inquired about the *rebbetzin* and how she was coping with the tragic loss of her beloved husband. I was informed that just a few weeks after his death, she also passed away. I was not surprised. It confirmed all that I sensed about them during the brief, yet memorable, moments I had spent with them.

In the years that followed, I came to believe that the efforts I made to bring couples together were directly inspired by seeing how Rav Simcha and his *rebbetzin* shared their lives. My goal with couples is to guide them to achieve this quality of closeness particularly in the earlier years of their marriage, when a home is filled with children and the promise of sharing many more years together. It is during these earlier years of marriage that there are countless opportunities to experience Hashem's many blessings for *shalom bayis*, love and closeness. However, this work is also intended for couples in their later years yearning no less for the blessings of *shalom bayis*, love and closeness.

I later came to understand that I was attempting to guide couples to share a marriage where they could feel emotionally protected, understood, respected and quietly intimate. There was nothing I encountered in any professional literature or through any existing approaches that comprehended the gentle flow of *tznius* (modesty) and love that emanates from a Torah marriage. It was many years later that Hashem guided me to understand that the one crucial element that could enable couples to develop these gifts emerged from the quiet power and inner strength of *menuchas hanefesh*.

This book has been written to guide couples toward internalizing the treasures of *menuchas hanefesh* and incorporating them into their individual and shared life experiences. It is based primarily on my efforts to help couples discover these strengths. In this sense, this work represents the essence of what I have found helps couples grow toward *shalom bayis*. As you learn to comprehend, practice and internalize the guidance of *Chazal's* precious gifts, you will enhance your own inner road to *shalom bayis*. It's a pathway that will enable you to understand and experience how *menuchas hanefesh* becomes the center of a marriage filled with true love and closeness. Moreover, with its acquisition, you will discover the *hashra'as haShechinah beineichem* (the presence of Hashem's *Shechinah* between you).

I have organized this book into the following sections, which are designed to teach these concepts and provide a comprehensive overview of how to transform relationships into meaningful shared experiences:

+ *Menuchas Hanefesh* as the Foundation of *Shalom Bayis* (Chapter III)

+ Five Dimensions of Experiencing *Menuchas Hanefesh* (Chapter IV)

+ Transforming *Pizur Hanefesh* into *Menuchas Hanefesh* (Chapters V–VII)

+ The EMBERS Program for Creating and Enhancing *Shalom Bayis* (Chapter VIII)

CHAPTER I

The Roots of
My Journey

◇ **A Couple's Last Resort**

Before I describe my process of discovery, I want to share a brief experience that will describe how teaching couples the principles of *menuchas hanefesh* has given many of them the opportunity to begin building a marriage.

> A *rosh yeshivah* called me to discuss a couple who were seriously considering divorce after seven years of marriage and four children. The marriage had been rocky from the very beginning, and over the years they had been to many marital therapists in an attempt to learn how to quiet the conflicts and stabilize their marriage. However, although their family was growing, instead of feeling closer, they continued to experience even greater marital stress and conflict. Before agreeing to help this couple end their marriage, the *rosh yeshivah* wanted my opinion on the matter. As a last resort, he asked, would it be helpful to send the couple to see me in New York, considering the long trip and expense involved in traveling from their hometown?
>
> I told the *rosh yeshivah* that I could offer no guarantees. The failure of marital therapists in today's environment reflects the complexities that challenge the talents of even

the best counselors. Conflicts arise from past life hurts, present financial pressures, religious differences, family tensions related to bringing up children, jobs, the Internet, and so many more dynamics. However, I had been expending my efforts in a direction that was proving beneficial. All I could do was suggest that before their final decision to divorce, the couple take the trip to New York.

Within a few days, I received a call from the husband to discuss this "last chance." Based on our conversation, the couple decided to make the trip. We set aside enough time to cover the areas of their lives that had been so challenging for them, as well as to share my own ideas about *menuchas hanefesh* and *shalom bayis*. In the short amount of time I met with them, I came to understand the areas of their difficulties and shared many of the ideas that will be articulated in this book. Both spouses were quite intelligent. They were able to comprehend the value of cultivating a state of mind that would enable them to transcend the emotional and spiritual morass that enveloped their lives and caused so much of the pain they were experiencing in their marriage.

Following our session, the couple returned home infused with a deeper sense of understanding and hope. Perhaps something *could* be done to make their marriage more stable, secure, meaningful and nurturing. Perhaps it *was* possible to escape the conflict and stress that had plagued their seven years together. Perhaps they *would* learn to experience positive emotions within themselves and toward each other, even after all these years of hurt and frustration.

A few days later, I received a call from the couple. Both confirmed their feelings that our meeting had been valuable and offered them hope for long-term benefits as a couple, as parents and as individuals. They understood that no ongoing change could be expected from a single visit. Yet their ability to comprehend what I was teaching them about their lives, their relationship and human caring had the power to create an attitudinal sea change that perhaps could spark the beginning of a long and meaningful journey toward leading the lives they both deserved. Since then, this couple has returned to New York to continue learning the concepts and skills to enrich their *shalom bayis* and create closeness in their marriage.

What I came to understand from this initial encounter was that when a couple can grasp fundamental concepts that address who they are at the core and their life's aspirations as Torah Jews, this new understanding has the capacity to transform their sense of themselves as individuals, as well as their shared lives as a married couple. And while it is certainly true that deep and lasting growth is a process that spans years, even the very beginning of this process opens new pathways offering direction, encouragement, and the understanding that regardless of what they are going through, there are answers waiting to be discovered.

Since I saw this couple, there have been many more like them. Each new experience is an opportunity to further refine and deepen my knowledge and ability to teach these concepts that have the capacity to transform lives. It is essential to express that the pathways in this book are not mine. They have been gleaned from the brilliant insights of how *Chazal* understand how a healthy Torah state of mind is experienced and how this state of mind is shared in a loving relationship between husband and wife, between *chassan* and *kallah* (groom and bride).

◇ **The Uniqueness of *Menuchas Hanefesh***

I realize that there are countless books and *sefarim* devoted to *middos*, relationship skills, communication, and how to behave in meaningful ways that deepen the bonds so precious in marital relations. Many are quite excellent and well thought out. If I were to ask couples what would bring them closer together in marriage, I would get many possible answers. Some hope to develop better communication skills, others feel they need to spend more quality time together and still others seek to develop better parenting skills, do more *chessed* or demonstrate greater appreciation for each other. Undoubtedly, all of these would contribute to the enhancement of any marriage.

However, what I have come to understand is that there exists an underlying dynamic that enables a couple such as the late Rav Simcha and his *rebbetzin*, and many other couples, to create lives of deep closeness and fulfillment regardless of the challenges that Hashem has placed in their lives. This underlying strength is the ability to deal with all of life's challenges, both large and small, while maintaining a sense of personal belief, security and balance. *Chazal* call this secure and strong sense of equanimity *menuchas hanefesh*. I have no doubt that this was a significant element that enabled Rav Simcha and his *rebbetzin* to forge such a close and quietly loving relationship during all the challenging years of their lives.

The more I learned and understood about *menuchas hanefesh*, the more I began to comprehend that this experience of deep personal security is generated from within. It is a strength with which Hashem endows us. Once we are aware of its power, and come to understand the efforts needed to acquire it, we can see its effect almost immediately, both in our personal and married lives.

When couples acquire this understanding, they begin to discover a greater sense of comfort and ease with each other that is at the heart of every close marriage. For along with *menuchas hanefesh*, they also develop the inner strength and resilience to overcome all challenges to the well-being of their marriage and family.

I also came to understand that this ability to remain close through all of life's challenges is at the heart of *shalom bayis*. For this inner strength remains intact through the moment-to-moment experiences of daily life that frequently ensnare couples and trap them into feeling hurt and resentful. I also realized that when *menuchas hanefesh* is not at the heart of a couple's experience of life, the marriage is as shaky as their next challenge they will face, even though it may seem secure to outsiders.

As we explore this underlying principle that lies at the heart of personal security and *shalom bayis*, we will discover the power of *menuchas hanefesh* to bring love, focus and peace into our lives. The absence of *menuchas hanefesh* creates an alternate universe of experience, leaving us feeling fragmented, troubled, hurt and alone. *Chazal* call this state of mind *pizur hanefesh*. In the presence of *pizur hanefesh*, a couple's experience of life is negative and superficial, regardless of their possessions, social status, looks or physical health.

There are many books that have been written on *shalom bayis* by authors who are far more qualified than I to share thoughts and experiences regarding this crucial area of Torah life. My goal in sharing my insights with you is not to replace the guidance these experts offer for improving *shalom bayis*. It is to open pathways to the inner road to *shalom bayis* by guiding you to the source that *Chazal* have offered for many centuries — the ability to deepen your own sense of *menuchas hanefesh*. I pray that you discover this inner road to deepen your marital and family closeness — a closeness that is Hashem's gift to *Am Yisrael*.

◇ Discovering a Treasure in My Own Backyard

How did I arrive at this understanding about the meaning of *menuchas hanefesh* as a force to acquire *shalom bayis*? Permit me to share the events of the past few years.

There is a well-known story about a man who had a dream that he would discover a treasure if he went to a certain bridge in a faraway town. Following the dream, he traveled to the bridge where he met a man who directed him back to his own house. Arriving home after the long journey, he dug up the treasure that had always been awaiting him right under his own feet.

This story rings true for me with bell-like clarity. For many years, in my work with married couples as well as singles attempting to marry, I had continuously searched for an approach that would enable couples to create and protect the delicate relationships that Hashem desires for each Torah marriage and family. In my search, I was determined to remain close to my professional training and experience, while understanding that I would always need to return to the Torah perspective on marriage and relationships. What was always clear was that *Chazal* had a very fundamental understanding of *shalom bayis* and marital fulfillment based on how a couple learns to understand and respect one another's deeply personal feelings and needs. Throughout my search, I was painfully aware of the ever-rising divorce rate, as well as the growing number of young people unable to successfully build relationships that lead to marriage. Professionally, I was being inundated with couples on the brink of divorce, while also receiving a steadily growing number of calls from engaged couples ready to break their engagements. It became so intense that I began to view my office as an emergency room.

In 2006, I became aware of the innovative approach of George Pransky, PhD. He and Roger Mills, both psychologists, had spearheaded the development of a revolutionary approach to treating personal and relational dysfunctions. It was based on the core principles that each individual carries a transcendent capacity for emotional and physical well-being that is ever present, regardless of background or life experiences. They called their new treatment methodology Health Realization. The Health Realization approach taught individuals and couples how to access this innately healthy dimension of self. When this understanding was applied and the obstructions removed, a deeper sense of personal strength, wisdom and security would naturally emerge, like a fishing float caught underwater by seaweed that is freed and rises to the surface of the water.

Pransky and Mills had acquired this understanding and philosophy of health and well-being through the teachings of Sidney Banks, a poet and theosopher living in Canada. Pransky would eventually offer his programs and approaches to individuals, couples, corporate executives, communities and even prisons — where prisoners would attend programs on Health Realization provided by Pransky and his associates. The center of the movement was at the institute he founded in La Conner, Washington, a small town about forty miles from Seattle. The Pransky Institute provided training programs that were designed to take about four days. Nearby lodgings were provided for attendees from distant locations.

While my initial exposure to this approach was through my readings of Pransky, Mills, Banks and others, as well as audio and video presentations, my first face-to-face encounter with Health Realization came through Rabbi Michel Twersky, *shlit"a*, of Milwaukee, Wisconsin. Rabbi Twersky had been introduced to Pransky's work by Rabbi Chaim Levine, who had founded the Center for Living Judaism in Seattle. Rabbi Levine had studied with Pransky for over a decade and had presented his ideas to Rabbi Twersky, who brought a group of professional and lay leaders to participate in a number of training programs in La Conner at the Pransky Institute.

In February of 2006, Rabbis Twersky and Levine organized a three-day conference in Milwaukee to open the Torah world to these concepts and introduce a fresh vision that would impact on our ability to reverse the processes that were undermining our marital and family lives. I was privileged to attend the conference, which featured Judith Sedgemen, who had been a central member of the Pransky staff in La Conner for over twenty years and was now teaching this approach at the University of South Carolina.

I came away from the conference filled with a sense of great excitement regarding the possibilities this approach held for our community, especially with its apparent congruity to Torah *hashkafos*. Energized by the conference and my growing commitment, I also actively sought parallel ideas and approaches that directly emerged from *Chazal's* writings.

I discussed my ideas with my son Dovid in Israel, with whom I conduct a daily learning *seder* (study session). About six months after the Milwaukee conference, he shared with me that he had discovered a *sefer* composed of the proceedings of *mussar vaadim* — small, interactive study groups — that focused on the concept of *menuchas hanefesh*. These groups were addressing concepts similar to those I had encountered in the Health Realization program. The difference was that these *vaadim* had been solidly entrenched in Torah life and the writings of *Chazal*. The leader of these study groups was the late Rabbi Chaim Friedlander, *zt"l*, the *mashgiach* of the Ponovezh Yeshivah in B'nei Brak. Rabbi Friedlander authored a series of works on the *yamim tovim* and *hashkafah*, under the name *Sifsei Chaim*. The volume referred to was entitled *Middos and Avodas Hashem*, and related to the acquisition of *middos* (personal attributes) to bring us closer to Hashem. In the volume were two rather large chapters on the concepts of *menuchas hanefesh* and *machshavah* (thought).

We began our explorations by integrating the *sefer* into our daily learning schedule. The more we learned, the clearer it became that what Pransky, Mills and Banks were teaching had been addressed by *Chazal*, and particularly the Mussar movement, over many centuries and on a level that truly led to acquiring the *middos* toward which Hashem desires us to aspire. Gradually I discovered that the experience of *menuchas hanefesh* was the underlying emotional state that enables us to become close to Hashem, our spouses, our families and everything else that makes life meaningful and significant. And the beauty and irony of it all was that it was always buried — waiting to be discovered — in our own backyard.

Our daily *seder* of studying the writings of the Sifsei Chaim led to my applying a growing understanding of *menuchas hanefesh* to my work with couples and singles, thereby enabling many couples to experience a significant enhancement in their *shalom bayis* and personal sense of balance and well-being. The result was the evolution of an approach that focuses on teaching couples *Chazal's* understanding of *menuchas hanefesh* as the foundation of personal balance and inner focus that could serve as the basis of a close and loving marriage.

Because all of what is presented here is a direct result of the insights of *Chazal,* I am particularly pleased to say that there is very little in this book that is original. Perhaps I have applied the wisdom and concepts in a manner that may not have been so apparent in the past; however, I proudly proclaim that none of these teachings are mine.

All that you will be reading is a distillation of the wisdom of great voices and luminaries of our past. They include Rav Chaim Friedlander, *zt"l*; Rav Eliyahu Dessler, *zt"l*, the author of *Michtav Me'Eliyahu*; the Sfas Emes, *zt"l*, the towering leader of the Ger Dynasty; the *Alter* of Kelm, *zt"l*; Rav Shlomo Volbe, *zt"l*, known for decades simply as "the Mashgiach," who left a legacy of wisdom that will be the source of our approaches to *chinuch*, personal *middos*, and relationships; Rav Avigdor Miller, *zt"l*; Rav Yerucham Levovitz, *zt"l*, the *mashgiach* of the Mir Yeshivah in Europe; Reb Levi Yitzchak of Berditchev, *zt"l*;

and others. I have attempted to weave my limited understanding of their teachings into this approach and offer my sincere apologies for assuming any grasp of their vast and overpowering genius. However, even with these limitations, the effect of teaching what I have learned to both married people and singles has enabled many couples to feel a sense of hope and mastery over the quality of their *shalom bayis* and relationships.

I have also incorporated a number of concepts that I respected and valued very much from the Pransky model. I was particularly impressed by Pransky's method of teaching his principles in a very coherent manner and ensuring that clients were able to understand and integrate them into their lives. While the principles that *Chazal* teach are significantly different, I have maintained the Pransky method of teaching these principles as a discrete body of knowledge. This has enabled my clients to review and master these concepts. The primary difference was that where Pransky taught the principles of Thought, Consciousness and Mind as the foundation stones of Health Realization, I had discovered *Chazal's* principles of *Chiddush, Tzomet* (Crossroads), and Mind as *Mishkan* as the principles governing this approach. All these principles represent pathways to continuously rediscover our personal freedom from the oppressive repetition of *pizur hanefesh* and will later be discussed in depth.

During this journey, I have discovered that *menuchas hanefesh* is essential to every Jew — whether relating to *shalom bayis,* how we experience Shabbos, the depth of our *tefillos* to Hashem, or the quality of our lives. Without cultivating our sense of personal security and trust in Hashem, we leave ourselves open to living lives continuously unbalanced by a sense of unpredictability and uncertainty.

◇ **Anecdotal and Case Histories**

Throughout this book, I have incorporated many anecdotes and case histories from my practice. In each of these examples, I have attempted to maintain two overarching guidelines. The first is to clearly demonstrate how the application of these principles has the ability to impact the marital relationship in a positive manner. The second is to preserve the anonymity of the couples I am describing. I achieve this by switching the gender, altering quotable phrases and changing the description of symptoms. However, the goal of providing the reader with clear examples is never compromised.

◇ How Couples Should Read This Book

Initially I wrote this book so that married couples, rabbis, therapists and anyone else who was interested could understand how *menuchas hanefesh* resides at the center of *shalom bayis*. However, after I completed the initial manuscript, I began to grasp that the real power of this book rests in having couples read it together and discuss it page by page, thought by thought. The results have been so impressive that I find it difficult to work with any couple that is unable to undertake the commitment to set aside daily time for this task.

Therefore, my recommendation is that for a couple to truly derive the benefits that these words of *Chazal* can have on their marriage and family life, I suggest committing to set aside five to twenty minutes on a daily basis to read, discuss and follow each of the exercises and assignments I have included in this work.

I wish you much success in bringing *menuchas hanefesh* and *shalom bayis* into your marriage and family life.

◇ My Gratitude and Acknowledgements

Every step in the writing of this book is the result of the loving guidance and *chessed* of Hashem. Along the way, Hashem has literally "spoon-fed" me one discovery after the next within the teachings of *Chazal*. Therefore, my first words are to express my deepest gratitude to Hashem for His loving guidance in every area of my life and in particular for helping me present these sublime concepts.

In writing a book about marriage, there can be no deeper feelings of gratitude than those I have for my beloved wife Vivian, who has been a continuous source of devotion, encouragement and support to all we have experienced through our shared lives since the beginning of our marriage. For forty-four years, she has taught me the meaning of everything I have attempted to convey to couples through this work. Through our marriage, all of life's precious gifts have unfolded, particularly through the endless *nachas* we are privileged to have from our children and their wonderful families.

I must express a special and loving *hakaras hatov* to my learning *chavrusa* (study partner) R' Dovid, who is also my son. As part of our daily learning *seder*, R' Dovid introduced me to the writings of the *Sifsei Chaim*, which enabled me to discover what I had been searching for throughout my entire professional career, and which serve as the central focus of this book. Studying these works has deeply enriched my understanding about our inner spiritual lives and marriage. May Hashem bless our *"chavrusashaft"* with many more productive years of shared Torah study.

While these concepts were introduced by and studied together with Dovid, it was in the Bais Medrash of Yeshivah Derech Ayson, under its Rosh HaYeshivah, Rabbi Yechiel Yitzchok Perr, *shlit"a*, and the Menahel, Rabbi Aharon Brafman, *shlit"a*, where my deeper understanding of *menuchas hanefesh* matured. Participating daily in the Yeshivah environment has enabled me to deeply comprehend how one's inner life can be cultivated through a close proximity to an *adam gadol* such as the Rosh HaYeshivah — a living embodiment of Torah, wisdom and unfathomable kindness. In such an environment, every *tefillah*, every learning *seder*, every Shabbos, all the Yamim

Nora'im and the Chagim have served to deepen my comprehension of *menuchas hanefesh*.

The very beginnings of this book actually germinated in another Bais Medrash, that of Yeshivah Sh'or Yoshuv. That is where I had the honor and privilege of presenting my initial thoughts in a series of *motza'ei* Shabbos lectures on *shalom bayis*. The Rosh HaYeshivah, Rabbi Naftali Jaeger, *shlit"a*, and his Rebbetzin had asked me to present some of my thoughts as part of a community service program in memory of their late daughter Ruchama, *a"h*. I am grateful to the Rosh HaYeshivah for offering me the opportunity to present these workshops, which served as an important catalyst in writing this book.

Rabbi Michel Twersky, *shlit"a*, and Rabbi Chaim Levine deserve special acknowledgement for initially introducing me to Dr. Pransky's work in the area of Health Realization. The conference they held in Milwaukee was my first intensive exposure to Health Realization and eventually led me to discovering the role of *menuchas hanefesh* in our lives. While I have never met Dr. Pransky, his pioneering work in personal and marital well-being is deeply appreciated and valued.

Aryeh Mezei and Nachum Shapiro of Judaica Press have been a great source of friendship and *chizuk* for me. Their rich experience and unequivocal support for what this book attempts to teach have made an invaluable contribution toward successfully bringing this work to fruition.

I wish to thank Mrs. Nina Ackerman Indig, whose gifted editing skills enabled me to express the complexity of these concepts in a coherent and articulate manner. Moshe Ibsen and Hadassa Goldsmith demonstrated great patience and precision in serving as proofreaders for the many iterations of the manuscript. I deeply appreciate their efforts and contributions to this work.

Justine Elliot is a graphic designer of great and deep sensitivity. Through her talent and artistic sensibilities, she has created a design that truly conveys in graphic form what the book attempts to convey through the written word. Thank you.

Two years ago, when I produced "The Foundations of *Shalom Bayis*," a CD recording of many of the ideas that serve as the foundation of this book, my dear nephew Rabbi Meir Kaufman heard the recording and vigorously insisted the CD be transcribed and published in book form. At first I resisted. However, his insistence and persuasiveness finally convinced me to undertake the project. What I thought would be a two-month project of transcription turned into a two-year labor of love. I am grateful for Meir's vision and persuasiveness.

Lastly, I want to express my profound gratitude to a dear friend whose generosity provided me with the funding to publish this work. During the long period I spent writing this work, I realized it would require financial backing to make it a reality. This dear friend, who shall remain anonymous, responded immediately and generously in a manner that enabled me to remain focused on the completion of this work. Without his encouragement and support, it is unlikely that my dream to publish this book would have ever been realized.

CHAPTER II

Marital Love as the Center of Self

Many years ago, I remember coming across a brief yet very poignant Chassidic gem about the Baal Shem Tov, the founder of the Chassidic movement, which has stayed with me over the years.

Shortly after the death of his wife, the Baal Shem Tov lamented that he always believed that when he died, he would rise toward the heavens in a fiery chariot like Eliyahu *HaNavi*. But now that his wife was missing from his life, he had come to accept that in losing her, he had become half a person. It seems clear that he was telling his followers that when he lost his wife, he lost half of himself.

The powerful reflections of the Baal Shem Tov are neither unique nor original. We all are aware that at the very beginning of *Beraishis*, the Torah tells us that Hashem never intended for Adam or any of his descendants to live alone, separated and apart: "*Lo tov heyos ha'adam levado* — It is not good for man to live alone." But the clear message from Hashem is this: Not only is it not a good thing for man to be alone, but the very design of how we were created promotes sharing and building our lives with one special person. And mankind has always recognized this as well. "No man is an island" are the well-known words of the poet John Donne.

◇ Understanding the Absence of *Shalom Bayis*

Because Hashem creates us all with this deeper need to build a home with our life partner, *shalom bayis* is not simply an option, but as necessary as the air we breathe. Its absence causes us to experience an internal pain that is deep and relentless, an inner condition of profound emotional confusion and chaos. It's not just that something is missing in our lives, like a new car or a vacation home. *Shalom bayis* is inherent to how we have been created; without it, we cannot feel whole and intact. This is because within the essence of our deeper selves, we all harbor the need for this close, safe and loving relationship. In its presence, we are fulfilled; and in its absence, we experience a sense of loss, isolation and emotional emptiness.

◇ In the Absence of *Shalom Bayis*

The absence of *shalom bayis* creates a deep and profound pain within ourselves because Hashem never intended for us to experience our lives in this manner. The pain may be indicated by a growing sense of alienation and disinterest. It may be seen in the continuous eruption of conflicts — typically struggles over control, finances and relationships with in-laws. At the outer extremes of these indicators we can see physical and verbal abuse, addictive behavior and even disloyalty. Sometimes couples seek other solutions and attempt to fill their painful marriages with more possessions and creature comforts. They may spend more and more time away from home and make other efforts to quell the pain and quiet the conflict. When all else fails, there is always the matrimonial attorney waiting so eagerly to "solve the problem" through the courts.

A couple can try to divert their attention from the pain in many ways, but none work for very long. Eventually the hurt resurfaces in countless forms and there is no real escape. It is crucial to understand that there is no substitute for *shalom bayis*. Hashem created the emotional and spiritual infrastructure of a husband and wife so they will be close and sharing. The countless interactions that a husband and wife continuously share must enable both to feel a sense of ongoing closeness, trust and comfort with each other.

◇ New Life Goals; Climbing Mount Everest

We may understand the meaning of *shalom bayis* in our lives; however, we also need to understand the profound impact of its absence. In my work with couples, I have encountered a number of reasons for this.

First, there are married individuals who feel that modern society has opened their eyes by inspiring them to live life to the fullest as individuals. In 2009, Mount Everest was conquered by Wendy Booker, the first Everest climber with multiple sclerosis. Wendy first learned of her condition at age forty. Determined not to permit the illness to prevent her from leading a full life, she divorced her husband of almost twenty years and set out to conquer the world's highest peaks. She succeeded, and we can all be inspired by her personal strength, determination and hopefulness. Yet, her achievement is alien to our own aspirations for the continuity of Torah life and to the meaning of *shalom bayis* as the emotional cornerstone of this way of life.

In our society, many couples do not need a reason such as MS to abandon marriage in pursuit of personal greatness. A growing number of individuals are very willing to jettison *shalom bayis* — and marriage itself — to pursue very superficial and infantile needs. In my work, I see an increasingly greater number of couples suffering as they relentlessly chase after money, power, fame, excitement and the fulfillment of sensory needs. Along the way toward these illusory goals, the seekers struggle with negative states of mind such as tension, anger, depression and moodiness; they feel obsessed and constantly beset by the external pressures generated by the relentless pursuits of life's more superficial goals.

Whether the causes can be directly attributed to the culture we live in or originate within ourselves, couples find themselves more frequently bumping into each other's personal agendas — and the result is always a clash. It's almost as if these couples view *shalom bayis* as an option that actually gets in the way of their busy and full lives. The refrain I hear so frequently is, "If only I could be left alone to pursue what's important to me." The result is that couples begin to adjust their lives to accommodate these private agendas and learn to stay clear of each other as they pursue their own dreams. Alternately, they become caught up in tension, anger, resentment and other negative feelings that may simmer until a crisis hits.

◇ **The Truth Beneath the Surface**

But the reality is that while many couples have learned to "adjust" to their distance and alienation, underneath the surface, there exists a profound sense of penetrating hurt. On the surface, they may be seemingly unaffected by their distance and isolation. However, within the *neshamos* of their being, the pain is unspeakable. In the language of our present experience, we have come to define our success through the achievement of life's superficialities, while deep within, we cannot articulate what it means to be leading lives devoid of love, security, acceptance, support, understanding and all the other factors that go into the deceptively simple concept of *shalom bayis*.

Once we get to the deeper level of awareness, we become profoundly conscious of how the absence of human closeness and the distance from the *Shechinah* impacts our lives. For Hashem has designed and created us to live together, closely and intimately — two people caring for each other and for others. While we are all unique and separate, our destiny is to become one. This need — to share a loving and secure life with one special individual — is at the very heart of our life's experience. It literally defines who we are. While our society has placed so much emphasis on personal agendas based on the pursuit of pleasure, achievement and acquisitions as the nucleus of life, the true experiences of our lives emerge from the *neshamos* within us.

I can recall countless occasions when a husband or wife first felt that nothing would really be lost if their marriage would end and then suddenly became overwhelmed and even frightened at the thought of being alone. There are two such moments in my own experience that I would like to share with you. One occurred even before a marriage had begun and the other was at the end of a long and loving life shared together. Both evoke a sense of the power of this voice that calls out our deep yearnings for our life partner, the voice that Hashem has placed in each of us.

◇ At the Height of a Career

The first event involved Michael, a man in his mid-30s who was a researcher for a well-known financial firm. I had been working with Michael while he was single and had been guiding him while he was dating Sarah. Over a period of about six months, he and Sarah had developed a close relationship. While marriage had been discussed, Michael was also a man on the fast track of life and felt he had places to go. His position kept him very busy and he was conflicted about committing to marriage. For him, marriage was desirable, but also very frightening. I had my doubts whether he would be able to take the next step. Then, without any explanation, Michael told me that he was ready to get engaged. I wondered what propelled him forward, but did not receive an answer at that time.

A few years later, Michael, Sarah and their son joined us for a Shabbos meal. When he and I were alone, he asked me whether I ever understood why he had decided to marry Sarah. I admitted that it was always somewhat of a mystery to me, realizing how conflicted and frightened he was about marriage. So he shared with me the following memory:

> Michael was an up-and-coming star and had been invited to give an important presentation at a conference attended by America's leading financial firms. He considered this invitation to be one of the most important developments of his career, a great honor that recognized his achievements. He packed his bags and went off to the conference with a great sense of personal satisfaction.
>
> His presentation went extremely well. After receiving great praise, he returned victoriously to his hotel room to bask in the glory of his personal and professional triumph. What more could he ask for? However, as he entered his hotel room, he was seized by a powerful sadness such as he had never encountered before — a deep sense of emptiness and aloneness. Michael had reached a milestone in his life, one he had worked so hard to achieve — yet there he was in a hotel room, alone, with no one to share his big moment.
>
> Beyond this feeling was an even more powerful one. His aloneness extended past this moment of personal triumph. It went past the present and stretched eternally into the future. He had no one with whom to share his life. The professional efforts that had been at the center of his life for so long were now satisfied. Yet along with achievement came an awareness of a deeper yearning.
>
> For years, Michael's pursuit of success had blunted his ability to hear the gentle voice within that recognizes Hashem's words, "*Lo tov heyos ha'adam levado.*" Now, with

a deep and unexpected force, this awareness rang within him like a bell suddenly pealing out and breaking the absolute stillness of night. In that moment it had become so undeniably clear that all this was of no real significance, neither the success nor the recognition. A life without someone to share it with would never bring him the fulfillment he deeply longed for.

Suddenly he had clarity and made the decision that had until now seemed impossible. The time for living life alone needed to come to an end. Instinctively, he picked up the phone to call Sarah. He heard her voice. He was reassured. He knew he would no longer be alone.

Shortly after returning home, Michael and Sarah were engaged. Their marriage has proven to be a blessing for them and their growing family. They recently celebrated the birth of their second child.

I remember Michael and Sarah when I am working with couples because, despite alienation and hurt, this voice within is always just a discovery away. Thinking of them when I'm with couples in conflict, my question is always, "What do I need to say or do to facilitate the awareness of this deeper truth that Hashem has planted in each of us?"

◇ **Seeking Solace in the Night**

Moving on from Michael and Sarah, when the voice is heard early in life, this moment reflects how our deeper awareness is experienced at the other end of life — the later years. In 1976, I attended a conference in Boston for Jewish Communal Service Workers. I was presenting a paper I had written on marital therapy with Orthodox families. While most of the presentations were given by mental health and communal service professionals, a keynote address was given by the late Rav Yoshe Ber Soloveitchik, *zt"l, Rosh haYeshivah* of Yeshiva University, who had resided in Boston for many years. I want to share with you what has never left my memory about that speech.

The *Rav*, as he was known, spoke to an overflow audience of conference attendees. He was describing the overwhelming power of loneliness that is part of our human condition, and how Hashem places within us the need for human closeness. Scouting for other yarmulkes in the audience, I spotted very few, perhaps ten percent. But the *Rav* was mesmerizing in his description of how Hashem has created us all with a need for a true life partner.

All his previous eloquence paled, however, when he shared an episode from his own life that left a life-altering impact on me and, I'm certain, on many others who heard him. Disclosing details about the final days of his late wife Tanya's illness, he vividly described the pain of sleeping alone in their bedroom while his frail wife was downstairs being cared for by an attending nurse in the enclosed porch.

> In the middle of the night, the *Rav* thought he heard his wife groaning in fear and pain. Fearing that the sounds of her agony indicated the end was near, he was filled with an overwhelming sense of vulnerability. At any moment, the woman with whom he had shared his life would be snatched away from him! He needed to see his beloved wife once again, perhaps to say good-bye for the last time or just to make certain that she was as comfortable as possible.
>
> He put on his robe and made his way down the darkened stairs. However, as he got closer, there was only silence and the porch was unusually dark. He entered the room, anticipating the feelings of relief he would feel at being with his wife of so many years on this dark and frightening night. But when he stepped closer, he suddenly became painfully aware that the bed she had

> been sleeping in was empty and there was no nurse. He then realized what he had forgotten. She had died three nights ago.

A frail and elderly *talmid chacham* had transmitted to a mostly secular audience of perhaps a thousand, in the most personal and intimate way, how Hashem has planted in our hearts the overwhelming human need to share our lives with one person. And when that person is no longer a part of our world, part of us is gone as well.

The audience and the *Rav* may have been from very dissimilar backgrounds, and few had any understanding of what his life represented, but in revealing this moment in his life, the *Rav's* message was poignant and penetrating. Hashem has created within us the need to share our lives with one special person. Through his words, every participant was suddenly faced with the stark reality of his or her own mortality and need for companionship, love and closeness throughout life with one special life partner. Suddenly there was a realization that at our core, Hashem has placed a profoundly deep and human yearning for a life partner within us all. The frail and deeply human voice of the Rav openly sharing his painful experience of loneliness gave new depth and meaning to *"Lo tov heyos ha'adam levado."* Hashem never wants us to be alone.

◇ The Spiritual Foundations of Marital Love and Closeness

I always tell couples who are experiencing emotional distress in their marriage that the reason the pain is so penetrating is that our deep yearning for love and closeness is at the center of our existence. It is only through a life of sharing *shalom bayis* on a moment-to-moment basis that we are able to feel complete and connected in deep and secure ways. In the absence of *shalom bayis*, the pain cuts deep and to the core, for Hashem has inscribed within our physical and spiritual DNA the awareness of this need for human completion and has made it as essential to our souls as water and air to our bodies.

◇ **Love in the Heart of Man**

Dovid *HaMelech* describes in *Tehillim* 131:2: "I swear that I silenced my soul like a suckling child at the side of its mother, like a suckling child is to me my soul ...." At the heart of all love is the primordial bond of love between mother and child. This serves as the foundation of our experience of love.

Hashem created us to build our connection to Him in this closeness. Twice daily we recite *"Shema Yisrael"* and then say *"V'ahavta es Hashem Elokecha ...."* *Chazal* guide us to cover our eyes to fully concentrate on the bond between us and Hashem. Ever since we were small children, we marveled at the heroism of Rabbi Akiva and the countless Jews before and after him who were able to experience life's ultimate closeness to Hashem. It is with this undistracted focus that Hashem wants us to relate to Him, with unwavering and unequivocal love. To experience this love, we utter the final word, *"Echad —* One," with a readiness to accept Hashem's One-ness. This personal encounter with Hashem's *"Echad"* enables us to realize the deeper essence of our spiritual selves.

We profoundly need this experience, particularly at times in our lives that call to us to pierce through barriers of separation — such as on Yom Kippur at *Ne'ilah* or when we are standing by the *Kosel* and feel the stirrings of the *Shechinah* in our midst. At these moments, the veils of separation are lifted, and just as an infant experiences trust breathing so effortlessly in its mother's arms, we too feel close to Hashem and realize that life and love are continuously emerging from Him.

For me, there is a distinct parallel between the closeness that we attempt to experience with Hashem and the connection that Hashem wants us to experience with our life partner. Creating a marriage balanced on the ongoing experience of *shalom bayis* is more than just the absence of loneliness and tension. It is the ability to create a continuous flow of trust, emotional closeness and security, shared at every stage and every dimension of marriage. Beginning with the early stages of dating, the *chasunah* and *sheva berachos*, it goes through *shanah rishonah*, continues with building a family and raising children, and extends into life's twilight years.

Therefore, when we are aware of this relationship through the emotional fulfillment of *shalom bayis*, in its loss we understand the pained expressions of the holy Baal Shem Tov or the deep expressions of human aloneness shared by the late Rav Soloveitchik in Boston more than thirty years ago. Since this need is innate to the DNA of our inner lives, we can also understand how a young man like Michael, returning to an empty hotel room, can become aware of a truth suddenly emerging in his consciousness that he had never before formulated.

Our awareness is even more heightened when a couple realizes, with great pain and fear, that this closeness that Hashem has placed in their lives is absent and may never be there. It is a sense of pain that says, "A crucial dimension of myself is missing. The very essence of who I am has been diminished. And even if I attempt to compensate for it through my career, possessions, success and all of life's external trappings, nothing can ever really make up for this part of my self that is missing." This is the awareness that accompanies us when we realize that our marriages are not filled with *shalom bayis*.

> Yoni and Chayah were considering divorce. Chayah felt
> very frustrated with many aspects of their lives and was

unable to control her strident criticism of her husband. She felt she was justified and was not giving in, even if it meant separation and divorce. After a few sessions, she was able to acquire skills that enabled her to control her criticism. She then asked me, "Do you think we can save this marriage? I'm suddenly feeling very scared that I may have pushed him over the edge. How can I bring our marriage back from the brink?"

All couples, whether at the beginning of their union, in the prime of marriage or in later years, need to acquire the understanding and skills to continuously create an environment of *shalom bayis*, where each can feel deeply cared for, emotionally safe and respected. This experience of *shalom bayis* emerges as couples feel that their deepest selves can emerge from behind the veil to be understood, respected and cared for in this most important of all human relationships. It is the ability of a couple to create an emotionally safe environment that allows each other to feel secure, while simultaneously enabling children to grow emotionally, physically and spiritually whole, appreciating the true wonder of growing up in a loving Torah environment. This is the environment in which the *Shechinah* yearns to dwell.

◇ The Soul of Silk

In my own attempt to comprehend why we long for a marriage rooted in the security of *shalom bayis*, I have come to appreciate the meaning of what Rav Yerucham Levovitz, *zt"l*, the *mashgiach* of the Mir Yeshivah, describes as the "soul of silk."

A number of years ago I was giving a presentation to married couples in Los Angeles. The workshop on marital sensitivity included an experiential exercise during which couples would focus on their feelings as they entered the door of their homes. Couples did a guided imagery exercise, wrote down their thoughts and feelings, and then shared them with each other.

After the workshop was over, a woman approached me.

> "The experience I just had," she confided, "answered a question I have been asking myself for almost a decade. For many years, as I walked up the steps of my house and turned the knob to open the door, I had a slight sense of anxiety and could even feel myself tremble. I was always aware that something at home was bothering me, but this exercise drew my attention to the symptoms. And even more than being aware of the feeling, through this experience I was able to remember the moment when it began."
>
> She went on to describe a difficult experience earlier in their marriage when she and her husband were very tense. The conflict quickly spun out of control and for a very brief moment, she experienced an outburst of unbridled anger from her husband. He said things she had never heard him say before and his shouting frightened her. He soon brought himself back under control, but she had never known he had this anger inside him. Then she said to me, "As I was doing the exercise, I realized that the fear I felt at that moment ten years ago was still inside me today. It's as if I'm afraid that such an explosion could happen at any moment again without warning. Just now, as we were doing the exercise, I realized that this is the feeling I still have when I'm approaching my front door."

I remember sitting with a couple who came to me after a fight during which the wife, in a fit of anger, took the car and left a family *simchah* in a huff. Her mortified husband had to concoct a story about why his wife had left early. A week later, he was still hurt. She apologized profusely, but to no avail. Finally she asked me, "Why can't he just get over it already?"

The answer is that Hashem created us all with very delicate feelings. When we are emotionally hurt, we feel our wounds in the very depths of our being. It's like picking up a hot frying pan by its hot handle. The handle leaves a burn mark that makes us sensitive even to warm water. When it comes to emotional pain, we are constantly reminded of the sting, whether a week or even a decade later.

Rav Yerucham, *zt"l*, was deeply sensitive to the inner core of our beings. He compared our inner selves to silk. He suggested that if you take a tiny pebble and place it under a piece of silk, and then run your finger over the silk, even the tiniest protrusion will be felt. His message was clear. Hashem has given us a soul of silk and every impediment can be felt, no matter how small.

With our soul of silk, every painful moment can be felt under the soft and delicate fabric of our hearts. And this is the reason why *shalom bayis* plays such a central role in marriage. Every moment of hurt and disappointment lingers, sometimes for hours, months or even decades. I call it the Chernobyl Effect, where emotional hurt experienced between two people who yearn to feel close and trusting leaves a radioactive contamination that never seems to go away. I say it has a "half-life of eternity." Perhaps this is why the punishment for embarrassing someone is eternal. The embarrassed or hurt person cannot recover from the emotional pain.

This helps us understand why *shalom bayis* is not an option or an upgrade, but a necessary part of our very essence. In its absence, we experience an inner pain that is deep and relentless, an inner condition of profound emotional confusion and chaos. It's not just that something is missing in our lives. Within our DNA, we all harbor the need for an environment of *shalom bayis*. The absence of *shalom bayis* causes us to feel out of sync, as if our body temperature jumped three points and just "doesn't feel right." For without love and *shalom bayis*, there is no way we can compensate for our loss. We can tolerate distance from people whom we know only casually because the distance has no deep meaning for us. However, we can never truly tolerate distance from those to whom we are close — a spouse, a child, a parent. For here the feeling that love and *shalom bayis* is missing creates a deep and profound pain within ourselves, because Hashem never intended us to experience life this way.

Our ability to adjust to life's disappointments is certainly true for the more superficial pleasures of life. Throughout life, we are always learning that we can survive without our acquired "necessities." I may not have my favorite coffee when the local Starbucks closes, but I'll certainly learn to get along without it in a very short period of time. When my car is sent to the shop, I will have to make do with public transportation, causing me great inconvenience, but I'll get by and perhaps even use the time to read or learn. However, when love and *shalom bayis* are missing from a marriage, the result is a profound sense of pain that is never assuaged or mollified by any adjustment.

◇ The *Bas Kol*

Perhaps this is why *Chazal* tell us that forty days before a child is born, a *bas kol* announces the future life partner of this soul. The reason, in my mind, is that the nature of this bond between husband and wife has to be so exquisitely tuned. These two *neshamos* will one day meet and begin to share a life together, and it is only through the delicate fine-tuning of their emotional and spiritual selves that they can guide each other and create an environment where Torah life thrives for both parents and children alike. For this couple to fulfill their roles in the long and unbroken chain of Jewish history, these two personalities need to be prepared in every way, beginning before birth. Then, as they grow, Hashem places each in an environment that prepares them for the task of weaving their lives lovingly together. Every moment is all in Hashem's hands. Nothing is accidental or without meaning.

This long period of growth and preparation that enables us to be ready to meet our *basherte* (destined life partner) is why, in the absence of *shalom bayis*, the hurt is penetrating and inescapable. I liken it to a little girl on the day of her birthday. No one has informed her of a party, but she has "a feeling" that a surprise is being planned by her best friends. When an invitation to play in her friend's house arrives, she's now sure that she was right. As she enters, expecting to be greeted by "Surprise!!!," she finds no party, just a family going about the mundane business of home life. No one is even aware that she's there, or seems to care. Who can describe her pain? This is the depth of the disappointment and hurt that couples experience on an ongoing basis in the absence of *shalom bayis*. We are raised and prepared from the very moment of our conception for the time when we will meet our *basherte*. We are promised that our lives will be fulfilling, inspiring and loving. When marriage arrives and is filled with hurt, there are no words that can describe the poignancy of the suffering.

◇ The Deeper Dynamic of *Shalom Bayis*

There are many factors that contribute to *shalom bayis*. These include appreciation, affection, the quality of communication, gratitude and many other essential *middos*. Each of these qualities and skills will always contribute to the well-being of a marriage.

Yet, we also need to reflect on what enables a husband and wife to gain the insight, personal discipline and commitment to practice these *middos* toward which *Chazal* are continuously directing us. We also need to become aware of a deeper personal dynamic that must be continuously present, just beneath the surface. *Shalom bayis* cannot be an external show of civility masking deeper feelings of hurt and resentment; the strength and stability to practice these *middos* needs to be present even when we are expressing our hurt or angry feelings.

What is this deeper dynamic? *Shalom bayis* is not the absence of pressures or tension; those are elements that all couples and families must deal with as a necessary part of life. Rather, its presence exists in the ability of a husband and wife to continuously discover a firm and stable sense of inner security, personal fulfillment and calm. *Shalom bayis* serves as a personal gyroscope to help each maintain his or her sense of balance through life's unavoidable storms. This inner balance enables both to keep their perceptions and experiences of life within a healthy and positive state of mind. We can restate this by saying that such a couple appreciates how their state of mind will lead to the strengthening or the undermining of their *shalom bayis*. Therefore, when one spouse feels that anger, hurt and isolation are beginning to well up within, this always signifies a state of mind that will undermine *shalom bayis*. Therefore, the greater our consciousness of our positive or negative state of mind, the greater our ability to preserve and cultivate *shalom bayis* in our marriage. Even though I may very much want to maintain a sense of peace in my home, if I am an individual who gravitates toward feelings of tension and being easily upset, there is no way I can achieve this peace and calmness in my home. I cannot create that which I have not learned to master within myself.

◇ Viewing Life from a "Jam Cam"

It is the fulfillment of our *neshamos*, or our inner selves, that is the true determinant of our *shalom bayis*, regardless of the external conditions in which we live. For example, traffic patterns in New York are frequently monitored by video cameras called "jam cams." We can set up one of these jam cams to observe a couple in a way that captures the flow and movement of their "quality of life." We can observe their home, car, kitchen, vacation home, health-conscious way of life, and all the external symbols of the "good life." Judging by an "aerial" view of their lives, they may seem to live in a veritable garden of comfort. However, if we were to use a kind of MRI to scan their feelings and experience of life from within, we may very well discover that instead of viewing the well-tended and orderly garden that the world sees, we would be looking at a distressed terrain of troubled thoughts and feelings, more reminiscent of the untamed wilderness of Afghanistan. For true *shalom bayis* is never solely a function of externals and even external gestures. How often have we all seen in our own lives how couples may be lacking in so many of the outer qualities and possessions, yet in their presence we sense a quiet, peaceful, verdant garden of two selves sharing their lives with great care, genuine love and trust.

The great danger we face is that in our society we have come to focus on the externals. We equate our outer lives with our inner lives. Therefore, we invest ourselves so deeply in appearing successful and happy on the surface, while underneath we can live in inner states of hurt and insecurity that continue unabated for decades of our precious lives.

There is a remarkable question that the *mashgiach* from Mir, Rav Yerucham, asks relates to the epic battle that Yaakov *Avinu* waged with the *sar* (angelic guardian) of Eisav. He asks us to consider: What did this *sar* of Eisav look like? Did he look like a hunter, a warrior, or a medieval lord? He answers that this heavenly representative of Eisav was dressed like a *talmid chacham*. Based on his outward appearance, he could have passed for the *gadol hador*. It took a Yaakov *Avinu* to understand that his outer appearance in no way influenced the corruption within. We can never understand the internal value of someone's life by using externals as the primary perspective.

◇ **Life on the High Wire: The Dynamic Balance of
*Shalom Bayis***

This book does not attempt to improve *shalom bayis* solely from
the outside. Rather, it equally focuses on learning to cultivate
an experience of life from within that is continuously aware of
the quality of our thoughts and emotions. This is what is truly
required to enable us to feel closer to our life partner. We learn
that *shalom bayis* means creating an inner sense of balance and
well-being that strengthens our shared quality of life.

There is a metaphor that I feel captures the nuance of this
phenomenon, one that has helped couples understand the
dynamic inner balance that needs to exist between husband
and wife, or *chassan* and *kallah*. I appreciated this concept many
years ago, and I have since shared it with many couples.

> When I was a young boy attending yeshivah on the
> Lower East Side, the arrival of *Nisan* and spring also meant
> that we would start seeing the subway and billboard ads
> for the Ringling Brothers' Barnum and Bailey Circus at the
> old Madison Square Garden. Since the circus always came
> to New York in time to coincide with the spring recess, it
> was frequently in town on *Chol Hamoed Pesach*. So we
> would pack our hard-boiled eggs and our matzos and head
> to Madison Square Garden. We would sit as high up as
> imaginable and munch away, mesmerized by the spectacle
> far below us in the three rings.
>
> Of all the attractions, I found the high-wire act to be
> one of the most fascinating. To a naïve child, it was incom-
> prehensible that two high-wire artists could be standing
> motionless on a thin wire high atop the Garden—even
> higher than we were. How was it possible, I wondered?
>
> As I looked up, I saw two "perfectly" balanced artists,
> each firmly holding a long, arched pole, high above us. We
> were locked in to their every move! After a drumroll, they

would begin moving toward each other as they somehow managed to maintain their balance and not fall.

When I was older, I realized that both my perceptions were neither complete nor accurate. First, to the child looking at the artists, it seemed that they were actually standing still. This, I learned later in life, was only an illusion. I came to understand that balance, whether on a high wire or in life, is a perpetual challenge. The more the artists appeared to be standing still, the more they had to keep balancing their muscles and their poles, continuously shifting their feet and posture ever so slightly. There were probably thousands of different balancing adjustments that had become unconscious and second nature. To my fascinated eyes, all these adjustments were not perceived. To me they were "standing still." However, for the artists, staying balanced was a very delicate and dynamic process that left no room for even a moment of casual relaxation. To remain on the high wire, each needed to monitor and adjust his or her inner sense of balance on a moment-to-moment basis.

My second perception — that of two independent people moving closer together — was also inaccurate. These two artists must have been very focused, not only on their own inner balance, but also on each other's balance. At any given moment, each could notice even the slightest tremor on the wire or any sign of tension in the other. They needed to be able to communicate with each other so that each could help the other maintain this balance. And when there was any sign of shakiness, each had the ability to deliver the message in just the right way. Perhaps the message would be to "straighten your shoulders, bend your knees, take a deep breath and quiet down," or many other similar reassuring messages. However, whatever the message, the ability to help the other could only emerge from the inner balance each had achieved on his or her own. This is what enabled them both to remain stable on the high wire. It is this same wisdom that serves as an internal frame of reference that enables two spouses to help each other at every moment of their shared lives.

Therefore, when someone asks me, "What is the most important quality a couple needs to maintain *shalom bayis?*," I think of Reb Simcha Wasserman, *zt"l*, and his *rebbetzin*, and relive that moment when I experienced the closeness of these two extraordinary people. Then I am able to answer, "The ability to help each other feel balanced, cared for and secure." Without these qualities, there can never be *shalom bayis*.

Therefore, this dynamic that we have been looking for is a couple's ability to truly balance and protect each other as they move forward, helping each other grow through the necessary and persistent march of life's challenges and struggles. This is what truly contributes to their peace and happiness. It's the satisfaction in knowing that they continuously help each other stay balanced and even learn to thrive while on this high wire of life.

CHAPTER III

The Link Between *Menuchas Hanefesh* and *Shalom Bayis*

◇ A Conflict of One

In contemporary society, we have come to accept the value of learning how to successfully resolve marital conflicts. The inherent message is that fighting is natural in the course of a marriage, and it's really not terrible if spouses fight — as long as they are skilled in the art of settling their differences. It's almost a way of saying that a couple is not truly well adjusted if they don't fight.

Over the years, I have come to a very different conclusion about marital conflict, and recently I expressed my position to a couple during a talk I gave at their *sheva berachos*. I suggested that arguing in marriage is unavoidable, and you have to accept it as a necessary reality. "However," I told them, "there is one condition you need to stick to: that is, to make sure that during any argument, one of you is not part of the fight. So as long as one of you can remain calm and neutral, I have no problem with your arguing ...." It took a few moments until the contradiction sank in. What I was saying was that in the world of *menuchas hanefesh*, conflict is neither valued nor inevitable.

I based this piece of wisdom on a story I was told by a friend, who witnessed the following event:

A well-known, elderly *rosh yeshivah* returned home after a long day, accompanied by a *bachur* who had been his driver. The *rebbetzin* had prepared dinner and was eagerly awaiting her husband's arrival. Wishing to ensure the *rosh yeshivah* a few uninterrupted minutes to eat and relax, the *rebbetzin* asked the *bachur* to please answer the phone and take all calls.

Just as the *rosh yeshivah* began his meal, the phone rang. The *bachur* answered and patiently informed the insistent caller that the *rosh yeshivah* was not available — exactly as the *rebbetzin* had requested. The woman was persistent, however, and would not take no for an answer.

The *rosh yeshivah* had been involved in a delicate matter of *shalom bayis* between this woman and her husband; now, hearing the *bachur* mention her name, he motioned to the young man to give him the phone. Left with no choice, the *bachur* handed the phone to the *rosh yeshivah*, who spoke to the woman for a few minutes, despite the silent displeasure of his wife.

Following the call, the meal resumed. When the *rebbetzin* left the room, the *bachur* carefully said to the *rosh yeshivah*, "Please excuse my *chutzpah*, but I would like to ask the *rosh yeshivah* a question about what just occurred." The *rosh yeshivah* nodded in a manner that signified he was actually waiting to hear the anticipated question. "I don't understand. A woman called the *rosh yeshivah* about a *shalom bayis* problem, but it seems that because the *rosh yeshivah* took the call, the *rebbetzin* may have become upset. Didn't this create the danger of a *shalom bayis* problem arising here?"

"There was no danger," answered the *rosh yeshivah*. "You see, over there, two people were upset, and here, perhaps there was one."

The *bachur* grasped that there was never a chance for the situation to get out of hand, and assumed that after a few moments the *rebbetzin* would accept her husband's judgment and all would be well.

We don't really know whether the *rebbetzin* was upset. And we are not at all clear about what it was like for the *rosh yeshivah* to handle his wife's understandable need to be protective while simultaneously attending to the call of a woman trying to save her marriage. But it was clear from the *rosh yeshivah's* answer that even in the face of pressure and tension, he was secure. He never wavered for a moment in his ability to maintain his sense of perspective and *menuchas hanefesh*. And once he was clear about his own sense of balance, the *shalom bayis* in his home was never at risk.

Yet, how did he know that throughout everything that was occurring he was truly caring about his wife and not simply driven to answer another call from a "woman in distress"? How many times does a husband say to his wife, "Please, dear, don't you understand that you have to back off? This call is very important." To this husband, his request that his wife accept his judgment on blind faith — that his decision is unquestion-able — seems very compelling and reasonable. But the wife who "has had it with his always putting her and the family second" may very well feel hurt and resentful. She may do her best to hold in her negative feelings, while quietly simmering inside. Her husband's request may even trigger the thought in her mind that "everybody who calls is important around here — except me."

There is an essential difference between the husband experi-encing *pizur hanefesh* or *menuchas hanefesh*. The one living with *pizur hanefesh*, as we will explore later, answers the phone out of a compulsive need to be busy and distracted. My own acquaintance with the *rosh yeshivah* in question and his *middos* gave me a clear sense that he was not shutting himself off from his wife's sense of concern, nor acting out of distraction. Rather, his motivation emerged from an understanding of the need of the moment, rather than a negation of his wife. It was his sense of clarity about all that was sacred to him that enabled him to feel secure enough to know that he would neither say nor do anything that would in any way hurt his wife or create a state of tension and conflict between them. Like someone holding a delicate jewel who does everything possible to protect it from theft, breakage or accident — so did the *rosh yeshivah* value his relationship with his wife. This clarity about their bond enabled him to trust that responding to the need of the moment would not end up causing a conflict, with a resultant loss of *shalom bayis.*

◈ Defining *Menuchas Hanefesh*

I have referred to the concept of *menuchas hanefesh* many times, but have yet to provide a clear and workable definition. For many of us, the concept of *menuchas hanefesh* conjures up visions of relaxation and being "chilled out." However, *Chazal's* definition of *menuchas hanefesh* involves our learning to coordinate all the powers that Hashem has granted us toward achieving our life's mission. For *Chazal,* the concept relates more to an ability to maintain a sense of focus, clarity and meaning that, in turn, produces the healthy and positive state of mind with which Hashem intended us to experience life. It is awareness that regardless of life's challenges, we are able to maintain a quality of consciousness that continuously addresses life's deeper and eternal priorities. Therefore, concepts such as being *dan l'chaf z'chus* (judging others favorably) or *hakaras hatov* (feeling gratitude) are states associated with *menuchas hanefesh,* because they enable us to see life closer to Hashem's perspective.

However, the ability to maintain our *menuchas hanefesh* does not come naturally. It must be continuously strengthened. Its acquisition can even be compared to developing a muscle. This awareness, which *Chazal* calls *rikuz* (concentration on a goal), is continuously strengthened to be on target and focused.

Consider this brief vignette that occurred almost a century ago:

> A commandant from the Bolshevik regime walked confidently and boldly into the *bais midrash* of the yeshivah in Kelm, fully expecting to be accorded the overt gestures of honor and respect due a representative of the revolutionary government. However, to his annoyance and anger, his entrance into the Kelm *bais midrash* caused not a stir. Not a single head was raised; no one even noticed him.
>
> With his pride sorely wounded, the commandant approached the *talmidim*, demanding to know the meaning of the disrespect shown a representative of the ruling government. The response was clear and reassuring. He was told, "This is certainly not a sign of disrespect. You see, here in our Talmudic academy, our students are taught the value of focusing only on what they are studying at that moment in time. Everything else is a distraction. They are taught that one never looks up from the Talmudic tract during the study session for any reason, not even for a moment. You were not noticed because we have trained our students not to see anything but the folio in front of them."
>
> Little did the commandant realize that he was being taught the value of achieving *menuchas hanefesh*.

◇ The Vilna Gaon's Definition of *Menuchas Hanefesh*

An even clearer idea of the centrality of *menuchas hanefesh* in Torah study and personal development is derived from Rav Eliyahu Dessler, *zt"l* — a student of the *Alter* of Kelm, *zt"l* — who shared how the Vilna Gaon described the focus required in Torah study to achieve *menuchas hanefesh*. Rav Dessler said that the Gaon made three suggestions to cultivate this quality of *menuchas hanefesh*. First, a student should imagine that the page or *daf* of the Torah he is presently studying is the only page or *daf* in existence; there is none that precedes or follows it. Second, he should realize that he is the only individual in the world who has been given the Divine responsibility to master this piece of Torah. Third and last, this is the only opportunity he will ever have to grasp it. Either he will master it now or the opportunity will be lost forever.

This is how the Vilna Gaon describes achieving the focus required for *menuchas hanefesh*. There are no distractions of the past, no worries about the future. There is only this very moment that carries echoes of eternity. The acquisition of *menuchas hanefesh* is acquiring the art of "living in the moment." As an *adam gadol* once told me, this is the essence of the prayer that we say in Maariv in the *tefillah* of *Hashkiveinu*: "*V'haseir satan mi'lefaneinu u'me'achareinu* — May Hashem remove the *satan* from in front of us and from behind us." We are praying for *menuchas hanefesh* and the ability to remain focused in the moment.

This concept of "living in the moment" defines a state of being wherein all is focused on being in the present as the key to achieving the goal at hand. We can be distracted neither by the past nor the future as we apply ourselves to the task of fulfilling our lives. There can only be the here and now. Worries and anxieties about the past and future play no role in the development of our ability to be focused and in the moment. They are actually impediments and distractions. Perhaps this is what *Chazal* mean when we are told "*dai tzarah beshayta* — worry about the problem later, if and when it arises, not now."

◊ *Menuchas Hanefesh* **as the Mayor**

The *sefer Sifsei Chaim*, by Rabbi Chaim Friedlander, *zt"l*, which has been my primary source for many of the concepts in this work, describes the development of *menuchas hanefesh* as similar to serving as the mayor of a city with its many commissioners and services. Each department head has his own domain, sphere of influence and budget. Each has his own operation to run successfully in order to keep the municipality capable of meeting the needs of the residents. The role of the mayor is to ensure that each executive does what he is supposed to do, without infringing on the boundaries or power of others. When all are working together under the guidance of the mayor, then the city is functioning well.

This is the same for a corporation, a government or any organized entity where all parts of the entity have to work together to achieve maximum results. And it is certainly true regarding the concept of *menuchas hanefesh*. For *nefesh* is a life force that Hashem places within each of us that enables us to fulfill our life tasks as Jews in this world. It has many dimensions, powers and drives, all of which are intended to work together to achieve life's most precious goals in the service of Hashem. When all of these forces place themselves under the direction of a unifying force — our Torah-inspired vision and aspirations — then all aspects of our cognitive, emotional and biological selves work together to achieve the ultimate purpose for which Hashem gave us life. The harmonization of these powers, guided by a clear and lofty focus, is what *Chazal* calls *menuchas hanefesh*. It is the synergistic blending of emotional, physical and spiritual forces within us that gives us a sense of profound security and well-being, all of which contribute toward achieving the goal at hand.

Menuchas hanefesh means that we have the perspective to handle the challenges that confront us, as depicted in the following scenario:

> You are holding a winning multimillion-dollar lottery
> ticket, but you could only cash it in if you travel cross-

country in a hurry. However, that would mean taking a very uncomfortable seat on a very uncomfortable plane to get from California to New York in time to cash in the ticket. During the trip, you may look a bit foolish to the other passengers, but your sense of security while on that journey would be very intact. It may very well be that on another occasion you would be bothered by the color of a drape, or a slightly recognizable odor that you didn't care for. But in this situation, you are very capable of dealing with great physical and even emotional discomfort to get to your desired goal to cash in this ticket. Through *menuchas hanefesh*, you learn to keep distractions at bay while pursuing your goal.

◇ A Lifetime of Desserts

Sometimes our *menuchas hanefesh* can help quiet the discomfort for much longer than just a few hours. It may even last over a period of decades.

A number of years ago, while I was waiting to *daven* Maariv in Yeshiva Derech Ayson, also known as the Yeshiva of Far Rockaway, a *rav* from Israel, who was recognized by one of the *rebbeim* as a well-known *talmid* of Rav Schach, *zt"l*, arrived early and sat to learn. He was scheduled to leave right after Maariv for nearby JFK and his return flight to Israel. In appreciation of the significance of his presence, the *rav* was asked if he would speak for a few minutes before Maariv. Reluctantly, he agreed. As this was the week preceding *Shabbos Parashas Vayechi*, when the last *parashah* of *Sefer Beraishis* would be read, the *rav* chose to speak about the *sefer* that was about to be completed.

Sefer Beraishis, he explained, is also known as *Sefer Hamiddos*, because of the *middos* of the *Avos* and *Imahos* that are mentioned throughout each *parashah*. With the closing of this *sefer*, he felt it was important for us to be left with the essence of what Hashem wants us to understand about the truly deeper strength of the *Avos* and *Imahos* that are described throughout *Beraishis*.

In his discussion of *middos,* he told a story of a *rosh yeshivah* he was close to, but whose name he did not reveal.

> While enjoying a Shabbos *seudah* at the home of this *rosh yeshivah,* a young *bachur* sat through the meal and ate the rather bland food of the *rosh yeshivah* and the *rebbetzin.* Although the food was somewhat tasteless, they spoke in Torah, and the young man appreciated the opportunity to experience every moment in the presence of this great man and his wife.
>
> At the end of the meal, the *rebbetzin* served stewed fruits, also known as "compote." The dessert promised to be a positive finish to a rather plain menu, so, with the expectation of ending the meal on a tastier note, the young guest took a heaping spoonful of the dessert. However, to the *bachur,* the fruits tasted intolerably sour and nearly inedible. He had to force himself to swallow them and make sure that he suppressed his instinct to vomit.
>
> As soon as the *rebbetzin* left the room, the *rosh yeshivah* gently took the bowl of compote and pulled it over to him. As he quickly swept the bowl away from the *bachur,* the *rosh yeshivah* said in a whisper, "I know. The compote can be a little difficult to eat. Let me finish it for you so the *rebbetzin* doesn't feel slighted. You see, I've been eating it this way for almost fifty years."

For the *rav,* this mundane story about cooked fruits portrayed the essence of the *middos* he was attempting to convey. For fifty years, a man whose greatness was known to the world of Torah had managed never once to complain about his wife's compote, even though he would have preferred it another way. Shabbos after Shabbos, there was never the slightest hint or gesture that he was displeased with her dessert.

What enables a man of great personal wisdom and profound depth and faith to be so vigilant over his wife's sense of dignity and self-esteem, even to the point of putting his own sense of taste second to her self-esteem? Some may even call him foolish for not letting her know. I can just hear them offering the well-known advice that is so rampant among marital counselors, "Why not be honest with her?"

We can say he was patient, self-denying, humble, self-effacing, or any number of descriptions that point toward his consideration for her dignity and self-respect. However, the one description that encompasses his ability to literally swallow her dessert unflinchingly for half a century while being able to subdue his need for a sweet dessert was the strength of *menuchas hanefesh*. And if we survey in our minds the countless stories of heroism on a giant scale such as the behavior of the Bluzhever Rebbe, *zt"l*, in the Nazi death camps, the fearlessness of the Brisker Rav, *zt"l*, walking through enemy lines, the gentleness of Rav Moshe Feinstein, *zt"l*, the courage and determination of Rav Aharon Kotler, *zt"l*, and countless other individuals who have come to represent how mortals can acquire Hashem's strengths and *middos* in this world, we will always discover the acquisition of *menuchas hanefesh* at the center.

◇ Acquiring *Menuchas Hanefesh*

The acquisition of *menuchas hanefesh* is a prerequisite for *avodas Hashem* and therefore cannot be the sole domain of *gedolim*. Consider the *tefillah* for Shabbos Minchah and you will become aware of how *menuchah* is at the heart of the *ruach* of Shabbos. The word *menuchah* is mentioned no less than ten times in a single *berachah* in the *Shemoneh Esrei* for Minchah. And along with each mention of *menuchah*, there are a total of nine separate descriptions of *menuchah*. If the Eskimos have multiple words to describe snow because of its centrality in their lives, then consider how significant the experience of *menuchah* is to Shabbos and the Torah experience of self. Later in this book, we will take a closer look at the inherent connection between *menuchas hanefesh* and Shabbos.

Menuchas hanefesh is not achieved through a passive process. While Hashem endows us with a *neshamah* that guides us when we are in a state of *menuchas hanefesh*, its acquisition and integration into our moment-to-moment experience of life is only the result of a determined and focused effort that permeates our existence. There are times when we discover ourselves feeling this sense of completeness and mastery. The challenge is how to be aware of its absence when we are not in this state. Once we are aware of its absence, we need to understand how we can access this healthier state of mind and return to a personal experience of self that brings us closer to how Hashem intended us to experience life and those around us.

In summary, our challenge is to know when we are experiencing it, when we are not, and how to return to it. We may feel very comfortable one moment with ourselves and others, and the very next moment we are feeling critical and hurt. The question is how to organize our lives so that we always have a portal that gives us access to this dimension of ourselves where the gift of life and *shalom bayis* truly lies.

◇ Returning to the Yerushalayim Within Us

This brings to mind a moving and memorable short story I read many years ago by the Nobel Prize laureate S.Y. Agnon. He writes of a young shepherd boy tending his father's sheep in the Carpathian Mountains. As he grows up, he hears his father's tales of the wondrous city of Yerushalayim where the *Bais Hamkidash* once stood and where the *kedushah* of Hashem's *Shechinah* still hovers. He dreams of reaching this Promised Land.

One day, a small lamb runs off into a cave. He runs after the lamb, which eludes him as it scampers through the labyrinthine trails in the cave. Finally, after a long and exhausting chase, the lamb leads him to an opening in the cave. He emerges to find the golden city of Yerushalayim. He cannot believe his eyes. He grabs the lamb and runs back into the cave to find his way back to where he began, to the grazing pastures of the mountainside. Breathless, he races home to inform his father that he has discovered the golden city of Yerushalayim. He grabs his father's hand and pulls him to the pasture and into the cave. However, when he enters the cave, sadly, he cannot retrace his steps. He knows it's there. He smelled its pine-scented air, saw its beauty and experienced its holiness. If only he would have left a trail to follow! Now he cannot find his way back.

The story is a metaphor for the Yerushalayim within us. Hashem places the golden beauty of Yerushalayim within us when we are brought into this world. It is an experience of life that enables us to feel whole, deep and secure within ourselves, and close to Hashem and all those we care for. It never leaves us. It's always there. We experience it when we are with people we love, when we are standing at the *Kosel* and when we are enjoying Shabbos *zemiros*, the joy of *yamim tovim* and the *smachos* that fill our lives. And even when we don't experience this elevated dimension of our lives, it never leaves us. It's always waiting to be rediscovered beneath the surface of our consciousness. And it's there even in our unstable moments. It's waiting for us to find our way back through the cave. But we need to leave signs along the trail, to drop pebbles and markers that remind us of the circuitous path we need to follow to retrace our steps to the *menuchas hanefesh* that Hashem has provided for us as a gift of life.

◇ The Portrait of Rav Chatzkel, *zt"l*

In our true selves that Hashem has placed within us, the sense of *menuchas hanefesh* brings us closer to Hashem, ourselves and those to whom we dedicate ourselves, such as our spouses and children. While the experience of *pizur hanefesh* and fragmentation pulls us away from Hashem, our deeper selves and those we long and need to be close to, *menuchas hanefesh* allows us to experience a sense of security, trust, humility and *hakaras hatov*. We are aware of life's many miracles. In this state, we understand the meaning and experience of human love and closeness to others. In it, we can study Torah, think clearly, make wise decisions and participate in every phase of life that is uniquely related to Hashem's world.

It is crucial to understand that *menuchas hanefesh* is not a state that is dependent on our physical, financial or social conditions. I remember so clearly visiting my close friend and *chavrusa* who was lying helpless in a hospital bed during the final stages of a long and torturous illness. It was clear that recovery was no longer within the realm of any natural process. Although he was wracked by unspeakable pain and realized that the end was near, none of this affected his ability to find meaning in every moment. There he lay, facing a portrait of his late *rosh yeshivah*, Rav Chatzkel Levenstein, *zt"l*, the former *mashgiach* of Ponovezh, whose *talmid* he had been more than forty years ago. He gazed at the picture and said, "He taught me to be prepared for all that I am experiencing." As he spoke to me, I realized that despite his condition and pain, he was in a state of *menuchas hanefesh* that was the result of a life lived — and still being lived — to its fullest.

Gratefully, the majority of us are not faced with such a great test of faith. Yet the need to acquire *menuchas hanefesh* is even more significant for the well-being of our lives and those we care for. Our focus is to use this state to achieve a fulfilling marriage and the fullness of life. This is where *menuchas hanefesh* plays its most important role.

◇ The Power of *Pizur Hanefesh*

Pizur hanefesh, on the other side of our spiritual universe, is characterized by emotional states of mind that could be described as confused, insecure, fragmented and impulsive — states of experience that contribute to marital discord, divorce and emotional imbalance.

The word *pizur* means to be spread out, scattered and unfocused. There is an aphorism that a ship without a port is always in a storm. This is why *pizur hanefesh* is usually accompanied by a sense of internal chaos. The world we live in today invites *pizur hanefesh* through its constant bombardment of distractions that invade our lives on a multitude of levels. It is a world that thrives economically and culturally on promoting *pizur hanefesh,* filled with electronic gadgetry, an array of addictive distractions that we call leisure, and the incessant and empty online and text-based chatter. What characterizes *pizur hanefesh* is that once we are in these negative states of experience, we are essentially imprisoned and frequently rationalize our right to feel insecure, worried, unstable, fidgety and depressed, and to wallow in many other similar states of negative personal experience. Over time, we learn to cultivate *pizur hanefesh* as an acceptable — and even preferred — state of mind.

◇ A Husband in *Pizur*

I recently received a call from a husband who told me, "We've been married for over thirty years, and I've had it. I'm ready for a divorce. I don't think I've ever cared for my wife or ever will." Here is a man who has cultivated an experience of self that has been thoroughly paralyzed by *pizur hanefesh* for almost his entire adult life. It has become his definition of himself. He may *daven* every day, learn, give *tzedakah*, help others with *chessed* projects and perform many other acts that will make him and us think of him as a Torah Jew. However, little does he realize that he is entrapped in the quicksand of *pizur hanefesh*. He has come to define his sense of self through his anger, hurt, deprivation and isolation. He is very unaware that beneath all of these very troubling thoughts and feelings, which have been aimed at his wife, for whatever reason, there lies a very different experience of self that Hashem has implanted in him. Unfortunately, his *pizur hanefesh* has become his default experience by which he defines himself. And with this he justifies his troubled feelings. He has never stopped to consider the presence of a deeper, healthier and more innate sense that has been hidden within him for the thirty years of his marriage — just waiting to emerge.

◇ Quieting *Pizur* at the Eleventh Hour

I distinctly remember working with a young woman who was about to become a *kallah*.

> It was only a few hours before she was going to meet her soon-to-be *chassan* and accept the ring she had been waiting to receive for as long as she could remember. However, as she prepared to meet him, she felt paralyzed by a sense of fear welling up within her. She began to obsess over a certain physical feature. "I know it's a minor thing," she said, "but it has bothered me since the first date." As they came to know each other, this feature had faded into the background. However, at the very moment when he was ready to give her the ring, her thoughts began to run wild. Once again she began to focus on this feature and obsess over it. "How can I live with this for the rest of my life?"

On one hand, we can certainly say she was feeling anxiety, "commitment phobia" and emotional distress, and offer many other similar terms. But whatever we call it, she was in a state of *pizur hanefesh*, where every moment of personal closeness that had led both of them up to this moment was no longer accessible. She was trapped in a perception influenced by a state of emotional chaos and insecurity that was wiping out her "emotional hard drive." At that moment, she was truly feeling the need to walk away from the young man who, she had said many times over, was the "best person I have ever met to spend the rest of my life with." She was willing to accept this momentary fear as reality and permit it to determine the rest of her life. For a brief yet critical period of time, she was telling herself, "I have the right to find a *chassan* without this feature that I'm not comfortable with. I'm entitled to have it better. And I'm even ready to walk away and wait for the right one." In this state, every moment of sharing and closeness had suddenly fallen out of sight.

Hearing her anxiety, I understood that my role was to help her regain her sense of *menuchas hanefesh* and to remember some of the moments they shared that brought them to this stage of their relationship. After following my advice, she was able to pull herself back to a clearer perception of *menuchas hanefesh* and retake control over the ship of her life. I can share that last year, she, her husband and their first child stopped by on *Purim* with *mishloach manos*.

◇ The Nature of the Crossroads

One concept I taught this young woman was that we should never make the mistake of thinking that we *are* the negative state we are in. We have been created with the potential to experience the dimension of *menuchas hanefesh* or *pizur hanefesh* at any given moment. In effect, at each moment of our lives we stand at a crossroads of our selves, where we are given the option of thriving in one state of personal experience associated with *menuchas hanefesh*, or in another state of personal experience that entraps us in the quicksand of *pizur hanefesh*. As the *Alter* of Kelm describes our options, we are always standing at the crossroads between these two states of being. Our perception and personal experience offer many different ways for us to define our present concept of reality.

This potential for either state of being is always in front of us. It's similar to how Rabbi Naftali Tzvi Berlin, known through his writings as the Netziv, *zt"l*, understands the opening *pasuk* of *Re'eh*, where Hashem says, "See that I place in front of you today a blessing and a curse." The Netziv says that we should be able to see both potentials as clearly as two distinctive mountain peaks standing in front of our eyes. The *Alter* of Kelm describes how there exists a continuous flow of conflicting and contradictory thoughts and feelings that fill our minds and hearts. Even when we may be in a seemingly quiet state, our thoughts and feelings are never at rest. At any given moment, our continuous flow of ideas and emotions can move us either toward or away from *menuchas hanefesh*.

◇ The Eternal Struggle Between the Two States of Mind

This challenge is one that has accompanied every soul that has every walked the earth and accompanies us at each moment of our lives, dividing two extraordinarily different states of personal experience. One brings us closer to a sense of wholeness and an ever-present appreciation of Hashem's countless gifts of life, while the other force takes us away from the sense of wholeness and covers our awareness of Hashem's gifts of life. In one we are closer to *Echad* (One-ness), and the other pulls us into the abyss of *pizur hanefesh* — the troubling experience of fragmentation. One brings a sense of *shalom bayis* between husband and wife, while the other creates conflict and hurt.

◇ The Glass Is Always Half Full *and* Half Empty

Consider being offered a glass of water that is filled to the half-way mark. At one moment, you may feel that the offer is for a half-full glass, and that gives you a feeling of satisfaction and gratitude. However, the next moment your perception changes and you now see the glass as half empty. Along with your perception, your feelings about the offer change as well. There has been no change in the quantity, only in the way you view it.

The reality is that both potentials exist simultaneously within us. They reflect the two mountains or the two states of *pizur hanefesh* and *menuchas hanefesh*. We always have the capacity to see the glass from the two very different perspectives. We are never trapped in any negative state, as Hashem gives us the power of free will, or *bechirah*, to determine how we will view the contents of the glass. One perception contributes to a feeling of *menuchas hanefesh*, while the other perception leads to a very different experience of self.

It is crucial to understand that the choice is not simply, "If you want to, you have a right to see the glass as half empty." That would be comparing it to which of two ties will be a better color match for your new suit. In the case of color preference, either could do very well. However, when it comes to a sense of wholeness and satisfaction, the choice is at the very heart of existence. For in our lives, Hashem is constantly challenging us to choose between two forces within. One choice brings us closer to Him. The other choice creates dark emotions that separate us from Him.

◇ The Shifting Sands of Perception

Recently, a wife called me to discuss her marriage. She divulged that for twenty-five years, she has felt a sense of emotional impoverishment in her relationship with her husband.

She then revealed that she was seriously considering ending the marriage after the wedding of their daughter in a couple of months. Yet, just a few days later, she called me once again, sobbing in her awareness of what such a break would do to her children and even her husband, and wanting to know if there was anything I could suggest that might help them at this late stage in their lives.

Her marriage did not change in the few days between the calls. However, our perceptions are continuously changing. Our understanding changes as we stand at the crossroads between *menuchas hanefesh* and *pizur hanefesh* and we continuously process the myriad of possible ways we can experience reality. If we choose one direction, it will bring us closer to our true selves, to Hashem, and to those we care for. If we choose another direction, we will become more distant from all that is precious in our lives.

There is a crucial understanding that resides at the very heart of this dynamic: At every moment, Hashem gives us the choice and the ability to escape the quicksand of emotions and perceptions that seemingly imprison us. And at every moment, we can transform ourselves to move from one state and experience to another. It is crucial for us as *baalei emunah*, who deeply believe in reward and punishment, that we truly believe we have this choice and ability. For if we really were trapped and imprisoned, then there would be no free will, no responsibility and no freedom. We are all very aware that Hashem never deprives us of our freedom.

CHAPTER IV

The Five Dimensions of Our Experience of Life

To introduce the five dimensions of our experience of life, we first need a brief review of what we've covered until now.

The ability of a couple to achieve *shalom bayis* is not based on an external issue, but on how we, as individuals, permit these issues to affect our inner sense of balance and clarity. *Chazal* define this inner road to personal security and balance as *menuchas hanefesh*. With it, we can feel close, safe and loved. Without it, we are isolated, emotionally alone and in conflict.

In our own lives, many of us have known couples who have created marriages and families based on their ability to cultivate this inner state of *menuchas hanefesh*. When we are in their presence, we can sense this closeness and the harmonious way their lives are interwoven. This quality is never a function of financial security, family size, age, health or attractiveness. It emerges from the inner security that both husband and wife share internally and with each other.

However, this state is not exclusive to great people. Each of us has experienced this state within ourselves many times. It could surface as we sit comfortably around a table with our spouse and family, in the calmness and *menuchah* of Shabbos, or even when we are walking in the woods or along the shore. We can be at work, in *shul*, or sharing an intimate moment together. We can even experience it during a moment of crisis, when we call upon reserves of wisdom and clear-headedness to make the correct decision in a defining moment of truth. The common denominator of *menuchas hanefesh* is that whenever and wherever we experience it, the feeling is always accompanied by a sense of security, inner focus and clarity.

On the other side of our emotional and cognitive universe, we also experience times when we are in a more troubled and distressed state of mind, when we are unfocused, insecure and frequently confused. We call this state of mind *pizur hanefesh*. It makes no difference whether we are at work, at home, driving a Lexus, on vacation or elsewhere. When we are in a state of *pizur hanefesh*, we are always alienated and emotionally isolated from each other. We can observe its effects through expressed anger, hurt, conflicts and long periods of silence when we simmer in anger, insecurity, mutual avoidance and many other negative experiences in marriage. In short, *pizur hanefesh* always deprives us of *shalom bayis*.

This is the struggle within us all: between *menuchas hanefesh* and *pizur hanefesh* that continuously impacts on our *shalom bayis*. One moment, we are clear thinking, rational, caring and related, and the next moment we may feel impatient, angry and critical. In marriage, a couple can feel very close and understanding, and suddenly — seemingly without warning — an argument erupts. No one wanted it, yet here it is, filled with hurts and abrasiveness between two people who just a few moments ago may have felt close to each other. And suddenly, regardless of their deeper feelings for each other, they can feel there is not enough room in their own home for them as a couple.

◇ **Defining the Dimensions of *Menuchas Hanefesh* and *Pizur Hanefesh***

What are the criteria by which we define the presence of

menuchas hanefesh and *pizur hanefesh* in marriage? While it may be possible to objectively look at a couple from the outside and judge whether they are secure and close, I believe that most of us would find that the externals are not a reliable litmus test. It never really tells us what's going on inside. You can be sitting in a restaurant when a couple comes in. On the surface, they look prosperous, well groomed and courteous. From an external perspective, everything looks very much in place. However, as we look at the deeper dimension of their thoughts and feelings, the picture may be very different. One woman shared with me, "When we have Shabbos guests, my husband is full of things to say and good-heartedness. Yet, when we are alone, we just sit there in stony silence."

Therefore, our measuring device of how a couple truly feels about each other is through the five dimensions that determine whether we are in a state of *menuchas hanefesh* or *pizur hanefesh*. These five dimensions comprise the tools through which we are aware of our experience of life. They are:

1. Thoughts
2. Feelings and Moods
3. Physiology
4. Behavior
5. Emotional Closeness and Intimacy

Let's look at each of these five areas from the perspective of the scale that either moves us toward each other or away from each other. Then, after we take a closer look at these dimensions, we can begin to consider approaches and strategies that help us transform each of these areas of our personal experience of life in a manner that brings us closer to *menuchas hanefesh* and *shalom bayis.*

THOUGHTS

The first dimension of our experience of life is the power of thought. The miracle of thought is with us all the time. We define our reality by thought. The philosopher Descartes said, "I think, therefore I am." Thinking is as natural as breathing or the beating of our heart. But what *is* thought? Is it a physical entity? Does it have a size, a footprint, a molecular weight, a quantum of energy? Where does it come from as we are aware of its presence and influence on our consciousness? And where do our thoughts go after they leave our field of awareness?

Chazal tell us that the power of thought is the gift from Hashem that makes us unique in the entire Creation. In *Shemoneh Esrei* we say, "*Ata chonen le'adam daas* — Hashem bestows on us the power of thought, wisdom and insight." Even beyond this, it is the power of thought that is actually the closest experience we have as human beings to emulating Hashem. For thought is, in essence, spiritual in nature. It is beyond the tangible and concrete, yet it has the power to define our reality. Consider where it exists as we are aware of its presence, as it passes through our consciousness — at the very height of our physical selves, in our brains.

Thoughts are our primary tools for defining reality. When we have a thought, we have a tendency to accept it as if it is the very essence of the world we live in. And in our lives, we come to accept these thoughts as the reliable guide to define our reality. However, we also need to understand that, as the *Alter* of Kelm tells us, many thoughts are flowing through our minds all the time. Some will bring us closer to *menuchas hanefesh* and others will bring us closer to *pizur hanefesh*. We cannot blindly accept our thoughts as reliable and trustworthy.

◇ **Unwanted and Runaway Thoughts**

Our thoughts have a way of challenging us in our moment-to-moment experience of life. They simply invade our consciousness like a swarm of mosquitoes on a summer night. One client asked me what he could do when he is davening *Shemoneh Esrei* and his mind seems to be roaming all over the place.

The question is not a new one. We *daven* three times a day, and *Chazal* appreciate the difficulty of maintaining our focus. Since many of us are not able to go through all nineteen *berachos* with *kavanah* (full focus and intention), *Chazal* suggest that, as a minimum, we attempt to stay focused during the first *berachah*, which contains only forty-two words. This sounds easy enough. Yet, when many people attempt to get through these forty-two words while maintaining their focus on the simple meaning of the concepts, they are invariably pulled toward countless distractions. Their thoughts are flying all over the place without any association to the meaning of the words. Regardless of their determination at the outset, before they realize it they have finished the first *berachah*, and once again their minds have wandered far and wide.

But what is even more important for us to understand is that not only are the thoughts distracting us from the focus of our *tefillos*, but they actually cause us to experience a sense of distress and disappointment over another missed opportunity to speak clearly to Hashem. We may even want to define the struggle by saying that when we are focused on each word and its meaning and feel a sense of clarity and accomplishment, we are in a state of *menuchas hanefesh*. And when we are distracted, disappointed, unfocused and feeling disappointed with ourselves, we are in a state of *pizur hanefesh*.

The difference between marriage and davening is that in davening we all attempt to maintain our focus and are disappointed when we discover once again that somehow we "lost our way." However, in marriage, we may experience very troubled *pizur hanefesh* thoughts about our spouse, yet claim that the criticism is an "objective truth."

A husband walks into his house after a difficult and pressured day at work. Upon entering the house, he looks at his wife, quickly assesses the situation, and almost automatically thinks to himself, "She really is stressed out. I really don't want to be here. I should have stayed in the office for a few more hours."

At this moment, he has a number of thoughts about his wife. They may occur even without his desire to have them. However, once they have entered his mind, they are embedded as very powerful arbiters of reality. They have taken the high ground and will not relent so easily. Even though they are untested and unchallenged, they have become his truth. And it may very well be that his wife really is stressed and waiting to "pounce on him" when he walks in the door. Or he may be off the mark and misinterpreting her mood. His perception may have been triggered by something he took home from the office, or a letter he received from a lawyer threatening a suit against him. What is important is that he is accepting that his troubled thoughts are the only possible interpretation of his reality. Thus, they will determine his attitude and behavior toward her.

He may insist that there is no other way of reading this situation. In his mind, his perception is justified by his belief that he has no other choice but to think this way, even if it leads him to *pizur hanefesh*. His claim is simply, "You may not be happy with my thoughts, but there's no doubt that I'm reading her mood correctly." However, whether his thoughts are an accurate perception of her mood or are fueled by other influences on his life, he is insisting that he is correctly accepting being in his negative state of mind, almost as if it is both an indisputable reality and a responsibility. In a sense, he has abandoned his obligation to choose between *pizur hanefesh* and *menuchas hanefesh*. And if *shalom bayis* is to be maintained, he will need to somehow emerge from the entrapment of his negative thoughts, regardless of how accurate or inaccurate he believes they are.

When we fall into this pattern of believing that our negative thoughts are justified, we become locked into negative thinking that becomes the norm. In other words, it becomes the "wallpaper" of our thinking. Just as we no longer consciously look at the wallpaper in our homes — we just assume it's always been there — we no longer see our thoughts as negative. "He's just a stingy guy" or "There's no getting away from it, she's a nagging wife" are typical kinds of negative thoughts that we come to assume are objective reality.

◇ Stuck in a Thought

There is nothing in life that is static and unchanging, especially our thoughts. They are always in motion. And there are moments when we are actually aware of our changing thoughts.

A young couple, Mordechai and Shoshana, came to see me to explore why they were stuck on a dating treadmill going nowhere. After speaking to Mordechai alone, I understood that he was considering proposing; however, there was something about the way she spoke that "irked" him. He had forgotten about this during the earlier stages of their dating. Now that they were in a more serious stage of their relationship, the thought of this feature kept popping up in his head and wasn't going away. He saw it as a "sign" that they were not meant for each other.

> After a deeply meaningful dialogue relating to how each understood the needs of the other, he began to grasp that she had a keen insight and empathy for the many challenges he faced in his earlier life experience. No one had ever articulated this understanding quite so

well before. After the session, he confided in me that "as we were talking, I actually saw how my perception of her changed. Somehow I began to feel closer to her and all my fears seemed to melt away."

◇ Our Ever-Active Minds

To have a better understanding of our choices, we must also realize that the thoughts we are aware of are not the only ones traveling through our minds. The *Alter* of Kelm tells us that even when we are sitting quietly and under the impression that our thoughts are at rest, our minds are filled with many varied thoughts. A number of years ago, I came across a psychological study that claimed there are about seventy different possibilities that our mind sifts through before we make a decision about our reality. Even if the number is a fraction of this, our minds are similar to a fiber-optic cable, with many thoughts simultaneously running through it. This means that I may be walking in the street, while deciding whether to cross the road. My mind automatically sorts through countless possible options until I make my decision and act. Yet, all the while, I am unaware of most of the considerations that I have internally processed.

But whether we have seventy different thoughts to choose from or just a few, it is clear that the thought we are aware of at any given moment in time is not the only one that the mind is considering. Some of these thoughts have the potential to evoke a state of clarity and *menuchas hanefesh*, while others will lead us to confusion and *pizur hanefesh*. Both are always within us. Therefore, when *Chazal* tell us to accept each person "*beseiver panim yafos* — with a favorable countenance and a pleasant disposition," it makes sense that within us at this very moment, we have the potential, and therefore the choice, to view that person either positively or negatively. Hashem always gives each of us the choice as to which perspective we wish to embrace.

However, we need to be clear as to which perception brings us closer to Hashem, and which creates distance and alienation.

I may walk into a very lavish home filled with the most exclusive possessions and immediately focus on all that I see that I don't possess. I may see a couple walking together on a Shabbos afternoon and think to myself how they must be so happy. Seeing them causes me to idealize their lives and assume that my thoughts are true and then think of all the problems I may be having in my marriage. What may begin with an invitation into someone's home or a pleasant walk on Shabbos afternoon suddenly places me at the crossroads between experiencing thoughts that are associated with *pizur hanefesh*, or others that elevate me to a higher level of perception.

When Mordechai's perception of Shoshana changed, it was not a new thought or perception. It was actually a *menuchas hanefesh* thought that was waiting to emerge to the surface — and *menuchas hanefesh* thoughts always unite couples. However, when Mordechai was pulled toward focusing on the way she spoke that he found "irksome," this was a *pizur hanefesh* thought that determined his perception of her and separated them. Just a few moments later, he was aware of thoughts that were emerging from the other dimension of himself.

Therefore, when *Chazal* tell us to *"dan l'chaf z'chus* — judge someone favorably," it is not only for the other person that we are exercising this effort to reframe our perception and assumptions. Achieving this positive perception has an immediate effect on our own sense of *menuchas hanefesh*. We begin to appreciate the preciousness of a healthy and positive thought, which is the way Hashem intended our minds and hearts to function. The shift in perception has an immediate impact on our sense of self. It is not as if we pulled another thought out of the air. The *"dan l'chaf z'chus"* thought was there all the time and it emerges because that's how Hashem intended us to perceive others. Under *pizur hanefesh*, we either assume that the negative thought was the "truer" one, or we're aware that it's not — but can't seem to shake its iron claws.

In no way am I suggesting that the behavior of a spouse that leads to hurt and conflict be overlooked by viewing it from a rosy perspective that denies its impact. Each of us has an internal sense of wisdom that can determine how to successfully influence the behavior of our spouse. But this wisdom can only be accessed when we are in a state of *menuchas hanefesh*. *Pizur hanefesh* thoughts only lead to the exacerbation and deterioration of a relationship. They limit our options and paralyze creative thinking and approaches toward improving our relationships. For this reason, my goal is to help you become aware that you are not your thoughts.

◇ **Five Principles about Thoughts**

Here are a few important principles to summarize our discussion on thoughts:

1. Many thoughts flow through our minds at the same time. Some will cause us to feel secure, and others will cause us to feel insecure.

2. The positive thoughts enable us to experience *menuchas hanefesh*, and the negative thoughts create a state of *pizur hanefesh*.

3. There are many possible reasons why we are aware of our *pizur hanefesh* thoughts; many are unrelated to our present situation.

4. Hashem always gives us the ability to drop our negative thoughts and become aware of our positive ones.

5. When we learn to drop these negative thoughts, we set the stage for *shalom bayis*.

◇ **EXERCISE 1. Defining Your *Menuchas Hanefesh* and *Pizur Hanefesh* Thoughts**

We each carry within us thoughts that bring us closer to *shalom bayis* and *menuchas hanefesh* and thoughts that drive a wedge between us as couples. Take a few minutes to write down some of these thoughts in the space provided. I have included an initial example as a starter.

My *Menuchas Hanefesh* Thoughts

+ I think about the day our first child was born and it helps me appreciate what we share.

+ _____

  _____

  _____

+ _____

  _____

  _____

+ _____

  _____

  _____

+ _____

  _____

  _____

The Impact on My Marriage and *Shalom Bayis*

When I am experiencing these *menuchas hanefesh* thoughts, how does my perception of you change?

_____

_____

_____

_____

_____

_____

My *Pizur Hanefesh* Thoughts

* I keep thinking about how much money you spent on that outfit and I think of you as irresponsible.

* _____

 _____

* _____

 _____

 _____

* _____

 _____

 _____

* _____

 _____

 _____

The Impact on My Marriage and *Shalom Bayis*

When I am experiencing these *pizur hanefesh* thoughts, how does my perception of you change?

_____

_____

_____

FEELINGS AND MOODS

Our thoughts frequently trigger our feelings. However, our feelings are a more intense and persuasive way of defining our experience of self and the quality of our relationships. I can say "I feel love and joy" or I can say "I feel low, alone and sad," and at that moment I experience life in just this way. There is no other possibility for defining myself at this moment. Our moods are similar to feelings, but tend to last much longer. Our feelings and moods are the second dimension that defines where we stand on the *menuchas hanefesh* and *pizur hanefesh* spectrum, so central to the achievement of *shalom bayis*.

Feelings are at the heart of our *avodas Hashem* and define the quality of our spiritual connection to Hashem. Each day, we say *Shema Yisrael*, where we declare the *mitzvah* of *"v'ahavta"* — to love Hashem with all our soul and all our heart. *Ahavah* is love, which represents the quintessential positive human emotion that we experience from deep within. We are told by the Torah to cultivate this and many other feelings in our desire to feel close to Hashem. Just as these feelings define our spiritual state of being, they also define the quality of our marital bond. I frequently hear complaints such as, "I just don't have the right feelings in this relationship." On the other hand, I may hear, "I deeply care for my husband/wife/*chassan*/*kallah*." The principle is quite fundamental. Just as feelings connect us to — or, *chas v'shalom*, isolate us from — Hashem, they also determine whether we experience our marriage as fulfilling and meaningful or as empty and even unsafe.

◇ **Defining Our Feelings**

What are feelings? When thoughts become more intense, they trigger feelings. The difference between our thoughts and our feelings is this: Thoughts are clear statements we make to ourselves and experience as originating in our brains, while feelings tend to flow from every cell of our beings and are experienced as all-consuming. We know that a thought is taking place at the top of our heads. However, we cannot pinpoint any special place in our body where we experience feelings or emotions, unless they take on a physiological dimension. And because they are so enveloping, they can be experienced as powerful, and even overwhelming, to our sense of self.

In marriage, and in all our meaningful and important relationships, our range of feelings is vast. We can feel close and secure, or distant and insecure. We can feel angry, contented, jealous, sad, depleted, lonely, hurt, resentful or happy. The list can go on with countless emotions that define our self and our relationships.

Shalom bayis suffers when one or both spouses carry a feeling that is troubled or negative. I recently saw a couple who were married for almost twenty years. In the very first interview, the husband told me, "During the first week of our marriage, she hurt my feelings by telling me that she really didn't know whether she felt love for me. I was very hurt and never forgot what she said. After that, she never really told me anything that would make me feel more secure about our marriage."

This husband was expressing a feeling that has been hovering for two decades and has deprived them and their children of the benefits of *shalom bayis*. Although the couple managed to raise five children, their home has been rocky and emotionally fragile during all this time.

Earlier in this book, I mentioned a wife who experienced a tremor of fear as she entered her home. During the workshop, she described how she would return to an experience of hurt that had occurred almost a decade ago, when her husband screamed at her and she was overcome by an intense feeling of fear. I happened to see her husband at the program. He appeared to be a caring and sensitive man. However, throughout the years, she has continuously returned to this feeling that has left her feeling insecure. And up until the very day of the workshop, as she turned the doorknob of her front door, she would almost instinctively enter a state of *pizur hanefesh* without any apparent external cues or stimuli. The feelings were always lying just beneath the surface.

These are two examples of long-standing emotions that have nested into the consciousness of individuals. In my work with couples, I find that this is a very common phenomenon. I hear painful emotions in situations related to early childhood hurts and losses. It comes to the surface when spouses feel uncared for and abandoned, and especially when they are frightened over threats of anger.

◇ A Midnight Fear

These feelings can emerge without warning and are overpowering.

> Consider a young boy who goes to bed feeling safe and sound. Suddenly he awakens at midnight. He sees the closet door open and is seized by the fear that there is a monster in the closet. He cries until his father comes in. His father brings him a glass of water, reads him a story, quiets him down and then, when all is calm, may even offer to open the closet and show his son that there really is no monster there at all.
>
> If the child is relaxed enough, he will allow his father to cautiously approach the closet, shine a flashlight inside

and say, "There, now, you see, there is no mean monster in the closet." The child will breathe a great sigh of relief.

When this little boy believes there is a frightening and sinister power lurking behind the closet door, he does not believe it will ever go away. It is there forever. The reason is that the monster exists within his own inability to control his imagination and fears. This is a form of *pizur hanefesh* because one aspect of his self, his imagination, is uncontrolled; he doesn't have the ability to self-soothe himself back to safety and to sleep. His father can help him, and does. Once he is soothed and safe, he can look inside the closet. In reality, he is looking inside himself and saying, "I'm no longer afraid of the monster within me."

It is the same way with couples. When either one or both experience negative feelings — whether for a short period of time or even years, long after a negative and hurtful experience has occurred — there is a sense that these overwhelming feelings will never subside. Couples believe that their painful feelings and moods are an understandable reaction to their hurt and don't believe they have a choice.

If I should ask someone, "Why are you breathing?" the answer would be, "I need to breathe! What else can I do?" This response is the same as, "Of course I feel this way; how else should I possibly feel?" This is why many couples are convinced they have no choice but to hold on to negative feelings; they cannot forgive.

The truer representation of the problem of feelings and moods is that they follow patterns that have been learned over time. We can call them neural pathways, where the slightest stimulus can trigger a patterned reaction. It may be a word, a look, an association, pressure or anything else that sets off the response. This is why our feelings are frequently so illogical. One man told me that he can get a statement from his bank informing him that his 401k lost a few percentage points — a loss amounting to thousands of dollars — and he'll just shrug it off. However, if he should get a parking ticket for $50, he'll feel deeply upset and carry his negative feelings around for days.

We are just beginning to understand that feelings play a powerful and frequently illogical role in life and in marriage. When they emerge, we are literally overwhelmed and helpless to quiet their impact. They are an even greater measurement of our reality than thoughts.

Let's return to the little boy who feels scared. In the end, his father soothes him. But where did the feelings of fear go? We all know, of course, that there never was a monster in the closet. It was all in the imagination of the child. And when the father comes into the room and quiets him down, the boy is soothed and calmed. But where does the quiet within this little boy come from? Does it come from the father? The father cannot give him anything that is not already there, within his son.

There are two sources of his inner quiet that enable him to fall safely to sleep. The first is that he has been soothed many times in his life; the experience of being calmed down was always within the child, even when he was experiencing his fears. He needed his father's reassurance to access these feelings of safety and security. The second source of his inner strength is his *neshamah*, the true fount of all inner tranquility and safety. Even when he was frightened, he carried both feelings — of fear, and of being soothed — simultaneously within himself. The problem is that at the actual moment of fright, he has no access to the other, quieter, and more secure side of himself. It takes the father's love and wisdom to bring his son back to feeling like a secure and loved little boy.

This same principle applies equally to couples. Even while experiencing their most distressed state of conflict, their ability to feel trusting and safe is present on the inside. It is just that they have no way of accessing this state of self.

I recently sat with a couple that had been battling for fifteen years over countless marital and family issues. During the second session, I enabled them to communicate in a manner that touched the deeper core of each. Following the dialogue, when the husband asked his wife how she felt, her response was, "I can't believe you could make me feel like I was understood." But as with our little boy, the ability for her to feel understood, and his ability to understand, was always within their reach, even after fifteen years of ongoing conflict. My role was to unlock the strength that was always within.

Couples take their feelings very seriously, and for good reason. Emotions are the weathervane that determines the quality of our experience of self and our relationships. This is especially so in our society, in which we pay homage to the unquestionable authority and power of our emotions. In this society, all emotions are sacrosanct. This is why we so often hear, "I know it's right. I can just feel it in my gut." I recently heard an NPR broadcast about a woman who was committed to spending the rest of her life single. She proudly exclaimed, "I prefer to live alone. I can do exactly what I feel like doing. I eat what I feel like eating, watch the TV programs I feel like watching, walk when I feel like walking, do whatever I feel like, and I just love to live this way."

However, this worship of feelings also extends to undermining married life. During a session, a young wife, Eileen, told me, "I believe that I need to talk about my feelings with Eric, particularly the negative ones. You know, we all have to be honest about our feelings." It's true that Eric should know how Eileen feels. But when and how she expresses them may very well be the difference between a failed marriage and a saved one.

In our society, so dependent on the fulfillment of personal needs, the focus is frequently on being aware of and expressing *pizur hanefesh* emotions. These include feelings of anger, deprivation, resentment, insecurity, jealousy, fear, inferiority, hurt and countless other negative feelings and moods. We see the result of this focus when couples gravitate so easily toward creating a home environment saturated with these negative feelings. Often they simmer beneath the surface until the "perfect storm" of events sets them off.

When couples experience these negative emotions and moods, they tend to see each other as the source of the problem. Yet, when we take a closer look at these couples and their complaints, it's often clear that many of these negative feelings are rooted in other experiences, such as earlier life experiences, work pressures, the challenges of daily living and the countless ways we are confronted by the many trials of our lives. And regardless of their source, these same feelings, whether having occurred earlier or recently, are frequently experienced as being a result of their marital relationship.

I sat with a couple, Moshe and Rivky, as they discussed each other's family. The conversation was pleasant and clear. Suddenly I heard Rivky choke up. Her eyes began to tear, and from nowhere she blurted out, "You always need to talk about my brother and my family that way. You just can't stop being so critical." I was somewhat surprised. I didn't understand where her emotions were coming from. His statements about her family were seemingly accepting.

As I came to understand Rivky's feelings about her growing up in a dysfunctional family, it was clear that she was still highly sensitive and conflicted about her relationship to them. Moshe's comments touched the hornet's nest that was always stirring. It reminded me of a tow truck parked on the side of the highway with the driver listening in on the police band for an accident to occur so he can be the first truck on the spot. These feelings are waiting to be expressed. And when they do emerge, they pounce out of nowhere with a ferocity that surprises and shocks.

The deep challenge for couples is when these feelings overwhelm them as with the power of Niagara Falls. When a husband feels angry and says, "I have a right to be angry," or when a wife feels unloved and says, "He makes me feel like I don't matter in his life and I don't think I can ever care for him again," these powerful emotions feel like they actually describe an objective reality — like the little boy in the dark experiencing his fears. Neither the child nor the couple experiencing the power of their *pizur hanefesh* emotions is aware of the fuller palette of healthier emotions that are alive within them, just waiting patiently to emerge and give them a truer sense of their real choices in life.

This principle of the power of our feelings resonates within us as a people, as well, throughout our history. As I write this, it is *erev Shabbos Parashas Ki Sisa*, when we read the Torah portion related to the Golden Calf. The *midrash* on this event illustrates how feelings of fear and abandonment caused a trauma and a tragedy that has cast its shadow over all our generations. After Moshe *Rabbeinu* was on Har Sinai for forty days, the *satan* caused *Klal Yisrael* to witness an image in the heavens of Moshe *Rabbeinu*'s funeral procession. The entire nation was gripped by terrible fear, alone in a wilderness without a leader. The illusion evoked a feeling of loss and helplessness. This was the desired effect that the *satan* wished to create. It was these compelling feelings that directly led to the building of the Golden Calf. *Chazal* tell us that each tragedy we face as a people is related to this tragedy.

◇ Living With our Feelings and Moods

Each year on the Ninth of Av, we fast to commemorate the tears that *Am Yisrael* shed through the night after the return of the *meraglim* (spies) with the news that they were powerless to subdue the enemies that awaited them in the Promised Land. Once again, the fears and feelings of hopelessness and powerlessness were overwhelming enough to obliterate any awareness that Hashem has placed within us other feelings that connect us to Him and to our healthier selves. We all are painfully aware of the results, the succeeding events that have plagued our people each year at this time: the expulsion from Spain, and the outbreak of World War I, which led directly to World War II. Each of these tragic events, and many other occurrences, all happened on *Tishah b'Av* (the Ninth of Av). During all these events, both national and personal, we were unable to overcome the tsunami of our feelings, and we believed that there was no other choice but to succumb. Yet the message that the Torah continually gives us is that feelings may be a tool to help us define reality, but are never to be accepted as reality.

In marriage and in our nationhood, we are all mortal. Yet, there is a spark within each of us that exists beyond the realm of nature and mortality. And while we may experience powerful negative emotions, Hashem has gifted us all with a *neshamah* that enables us to place these emotions in perspective. The miracle of our ongoing existence as a people has always been dependent on being able to live in a state of personal experience that transcends the moment and enables us to maintain our bond to Hashem.

Today, marriages are suffering in their ability to sustain a state of *shalom bayis* because we have succumbed to the belief that our negative feelings are justified. I once told a husband who was complaining about his wife's critical nature, "You can line up a thousand men and all may agree with you that your wife is a critical person. However, your own perception of her in these negative terms that you have harbored for more than twenty years is more damaging to you than anything she can ever do to you. It entraps you and it entraps her. No one has a chance." My message to him was that our perception of reality should never place us in an emotional state of *pizur hanefesh*.

In marriage, in our personal lives and in our lives as a people, Hashem endows us with a *neshamah* that continuously strives to experience the true blessing and fullness of life. This fullness is achieved through cultivating feelings related to *menuchas hanefesh*, such as trust, joy, security, modesty, love and closeness. These and other experiences are the emotions that enable us to feel whole and complete. This is the only time we can feel close to Hashem, each other and our own innate and exalted selves.

◇ **EXERCISE 2: Assessing Your *Menuchas Hanefesh* and *Pizur Hanefesh* Feelings**

We each carry within ourselves feelings that bring us closer to *shalom bayis* and *menuchas hanefesh*, and feelings that destroy our marital harmony. Take a few minutes to write down some of these feelings in the space provided. I have included an initial example as a starter.

My *Menuchas Hanefesh* Feelings

+ There are times when I feel very grateful that I have you as my life partner.

+ _____

_____

_____

+ _____

_____

_____

+ _____

_____

_____

+ _____

_____

_____

The Impact on My Marriage and *Shalom Bayis*

When I am experiencing these *menuchas hanefesh* feelings, how does my perception of you change?

_____

_____

_____

_____

_____

_____

My *Pizur Hanefesh* Feelings

+ Sometimes I feel very frustrated by your inattentiveness to my needs.

+ _____

_____

_____

+ _____

_____

_____

+ _____

_____

_____

✦ _____

_____

_____

The Impact on My Marriage and *Shalom Bayis*

When I am experiencing these *pizur hanefesh* feelings, how does my perception of you change?

_____

_____

_____

_____

_____

_____

PHYSIOLOGY: *Our Physical Selves*

The third dimension of our experience of self that determines our position on the spectrum between *menuchas hanefesh* and *pizur hanefesh* is physiology, the way our experience of physical well-being is affected by our state of mind.

> Ben and Cindy had been married for three years and had a two-year-old son. They undertook a difficult challenge when they decided, for family and social reasons, to leave the small community in which they lived and move to New York. The combination of adjusting to life in the big city and having to deal with the conflicts of their respective families, who now lived nearby, created significant stress in their own marriage. They found themselves fighting and experiencing long periods of anger and resentment.

The results of their arguments were not only emotional but also physiological. Ben began to develop intense headaches, while Cindy felt increasingly lethargic and listless. Neither had had any previous symptoms in the past, and medical examinations could not define the source of Ben's headaches or Cindy's exhaustion.

As we began to unknot some of their complicated family and marital issues, the young couple began to understand how their symptoms were linked to the new stresses in their lives. Over time, along with acquiring the skills and wisdom to maintain balance and emotional support in their marriage, they both began to experience a diminishing of the physiological symptoms as well.

What contributed to Ben's headaches and Cindy's loss of vitality? To my understanding, the answer lies in that almost mystical area where self meets soul. It's almost as if we are looking over a broad ocean vista and see a distant mist over the waters, which is actually a rainstorm. However, it's impossible to discern where the ocean's water begins and the rainy atmosphere above it ends. From the distance, the two are indistinguishable.

In terms of our physical selves, Hashem has placed a delicate homeostatic mechanism within each of us, where our physical and emotional well-being are delicately balanced and mutually interdependent. This elegant and sensitive system maintains the stability of our physical functioning. It enables our body temperature to hover at around 98.6 degrees, our blood pressure at around 120/80, and our heart rate, breathing rate, blood sugar, digestion, excretion and countless other functions and indicators of our physical well-being to function optimally. From a distance, the human body seems to "operate by itself," with the uncanny ability to know exactly what is required to maintain healthy physical functioning. In contemporary language, we relate to these as our immune, respiratory, cardiovascular, digestive, nervous, glandular — and other — systems. They make up the ongoing miracle of our existence.

However, we understand these functions as being under the moment-to-moment *hashgachah pratis* (Divine supervision) of Hashem. Through this continuous caring, each of us is a personal recipient of the love and wisdom Hashem has placed in our *neshamah* and in our body. There is nothing accidental or automatic about our ability to function, from being able to move a limb — which we can do with intent and great accuracy — to our autonomic systems that function seemingly on their own. All are part of the miracle of Hashem's ongoing gift of life, lovingly implanted in each of us. When we are performing optimally, this wisdom within us sends its healing and nurturing powers to every part of our physical selves. We feel alive, we heal quickly, we are resilient and we have stamina, energy and a sense of vitality that makes life so special and precious.

◇ **Upsetting the Delicate Balance**

This balance can be upset by many forces. Some people get more depressed and lethargic in the winter months. Blood pressure can rise during an exciting sporting event. With aging and illness, we find that we require medications and other means to maintain the healthy range of our vital signs and functions. For Ben and Cindy, the conflicts unleashed in their marriage had upset this delicate balance in each of them and contributed to their sense of physical discomfort.

The dynamic is that when we are not functioning well emotionally, the list of aches, pains, weaknesses and other troubling symptoms grow exponentially longer. The Torah itself alludes to this in reference to our breathing. When *Am Yisrael* was in Mitzrayim enduring the hardships of slavery, the *Chumash* tells us that they were suffering from *kotzer ruach* (shortness of breath). Rashi explains that when an individual cannot feel free to be spiritually and emotionally expressive, it leads to the inability to take a deep and natural breath. So while Hashem has lovingly placed the power of vitality and healing in us all, the cardinal principle is that our bodies function in a healthy and healing manner when they are unimpeded. Otherwise they are thrown out of synchronization and harmony.

For example, you may have a paper cut. If you dress the wound before you go to bed at night and keep it protected, you will probably notice by the next morning a closing, and even a slight scabbing, of the area. This is a sign of the healing process that occurred during the night while you were resting. However, if you leave the small wound open and unprotected, chances are the healing process will be delayed. The wisdom of the healing process has not been lost. Your body still has the ability to heal the wound. However, in the presence of impediments, such as exposure to the cold or dirt, this healing process is neutralized and cannot perform properly.

In spite of the predominant evidence, many of us tend to view physiology as independent of our emotional and cognitive states. A close friend who is a physician shared with me that when he checks a patient's blood pressure, the initial measurement will frequently be higher than later ones. Physicians understand that the anxiety produced by measuring such an important indicator will frequently drive up the blood pressure, so they repeat the test. After a few minutes, when the patient has had a chance to calm down, the blood pressure will frequently return to its normal level.

Let us return to the continuum of our experience of self. Our thoughts flow into feelings as they intensify, and feelings become moods as they are prolonged. Physiology then flows from feelings and moods as our emotional imbalance triggers us to react physiologically.

When our thoughts, feelings and moods unbalance our

sense of physical well-being, the impact on *shalom bayis* can be very destabilizing. If a husband or wife feels that his or her health is being undermined, an accusatory finger will naturally be pointed in the direction of the conflict. I frequently hear comments that include: "You give me a headache." "You make me tense." "Because of you, my nerves are shot." "Sometimes I get so upset with you that my stomach is out for a week." "My blood pressure/blood sugar is sky-high because of this fighting." "We had an argument last week, and I was shaking like a leaf." "My heart was palpitating like a kid banging on a bongo drum. I thought I was having a heart attack." The list is inexhaustible.

What is important for us to understand is how physiology contributes to the strengthening or weakening of *shalom bayis*. The process is that *menuchas hanefesh* will enhance our physical sense of well-being, and *pizur hanefesh* will usually diminish our sense of physical comfort and our ability to tolerate discomfort. The closer our lives move toward *menuchas hanefesh* and *shalom bayis*, the healthier we will feel physically. This opens the door to create the kind of home environment and marital relationship where husband, wife and children experience the essence of well-being and security.

◇ EXERCISE 3: Assessing Your *Menuchas Hanefesh* and *Pizur Hanefesh* Physiology

Our body understands the language of our heart. The closer we are to *shalom bayis* and *menuchas hanefesh*, the better and healthier we feel. And the more we move toward *pizur hanefesh*, the greater our sense of physical discomfort and lack of well-being. Take a few minutes to reflect on those physical states that enhance *menuchas hanefesh* and those that create the opposite effect. I have included an initial example as a starter.

My *Menuchas Hanefesh* Physiology

There are times when I feel physically sound and good about myself and our marriage, like when:

- ✦ We take a walk on the beach and have a chance to talk.
- ✦ _____
  _____
  _____
- ✦ _____
  _____
  _____
- ✦ _____
  _____
  _____

The Impact on My Marriage and *Shalom Bayis*

When I am experiencing these *menuchas hanefesh* feelings, how does my perception of you change?

_____
_____
_____
_____
_____

My *Pizur Hanefesh* Physiology

Sometimes I feel physically low, like when:

- ✦ We have an argument.

+ _____
  _____
+ _____
  _____
+ _____
  _____

My Symptoms May Be:

+ An upset stomach
+ _____
  _____
+ _____
  _____
+ _____
  _____

The Impact on My Marriage and *Shalom Bayis*

When I am experiencing these symptoms of my *pizur hanefesh*
physiology, how does my relationship with you change?

_____

_____

_____

_____

_____

_____

BEHAVIOR

The fourth dimension of our experience of self is how our state of *menuchas hanefesh* or *pizur hanefesh* affects our behavior — the way we act. At one moment, we may be able to perform a great *chessed*, set aside our own self-interest and behave in a manner that enriches our own life and the lives of others. This form of inspired behavior is always a result of *menuchas hanefesh*. Then there are other times when our behavior is self-centered, uncaring and impulsive. This is the domain of *pizur hanefesh*.

◇ **An Ideal Setting for a Tragedy**

I received a call from David, a man in his late twenties, who told me that he needed to make an appointment to "save his marriage."

> David and Shana had been married for five years and had two children. When we met, they came across as a *frum*, affluent and well-groomed couple – the type upon whom others gaze with a sense of wonder about what it must be like to have beauty, charm, wealth, children, a lovely home and all the other accoutrements of the "good life." However, their presence in my office indicated that life was not as it appeared on the surface.
>
> As we spoke, their story unfolded. Both came from affluent families and had spent the first five years of their marriage dealing with the many areas of dissimilarity they discovered between them. And while differences led to arguments, the fights would die down after a few days. Recently, however, a conflict hit them that would not go away.
>
> It was a warm summer evening, and David and Shana had invited several couples over to celebrate David's twenty-sixth birthday. Shana had asked David not to serve

alcoholic beverages. However, David was insistent that nothing would happen—and it was his party, after all. "You always have to rain on my parade!" he griped. Shana watched as David made *l'chaim* after *l'chaim* with his invited guests, drinking only the best single malts available. The more he drank, the more erratic his behavior became.

An hour or two into the party, David had the brilliant idea to take the guys for a spin in his new SUV. Shana protested; David insisted. The guys all piled in. Within two streets of their home, David missed a turn and crashed the car into a tree. Were it not for the tree serving as a barrier, the car would have gone through the front window of a house. And while no one was hurt, Shana now realized that David's lifestyle was dangerous for everyone, including their marriage.

At first, David thought Shana would quiet down, but she was not accepting his calls. He realized that this time he had crossed the line. His behavior had clearly created a crisis in their marriage, one that had the power to overturn their lives. He was in over his head, and he needed guidance to patch things up. He received my name from a local rabbi and called me.

When they came in, I spent a few minutes alone with each spouse. Shana was very clear about her position. "I've had it with his cars and his SUVs, his endless hours at the office, his pampering himself, his Facebook friends, and especially his drinking. If he can't control himself, I can't go on."

Even in the larger society, there is no defense for the lethal combination of drinking and driving; that matter would need to be dealt with separately. However, at this moment of crisis in David and Shana's relationship, the more pressing issue was David's right to "be with the boys" and have a "good time" because it was his birthday.

From my perspective, David's behavior was an expression of his ongoing state of *pizur hanefesh*, a condition which has become accepted as the norm in our society. I believe the reason is that we now live in a world of birthday barbeques, performance cars, the ready availability of world-class single malts and lots of expendable income — and this is where *pizur hanefesh*, with all its distractions and impulsive behavior, thrives. These distractions divert us from focusing on our deeper inner life, which is necessary for achieving *menuchas hanefesh*. Instead, the Davids among us become addicted to a lifestyle that thrives on a continuous need for excitement and chaos that frequently accompanies *pizur hanefesh*. Serious problems arise when these feelings are equated with security.

When someone tells me "I need a smoke to relax," I understand that he is confusing the false sense of security that comes with an addiction such as cigarettes with a deeper sense of security. For example, I vividly remember witnessing the following scene on a subway platform many years ago.

> A young woman was in a panic because she could not find her child. She was running up and down the station calling his name. A police officer approached her and began alerting other officers about the missing child. Suddenly the woman said, "Officer I'm really scared and shook up. You don't mind if I have a smoke, do you?"
>
> She knew it was illegal to smoke on a subway platform. However, she felt the cigarette would give her a sense of security. How could the officer refuse such a request? He agreed and she lit up and took a long deep drag on her cigarette. As I observed her, I wondered to myself, "What kind of security is she getting now? She wants her child back. The cigarette makes her feel better but won't produce her child."
>
> The deeper security she was seeking was to achieve

some assurance that her child was safe. All she could give herself was the sensation of a column of smoke entering her lungs. Watching her nervously suck in the smoke was a pitiful sight. That's how all addictions fuel our illusions of security. Feeding an addiction calms the panic but never really relaxes. However, in *pizur hanefesh*, we never really understand what true relaxation and calmness is, so we accept satisfying the deadly addiction as the "real thing."

Therefore, when I am told that cigarettes "calm me down," I always remember that woman on the subway platform and tell the smoker that it's simply not true. It is well documented that they clog arteries and escalate tension and anxiety. Yet the dependency is so great that there is little awareness of the rising sense of inner tension. When this occurs, whether because of an addiction to cigarettes and other harmful substances or the "exciting lifestyle," there is very limited awareness that real security is only experienced within our truer and authentic selves. This only occurs when we can experience a calmer, deeper and more meaningful experience of self.

Let us consider another situation where a different young couple was experiencing a crisis in their marriage related to behavioral symptoms of the *pizur hanefesh* lifestyle:

> Mendy and Shari had been married for just a few months and were seriously considering divorce at this early stage of their marriage. When I first met them, Shari was dressed seductively in a tight-fitting outfit and stiletto-heeled, pointy-toed shoes. Mendy's look was more casual; he wore a stylish polo shirt and designer jeans. Both held on to their Blackberries throughout the interview, continuously checking for incoming calls and e-mails.
>
> Within a few minutes, the arguing erupted. Apparently Mendy objected to Shari's need to maintain contact with her old friends — including young men — through Facebook

and e-mails, and to her enjoyment of "clubbing." For her part, Shari took issue with Mendy's consuming interest in sports. At every possible moment, he was tuned in to the Yankees, Rangers, Knicks or Giants, to college football or basketball, or to any of countless other sports programs that ESPN and Dish Network had to offer. Shari claimed she was a sports widow, and Mendy accused Shari of being busy with everyone but him.

The interaction between the couple was angry and hurtful and quickly turned to accusations over parents, siblings, money and many other areas of their lives. What was very clear was that every inch of this couple's emotional life was consumed by behavior fueled by *pizur hanefesh.*

The reality is that Mendy and Shari's behavior and lifestyle could easily be accepted in our society as a valid form of "self expression." Each area of their personal preferences was the result of their being successfully targeted by the leisure industries of America. Their respective interests in clubbing, Facebook friends and the ESPN sports network were all in lockstep with a vast group of young people who are essentially cut off from life's deeper treasures of marital love, fulfillment in family life and the development of their spiritual dimension.

Their "self expression" was a form of imprisonment within the *frum* America success story. Externally they called out to the world to celebrate their empty expressions of happiness. Inside they suffered from the insecurities that drives all of Western pop culture.

As I sat with them during the initial session, my impression was that this couple was trapped behind enemy lines. They had come to adopt an imitation of life and marriage, saturated in *pizur hanefesh* behavior. All their interests continuously entrapped them in empty patterns of behavior and painful emotions that would eventually draw them further apart until they would eventually reach a level of mutual hurt and alienation that would result in separation, and divorce.

In a sense, their behavior flowed inevitably from their troubled thoughts, feelings and even physiology. The primary difference between behavior that is a consequence of *pizur hanefesh* and that which flows from *menuchas hanefesh* is very apparent. Behavior guided by *menuchas hanefesh* is always directed to the well-being of others. *Menuchas hanefesh* behavior is never "It's you or me." It emerges from a deeper and more secure experience of self. This is the state of mind that enables us to feel centered and intact. And when we experience our stable and integrated selves, our physiology is under control. Under these conditions, our behavior is always informed by the precious meaning and value of our relationships — and particularly marriage. This is why in a home where there is a greater sense of *shalom bayis*, there is always an abundance of thoughtful, caring behavior — the ability to share, physically help and enhance the lives of others. The couple that understands this direction of life will always pursue forms of behavior rooted in *menuchas hanefesh*, such as caring, kindness and *chessed*.

However, when behavior emerges from *pizur hanefesh* — a state in which thoughts, feelings and physiology are fragmented, and life is pulled in different directions — the stage is set for actions that instinctively and impulsively serve the limited needs of self, usually at a cost to others. In this form of behavior, we are driven compulsively to satisfy our needs, even at the most primitive and selfish levels.

⬦ Experiencing *Pizur Hanefesh* at a Wedding

I had a personal experience recently in our world of excess that helped me understand what it's like to have behavior determined by an "acceptable" form of *pizur hanefesh*.

I arrived at the wedding of a close friend's child. The lavish smorgasbord was in full array. Men with high chef's hats were proudly manning their carving tables, while ever sharpening their gleaming knives. Wannabe Samurai warriors were whizzing through their elaborate sushi creations. All the signs were there: What our culture has come to view as a wonderful wedding was about to unfold.

After quickly wishing *mazal tov* to the *chassan, kallah* and their parents, I selected a plate of veal covered with a very delicate sauce. As soon as I sampled the first mouthful, I knew this was the "real stuff." However, before I could take a second bite, my mind was distracted by what I was missing at the other food stations. There I was, standing with my plate of tender veal — yet I couldn't wait to finish it so I could sample whatever else caught my hungry eyes! Even as an old friend approached me, I remained distracted and kept looking around for the next chafing dish to attack. My impatience was palpable. I disappointed myself.

"I'm not enjoying my friend's company," I realized. "I'm not enjoying the veal, and I won't enjoy the next dish any more than this one. And I am certainly not fulfilling any *mitzvah* by being here."

Then it dawned on me. My behavior of running from one food station to the next was pure *pizur hanefesh*. Whereas I should have been more focused on the *mitzvah* of *simchas chassan* (enhancing the *chassan's* joy) or some other worthwhile activity, instead I felt like a kid running frantically through Toys 'R' Us with a hundred-dollar bill in his hand. Where does he run to next? What can he grab next? This realization helped me understand more deeply how *pizur hanefesh* has become so rampant in our generation.

A short time later, I was reminded of this wedding experience after I came across a Torah thought by Rav

Yerucham Levovitz, *zt"l*, who suggested that the only purpose for attending a wedding is to bring joy to the *chassan*
and *kallah*. I wondered what he would have said about my
urge to run from one chafing dish to the next.

Our challenge is that we live in a society that has created more
opportunities for distracted behavior than ever before. And
where it really gets problematic is when our *pizur hanefesh*
behavior embeds itself into the core of our *mitzvah* observance.

Recently, I was in *shul* next to a gentleman who was
davening *Shemoneh Esrei*, apparently quite devoutly.
When he finished, he took three steps back, followed by
a deep and very long bow. Curiously I peeked over to see
why his head was down for so long. Then I saw the object
of his true adulation. As he was ending the *tefillah*, he
was receiving and sending e-mails over his Blackberry!
I said to myself, "He is saying *oseh shalom bimromav* (a
prayer proclaiming that Hashem makes peace on high).
However, for this poor fool, there is no peace on high
or down here below—just a lot of distractedness and
insecurity."

At a moment of great closeness between him and Hashem,
this man was unable to control the urge to *daven* to his Blackberry. (Perhaps that's why it's also known as the "crackberry.")
He had incorporated his classic *pizur hanefesh* behavior into
his most intimate moments of davening to Hashem. In *pizur
hanefesh* behavior, there is no peace, just tension, distractedness
and insecurity. And for this fellow, the only pacifier that quiets
these down is his Blackberry.

I have also observed that the behavioral patterns that undermine *menuchas hanefesh* and *shalom bayis* are often related to
our incessant drive for acquisitions.

A young woman came to see me about her failing marriage. It troubled her very much that her husband was never home; he was always on the go and never had any time for her or the kids. Clearly she was tense and depressed. Along with these problems, she proceeded to list many other areas of his life that evidently indicated a young man out of control.

On one level, I empathized with her in her suffering and perhaps even abuse. Yet, on another level, I took note of her statements of personal success and the obvious signs of her extravagant lifestyle. She parked her gleaming luxury car — valued in the $100,000 range — outside, while she clutched her overpriced designer handbag close to her and spoke despairingly of her unnecessarily opulent lifestyle. All these symbols of comfort placed her in an enviable position when viewed from an external and superficial perspective. Yet no one would realize how she and her husband had become helpless prisoners of a lifestyle driven by *pizur hanefesh*.

I see this so frequently with couples whose lives are devoid of *shalom bayis*, yet they own well-appointed vacation homes, take cruises, spend large amounts on *Pesach* resorts and vacations, and insist on large luxury cars. For this group, the lack of *menuchas hanefesh* and *shalom bayis* is never compensated for by the quality or quantity of their possessions. However, it is difficult to break free of this pattern when we live in a culture that says, "I own, therefore I am."

◇ **A Plethora of *Pizur***

My own list of what I call *pizur hanefesh* behaviors in our society seems to grow daily. It includes unnecessary consumption, overeating and addictions that include substance abuse, cigarettes, gambling, work, Internet, media, pornography and the compulsive need for sex. Aside from these, there are interpersonal behaviors, such as anger, reckless driving, the use of foul language, compulsive habits and many other behavioral expressions of *pizur hanefesh*. All these behaviors are self-perpetuating because the interactive nature of our thoughts, feelings, physiology and behavior keeps us entrapped in inescapable repetition.

The irony is that *pizur hanefesh* behavior never really satisfies. *Pizur hanefesh* behavior is always directed toward "me," which heightens emotional isolation, alienation and insecurity. The more we behave this way, the emptier we feel; and the emptier we feel, the more we behave this way to compensate for the hollow feelings. It creates an empty black hole that just grows larger and larger. On the other side of the spectrum, *menuchas hanefesh* behavior is always directed toward the big picture, toward relationship growth, trust, caring and *shalom bayis*.

Probably the most destructive of all behaviors that emerge out of *pizur hanefesh* is behavior that is designed to seek attention from someone other than one's spouse. It seems as if this feeling of insecurity and imbalance can only be corrected by attracting the attention of someone of the opposite gender.

> One couple was trying to resolve the conflict created by the wife's jealousy over how the women in her husband's office were always hovering around him. The husband's response was, "That's right, they know how to give me the attention I deserve!" Little did he realize that his need for attention was driven by a deep sense of insecurity that would only lead him down the slippery slope of marital tragedy.

The level of overt religious commitment may have very little effect on the inappropriateness of this type of behavior.

> I sat in the conference room of a large financial equity firm waiting for a meeting to begin. The heads of the firm

are known throughout the world as generous supporters of worthy Torah causes and *chessed* initiatives. Sitting there, I understood that the money that flowed from this corporation was in a league far beyond any that I could fathom.

Suddenly I heard loud noises coming from the inner office. The noises increased in volume, and I began to recognize the sounds of rage punctuated by what may have been the angriest and most profane language I can ever recall hearing. The verbal sewage flowing from the office saturated every square inch of the vast organization. Obviously someone had "messed up" and was getting "dressed down."

But what became clear to me at that moment was that these sounds were not unusual in this environment. They had to have been a commonplace occurrence. This was a place where *pizur hanefesh* reigned supreme. I understood that this form of outburst was not simply the way these bastions of success and support "stay on top," but they were trapped in their own inability to control themselves. This environment reflected their ongoing state of *pizur hanefesh*. All this was occurring while they were seen as the financial savior of so many worthy Torah institutions.

Chazal point out that if we have a hundred dollars, we want two hundred. We are never really satisfied when it comes to acquisitions and fulfilling our needs. Perhaps that's what I was feeling when I had the urge to gather as much food as I possibly could at that wedding. When we consider the *"askanim"* who are so driven by their compelling need to make lots of money, they can even justify their dehumanizing rage. Neither the food nor the money leads to any deeper satisfaction. Behavior that is driven by spiritually empty compulsion never gives us deeper satisfaction.

When these forms of behavior rooted in insecurity and compulsion occur between a husband and wife, they inevitably destroy *shalom bayis*.

◇ **EXERCISE 4: Assessing Your *Menuchas Hanefesh* and *Pizur Hanefesh* Behavior**

There are times when we are inspired to behave in ways that are beneficial to our marriage, our family and even *Klal Yisrael*, even if it entails self-sacrifice. This behavior always flows from *menuchas hanefesh*. There are times when our behavior is not only self-centered, but even more so — uncaring about the well-being of others, even those who are important to us. This form of behavior flows from *pizur hanefesh*. Take a few minutes to write down some of these forms of your behavior in the space provided. I have included an initial example as a starter.

My *Menuchas Hanefesh* Behaviors

There are times when I am ready and able to demonstrate my caring for my spouse, such as when:

+ I call you just to stay in contact.

+ _____

_____

+ _____

_____

+ _____

_____

The Impact on My Marriage and *Shalom Bayis*

When I am acting in a manner that is rooted in my me*nuchas hanefesh* thoughts, how does our relationship change?

_____

_____

_____

_____

_____

My *Pizur Hanefesh* Behaviors

There are times when I behave in ways that demonstrate my inability to care for my spouse, such as when:

+ I tell myself it doesn't make a difference whether I call.

+ _____

_____

+ _____

_____

+ _____

_____

The Impact on My Marriage and *Shalom Bayis*

When I am acting in a manner that is rooted in my *pizur hanefesh* thoughts, how does our relationship change?

_____

_____

_____

_____

_____

EMOTIONAL CLOSENESS AND INTIMACY

The fifth and perhaps most important dimension in which *menuchas hanefesh* and *pizur hanefesh* impact on our experience of *shalom bayis* is our ability to experience love and caring for the special individual with whom we are sharing our life. This last dimension is focused on the ongoing comfort and closeness of our day-to-day marital relationship, and is a direct result of the previous four dimensions of thoughts, feelings and moods, physiology, and behavior. It is the combination of all these that enable us to achieve this shared state of *menuchas hanefesh*, which culminates in the experience of marital love and closeness.

◇ Love in Our World

A Google search of the word "love" brought up 1.5 billion entries; it was only exceeded by the word "life," which had 1.8 billion entries. Love is so central to marital life, yet how do we define this experience between husband and wife, and how does this emotion emerge within a marriage?

First, to clear a misconception, when I say "love" I am not referring to feelings of passion. Rather, I am more focused on the love of compassion. Passion is focused on an overwhelming emotional and physical experience of "me," where individual pleasure is the essence of what is shared. It may even be a necessary component in marriage. But it can also be shared and experienced by two strangers who have never before met and will never meet again.

◇ An Instant Romance

Many years ago, during the Vietnam War era, when hippies flocked to the Lower East Side where I lived, I walked into a store to purchase some candy. In the store was a young woman wearing a headband that signified her anti-war allegiance. A young man then walked in with similar "peacenik" symbols. They looked at each other, embraced, hugged and kissed passionately – and the young woman left.

> I turned to the young man, who was now alone with me in the store, and asked, "Your girlfriend?"
> "No," he answered. "I never met her before."

Passion can be shared by anyone. It is essentially a biological response, and it has come to define our infantile wishes for love. It rarely, if ever, contributes to marital stability and closeness.

Compassion is much closer to our definition of love. It is where "you" are at the center, and is the very core, strength and nucleus of a marriage. It grows out of *middos*, understanding, patience and a deep respect for the life and well-being of our marriage partner. It never causes hurt as a result of fulfilling our personal needs.

◇ Where Does Love Come From?

I had the opportunity to sit in the *sukkah* of Rav Yitzchak Berkowitz, *shlit"a*, in Yerushalayim, and discuss some of my questions about marital love and affection. One question I asked him was, "Where does the love between a *chassan* and *kallah*, or a husband and wife, come from? Do *Chazal* view it as innate, or does it emerge from the nature of the relationship?"

His answer was quite simple and direct. He told me, "Just look at the last of the *sheva berachos*. It reads, '*Asher bara sasson v'simchah* ([Hashem] creates joy and happiness)' and then continues to include '*ahavah* (love).'

"It's simple," he explained. "Hashem creates love and then gives it to the *chassan* and *kallah* as a gift."

I realized that for Rabbi Berkowitz, the answer was that the experience of love between a *chassan* and *kallah* is bestowed by Hashem in order to bring this couple even closer. It seems so logical when we understand that everything comes from Hashem. Yet this idea is so strange to many of us who were brought up on Hollywood and Broadway tales, in which love somehow just happens magically.

I remember, as a young boy, listening to the show tunes of Rodgers and Hammerstein. "Some enchanted evening, you may meet a stranger across a crowded room …." The song speaks of strangers "falling in love" at the very first moment they see each other. This "love at first sight" idea has corrupted our understanding of the meaning and experience of love. Today, the music and media portrayal of love is so much cruder, distorted and self-centered. Yet, so many couples I have met have internalized these definitions of love and insist it's their "right" to experience this feeling of love in their marriage. The difficulty is that none of these definitions appreciate that love is not a state of mind that we acquire. It's an experience that is a very precious gift from Hashem, and the result of deep emotional and spiritual maturity.

Love is at the heart of our lives as Torah Jews. We are commanded to love Hashem with all our heart and all our soul. In the morning davening, between the *berachos* of *Krias Shema* and the end of *Shemoneh Esrei*, the word *ahavah* is mentioned thirteen times. And it's most prominent and most concentrated in the *berachah* preceding *Krias Shema* and during the *Shema* itself.

I have already cited that the *Alter* of Kelm teaches that the foundation of our experience of love for Hashem emerges from the experience of love we absorbed at the bosom in our infant years. This primordial bond of love between mother and child serves as the foundation of all of our ability to give and receive love.

The cultivation of our ability to understand and appreciate love is so central to our personal development that Rabbi Elimelech Bar Shaul, *zt"l*, the former chief rabbi of Rechovot, describes it as the basis for the *mitzvah* of *shiluach hakan*. This is the *mitzvah* of chasing away the mother bird from her nest before taking the egg or infant bird in the nest. He explains that the mother bird will give her very life to protect her chicks, even against a towering and powerful enemy. At the moment when her offspring are endangered, her love for them knows no fear or limits. This is the power of love. Each of us needs to deeply respect the self-sacrifice of a bird protecting her young as nature's profound and touching demonstration of the commitment of love. When we attempt to capture a young bird or egg in front of its mother, we show callousness to this love that Hashem has placed in all of Creation and in each of us. When this most precious of all human bonds — that of mother and child — is not deeply respected, it can not be respected between man and wife.

We take this concept and incorporate it into our lives on a daily basis. Even as I put on my *tallis* in the morning, I recite how an eagle hovers over its nest, gently stirring and alighting onto the nest of its young in its loving and protective manner. This is how Hashem hovers over the People he loves, lovingly and gently. This is how a bird and a mother hover over their beloved offspring. And this is how Hashem wants us to care for those with whom we are sharing our lives. Once again, this is compassion, not passion. Love is delicate, soft, sweet and very protecting of those we love and care for.

Love begins at life's earliest moments and progresses until we can share and experience this emotion in marriage and in bearing and raising children. I have always been moved and fascinated by the Torah's description of how Yitzchak *Avinu* first meets his new bride, the young Matriarch-to-be Rivkah, and brings her into the tent of his late mother Sarah. Rivkah's presence consoles Yitzchak for the emptiness in his life that was occasioned by the painful loss of his mother. Once again, in his bride's presence, his life is filled by a woman whose *middos* and *kedushah* create an aura of beauty and kindness that envelops their home and lives. This is the Torah's description of the growing experience of human love.

It is the essence of human compassion and emerges when two people are deeply committed to the same inspiring vision of their lives, and when they fill the deep needs for caring, fulfillment and comfort within each other.

These are the conditions necessary for a *chassan* and *kallah* to be receptive to Hashem's gift of love. It can only be received when they are emotionally and spiritually suitable for this gift. This is when each has learned to cultivate a sense of inner peace and calmness, which we call *menuchas hanefesh*.

Love emerges when there are two distinct "selves" — a *chassan* and *kallah who* are emotionally and spiritually prepared to receive Hashem's gift of love. This self of each individual evolves and is nurtured through early years of loving parental care, or the care of others who have devoted themselves to our development. And as we mature and enter into young adulthood, we patiently wait to discover who the special individual will be to share our life as our *zivug* (life partner). This, then, is our opportunity to share experiences of deep closeness and delicate intimacy. As we grow together, we learn to appreciate that throughout this vast universe, Hashem has led us to the only individual destined to be our true life partner. Perhaps this is why *Chazal* say that forty days before birth there is a *bas kol* (heavenly voice) announcing the names of these destined life partners. We are open to Hashem's gift of love when we recognize that we have truly met our *basherte* and our deeper and truer selves can emerge. And the emergence of this self only occurs through *menuchas hanefesh* and *shalom bayis*.

However, when couples live in *pizur hanefesh*, two selves are too chaotic to draw closer together and feel safe within either physical or emotional proximity. The result is that they live in an ongoing state of tension and alienation, because their deeper selves need to be protected and hidden away. And there is no limit to the ways in which this fear and insecurity over closeness is expressed. Here are a few examples:

Avromie needs to control the way Chavie spends her money. Each month, he goes over her credit card bills and bank statement item by item, and expects an accounting for every dollar she spent.

Katie and Shimon have been married for over a decade. Although they have two children, Katie is fearful of almost all physical closeness and places extreme restrictions on Shimon's behavior during physical intimacy.

Yaakov and Malkie have been married for twenty years. Yaakov is a software developer and is obsessive about the house being clean and in order. While he is careful not to show his anger, he frequently simmers inside for long periods of time when his standard of cleanliness is not met. Malkie is aware of his silent anger and brooding and it makes her feel tense or hurt within.

Allen and Pearl have been married for ten years. Most of the time, Pearl, a lawyer, has felt that her marriage to Allen was a hasty decision. As she admitted to me, "We've been married for ten years, and sometimes I feel that marrying him was the biggest mistake of my life. I feel sad, hopeless and cheated out of a life." Allen senses her unhappiness and makes efforts to understand the source of Pearl's complaints, but has no idea what he can do to remedy her disappointment.

In each of these and countless other situations, we can point to a sense of anger, obsessive thinking, anxiety, fears, unrealistic expectations and many other clear causes for the marital hurt and emptiness. However, beyond all of these, there is a deeper dimension that needs to be understood and addressed.

None of these couples have the ability to experience closeness and love when they are together. They can love their parents, children, nieces, nephews, siblings and even friends and teachers. They can wish each other a *shanah tovah* and ask forgiveness from each other before Yom Kippur — and deeply mean it. They can feel *simchah* together at a *bris, bar* or *bas mitzvah,* or wedding, and cry together over a loss. All these opportunities to share and experience affection are certainly aspects of love. But when they are face-to-face, physically or emotionally, their selves are in hiding. They experience a sense of fear and anxiety over exposing their emotions and their vulnerabilities. They may care for each other but can no more sustain feelings of closeness and love for each other than they can hold their breath under water. This fear of closeness creates a vacuum in their home environment. What should be an atmosphere filled with gentle caring and concern about each other's well-being is filled instead with negative thoughts, feelings and behaviors. For this reason, out of nowhere, the slightest incident can trigger off a series of highly charged feelings and emotional exchanges that can have tragic consequences.

Therefore, this last dimension focuses very squarely on the level of closeness that we experience with our spouses, whether in the kitchen, in the bedroom, on a walk through a garden, or with our children. If we should stop for a moment and ask ourselves, "Can I feel close and caring at this moment, or do I feel distant and upset when we are together?" — the answer will determine whether our relationship of love and closeness is experienced in *pizur hanefesh* or *menuchas hanefesh.*

◇ **EXERCISE 5: Assessing Your Love and Closeness from the Perspective of *Menuchas Hanefesh* and *Pizur Hanefesh* Behavior**

At this stage, I suggest that you take a few minutes to write down in the space provided some of the thoughts and feelings that enable you to feel either love and closeness or isolation and conflict. I have included an initial example as a starter.

Thoughts and Feelings of Love and Closeness

+ There are times when I am really grateful that we are spending our lives together.

+ _____
  _____

+ _____
  _____

+ _____
  _____

+ _____
  _____

The Impact on My Marriage and *Shalom Bayis*

When I am aware of feelings that bring us together, how does our relationship change?

_____

_____

_____

_____

Thoughts and Feelings of Separation and Conflict

+ Sometimes I just feel that I made the wrong decision by deciding to marry you.

+ _____
  _____

+ _____

+ _____
  _____

  _____

+ _____
  _____

The Impact on My Marriage and *Shalom Bayis*

When I am tormented by thoughts and feelings that divide us, how does our relationship change?

_____

_____

_____

_____

_____

CHAPTER V
Transformations

◇ **The Miracle of Transformation and Change**

Transformations are about the ongoing miracles of human change and growth that Hashem has placed within the moment-to-moment experience of our lives. Within Torah life, each transformation represents an opportunity to redefine and deepen our relationship to Hashem and the world around us. Each *berachah*, *mitzvah* and *tefillah* throughout our day is an opportunity for growth and renewal. Every Shabbos, *chag*, Rosh Hashanah, Yom Kippur and other special days of our calendar year — all represent spiritual environments for transformation. The transformations of this program are rooted in these same principles of growing and changing. The difference is that our focus is dedicated to learning to transcend states of *pizur hanefesh* to *menuchas hanefesh*, and from marital hurt and divisiveness to *shalom bayis* and marital love.

Transformations mean that each of us carries the strength and ability to change in each of the five dimensions that comprise our experience of self. Regardless of how troubled our thoughts, feelings, physiology or behavior are, or how great our sense of distance from our life partner, Hashem never deprives us of the ability to transform these negative experiences of *pizur hanefesh* into a sense of balance and well-being that is inherent within a *menuchas hanefesh* state of mind.

You may ask: If our lives are always engaged in an ongoing challenge of transformation — from states of anger to inner peace, frustration to acceptance, depression to joy, destructive behavior to *chessed* — how do these states of mind change? Where does one state come from and the other one go? The answer is that *menuchas hanefesh* is a naturally inspired awareness of a deeper and truer self that is always within us. It is inherent in our spiritual design. Once it emerges, our state of *pizur hanefesh* recedes, no longer creating insecurity and helplessness.

◇ The Fox and the Wolf: A Fable about Transformation

The *gemara* in *Avodah Zarah* relates a fable, which I took the liberty to modify for the purpose of my work with couples. It gives us an insight into how *Chazal* understand our ability to transform ourselves from one state to another.

> A tired and thirsty fox searched the forest for water and finally came across a well. He looked down into the bottom of the well and his heart jumped with excitement. There, at the well's bottom, sat a pail of clear, cold water to slake his thirst. At the top of the well was an empty pail. When he would lower the empty pail, it would bring the water-filled pail to the surface.
>
> When the fox attempted to lower the empty pail that would bring up the full one, he discovered he had no strength. So he circled the well for hours, looking for a solution that would save his life.
>
> Time passed and the sun set, giving way to darkness. The moon rose, shining its beam of light right down the well and onto the surface of the water sitting in the pail. The effect of the moon's reflection in the water was mesmerizing.

Just as the fox saw the reflection of the shining moon on the water, a hungry wolf passed by. The wolf saw the fox standing by the well and was relieved. He had not eaten all day. This fox was going to be his dinner.

"Hello, fox," said the wolf. "I'm going to eat you."

The fox was weakened by thirst and was clearly no match for the wolf. He seemed destined to either die of thirst or be devoured by the wolf. However, just at that moment, the fox had a sudden insight. He realized that the wolf's arrival was really a very positive event.

"I understand, wolf," said the fox. "You must be hungry and I'm in no shape to fight you. But I want to tell you that if you eat me, you will never be the world's richest wolf."

"The world's richest wolf? What are you talking about?"

"Look down into the well," said the fox. "What do you see?"

"That's the biggest diamond I ever saw!" said the wolf.

"That's right," said the fox. "But if you eat me, I can't help you get it."

"But how am I going to get down there to retrieve it?" asked the wolf.

Suddenly the wolf had a great idea. "I know!" he exclaimed. "I'll jump into that empty pail, you'll lower me down, I'll get the diamond and you'll pull me up."

"That's brilliant!" said the fox.

And so that's what happened. The wolf jumped into the pail. The fox lowered the wolf down the well, and the wolf's weight was enough to send the full pail at the bottom up to the very top of the well. Now the fox's situation was very different. The cool, life-giving waters were in front of him, and the dangerous wolf was safely at the bottom of the well, never to bother him again.

Take a moment and consider the turning point in this fable. One minute it seemed that the fox was finished. He was thirsty, weak, and soon to be overpowered by a hungry wolf. His fate seemed sealed. But the next instant, he had an insight that changed everything. Suddenly he had an answer that freed him from his fate.

The fable is very clear in its message. Change can always occur, even when there seems to be no way out. Even more than this, the *Alter* of Kelm actually tells us that the answer is found in the very threat itself, a concept that we will also explore later. But for now, it is clear from this fable that the energy behind the solution is the wolf. When it comes to learning to transform our negative states of personal experience, Hashem has created us with the ability to always discover the right approach that elevates us from the emotional quagmire. And each time we discover that there is an answer to the problem, we come to deeply believe that we are never truly entrapped by our thoughts and feelings on an individual level, and certainly not on a marital level.

◇ **Transformation in Nature**

Before we venture into understanding what we can do to bring the gift of transformation into our lives on a moment-to-moment basis, it is crucial that we understand the meaning and significance of change and transformation in the world of nature. Within our natural surroundings, we observe how a caterpillar transforms itself within its cocoon and emerges as a butterfly, a snake sheds its skin, and the plant world is continuously reborn in the renewal of each spring. However, transformation in nature is different than it is within us. Transformation in the world of nature is always meticulously guided by the irrevocable laws Hashem has designed for it. The same crawler always creates a cocoon around itself and emerges some time later as a moth or a multicolored butterfly. Whatever variations exist are always coded into the genetic tapestry of a specific creature.

There is no awareness, no choice, no growth of self.

In contrast, human transformation is based on the ever-present struggle for a true and authentic self to emerge, one that is in deep harmony with Hashem and the world around us. We call this growth *bechirah chafshis* (free choice). It is a gift that Hashem places in each of us; it at the heart of all transformation and growth, and is never denied to us. At the heart of this approach is understanding the difference between the immutable rules that govern the world of nature and our world as individuals created *b'tzelem Elokim* (in Hashem's likeness). This is the essence of appreciating our potential for growth and change.

◇ The Snake and the Bird

Rav Avigdor Miller, *zt"l*, in discussing how many of us may at times feel trapped in feelings of anger, shares a story about a bird and a snake. I later came across a similar story in the *sefer Cheshbon Hanefesh*, which was written by Rabbi Mendel, *zt"l*, of Satanov, published by Rav Yisrael Salanter, *zt"l*, in 1845. However, I prefer to present the story as I heard it from Rav Miller, while adding my own embellishments.

> A zoologist was in the Amazon rain forest studying the behavior of a rare snake and a particular species of bird. It was widely know that this snake fed off the bird, but no one had ever really understood how a reptile that slithers along the jungle floor could subsist by eating a bird that makes its nest high above in the canopy of trees.
>
> One day, the zoologist spotted the snake making its way through the jungle and followed it, hoping to solve the mystery of how the snake reaches the bird. Suddenly the snake stopped dead in its path, raised its head and looked straight up. There, perhaps a hundred feet above, was one of these birds, sitting innocently and seemingly

protected from its predator and joining in the riot of song and sounds of the rainforest. From the perspective of the researcher, there was no way the snake could ever reach the bird. So he just waited patiently to observe the next moments.

The snake opened its jaws and extended its fangs toward the bird sitting comfortably and safely out of range. At first, the bird was oblivious. Then it caught sight of the menacing snake, with its fangs extended, and began staring at its predator. Within a few moments, the mesmerized bird had become motionless. The singing stopped, and soon the zoologist noticed the bird's first slight tremors. The trembling became more pronounced until the bird was shaking and shivering uncontrollably. Within a few moments, as if already dead, the helpless bird fell from its safe perch atop the jungle canopy and into the waiting jaws of the triumphant snake.

Rabbi Miller's message was very clear. Just as the bird had lost its ability to fly away from the snake and was trembling fearfully until it helplessly fell, we, too, become mesmerized by our own anger and lose our *bechirah*. After hearing Rav Miller describe this scene, I asked myself, "What if I cared about this bird? Perhaps it was my pet. Or perhaps I could speak the language of birds and, witnessing this macabre scene, felt the need to rescue this helpless prey from the waiting jaws of the snake. What would I say or do?" I realized that I would want to tell the bird, "Hey, bird, wake up! Don't you realize that the snake has no power over you? Don't you remember that you have wings and you can fly? They can carry you safely upwards toward the heavens. Don't you remember that Hashem gave you those wings, just as He gave the power to fly to every one of your ancestors since the very first days of Creation?"

Perhaps that bird would hear me and suddenly realize that

he did have this wonderful power of flight. And even as he hurtled down toward the waiting jaws of his fearsome predator, he would suddenly remember his ability to fly. He would shudder, snap out of his trance, spread his wings and pull out of his death dive just in time to save himself. Then he would triumphantly soar upward to life and freedom.

However, my image is all fantasy. The laws governing nature are very different and follow very precise, immutable rules. Although the bird was born with the innate capacity to fly, and never lost it, under the influence of his paralyzing fear, he was not capable of using his gift of flight. It's as if there was a band of steel around his wings; he no longer had the ability to fly. Even though the wings were there, without the knowledge of how to use them they were as useless to the bird as two lifeless wooden boards attached to its body.

◇ Courage for a Princess

Our own free will, however, is different from the world of nature. We are created *b'tzelem Elokim* and therefore are never deprived of our ability to discover the innate gifts that Hashem has implanted within our being. For us, the power to overcome the mesmerizing effects of fear is very different. The power of the human will is limitless and never constricted by the same ironclad laws of nature. Hashem always gives us the ability to transcend our limits if we deeply believe and are committed to the purpose of our lives to serve as *ovdei Hashem*.

To illustrate this, I want to share a tale, as told by the Baal Shem Tov, that can offer great insight into how our own human determination has the potential to transcend what appear to be obstacles that are seemingly unconquerable.

> There was once a king with a very beautiful daughter. When it came time for her to marry, the king could find no

husband courageous and intelligent enough for her. So he decided to permit every able-bodied man in his kingdom to compete for the right to win her hand. He placed her high up in a castle where she was in full view of the kingdom. Around the castle he placed a fence, and within the fence protecting the castle, he informed his subjects that he would be placing fierce beasts and destructive forces to prevent anyone from reaching her. Then he proclaimed throughout the kingdom that even though it seemed impossible, there was a path to reach the princess, and anyone who could reach her would be rewarded with her hand in marriage.

From throughout the kingdom, able-bodied men seeking the prize of the princess's hand in marriage were drawn to the castle. Each arrived at the castle's perimeter, but no one dared advance through the fence and into the field of horrors beyond. Each man simply melted in fear. For endless days men arrived from every corner of the country and helplessly observed the princess from afar, as she remained secluded and waiting for her suitor. But not a soul dared battle the forces blocking their access to her.

One day, a young man arrived. He observed the teeming crowd of men, saw the princess, and understood their fear. As time passed, he became more enchanted with the maiden. Overcome by her beauty, he was determined to succeed in reaching her. "Such a beautiful princess must indeed be reachable," he thought. Finally, understanding that ahead of him there was a hidden path to the castle, he ventured through the fence. Nothing would stop him.

With great effort, he summoned all his powers to race through the field of destruction—dodging, leaping and striking with all his might. Somehow, miraculously, he found himself triumphant and unharmed at the castle's entrance. He opened the door and made his way to the room of the waiting princess, who had observed his heroic advance.

When he entered her room, she greeted him as the bravest of all men and the one she had been waiting for to take her hand in marriage. Then she said, "Now you can turn around to see the truth." He turned around and gazed through the window. He saw the throngs of frightened men assembled and standing helplessly at the periphery of the castle. However, to his shock, on the inside of the fence, between the men and the castle, there was only empty space. There were no ferocious beasts, no destructive forces.

"Where did they all go?" asked the young man.

"They were never there," answered the princess. "They were all illusions of everyone's imagination. From where they stand, the beasts are still there. Now only you know the truth. Now that you are standing within the castle, only you can see those dangerous monsters for what they truly are. Only you know what the others never will know. The monsters only exist because of their fears."

In effect, the tale is a metaphor for what occurs continuously throughout our lives. We feel ensnared by a painful feeling, by our anger, hurt, resentment or any other overwhelming feeling or thought. We believe there is no other way to experience life. Then we become aware of a higher understanding of life, a deeper vision — and suddenly we find ourselves in the castle with the princess. We are free once again.

I once told this Chassidic tale to a young man who was single and had been suffering from paralyzing anxiety that was keeping him from becoming engaged. I taught him a number of approaches to help him handle his anxiety; soon afterwards he became a *chassan*. I was invited to his *vort* (engagement party), and when I arrived, he asked me to walk outside with him for a moment. When we were outside, he told me, "There is no way for anyone to understand how the monsters in that tale can seem to be so real and ferocious. That was how I viewed life before the engagement. But now that I am here at my own *vort*, I can look back and see that the monsters were all only in my imagination. They are just empty threats and never had any real power."

The difference between these two stories lies in the contrast between the laws that guide change and growth in the world of nature and the power of free will in our lives. In the first story, the bird cannot fly because the laws that Hashem has created to guide the world of nature are, in fact, immutable. The animal world possesses no ability to think. It is compelled to follow, without choice, the path that has been laid out for it. The second story, however, portrays our human gift of thought, hope, belief and the power that enables us to transcend the illusion of our helplessness and self-imposed limitations.

◇ Discovering My Own Free Will

The power of transformation is always in the air, and at times transformation can even occur in an instant.

> When I was growing up, cigarettes were just beginning to be considered a health hazard. At the age of about sixteen, I had begun to experiment with smoking. I had no father to guide me; he had died when I was ten. For me, that cowboy on the horse smoking Marlboros was a man to be admired and emulated. He was strong and free to roam, unfettered by life's limitations. So, like other foolish boys and men, I swallowed the message — tar and all — and believed that like the man on the horse, I would grow up to be strong and brave.
>
> I began smoking Marlboros and the habit stayed with me for decades. Sometimes I would smoke a pipe and other times I would revert to cigarettes. I tried to stop on many occasions, but was always drawn back by the chemical and social tenacity of the habit. Then, one night, when

I was about forty and had been smoking for a quarter of a century, I had a dream. In it, I saw my children walking around a grave. I looked closely at it and saw ... guess who? I woke up in a cold sweat. The message had finally entered my brain. It frightened me as no warning on the cigarette package or Cancer Society commercial ever could. Nicotine had suddenly lost its power over me. I had a chance to be free. I saw it as a true gift from Hashem, and from that day on, I never took another cigarette.

Today I look around at young men—and even boys—smoking. I feel a sense of pity for how they have relinquished their free will to the power of cigarettes and nicotine. And each time I see that cowboy on his horse, it is a powerful reminder of how we live in a society that takes our freedom away and replaces it with a childish fantasy and an addiction to black tar.

This potential for transformation is the inner strength that I consistently attempt to transmit to couples I am working with. Sometimes it takes laboriously hard work, and other times, an insight similar to my own graveyard dream can make a critical difference in a marriage.

◇ Transformation in Marriage

The challenge that many face in our personal and married lives is that we continually see a field of obstacles that distract us from *shalom bayis*. They may be our fears, anxieties, moods, sensitivities or hurts. Whatever they may be, these are the illusions of the "fierce beasts" that prevent us from reaching the castle of *shalom bayis*. The real power of these illusions is that we believe that we cannot overcome our negative feelings of hurt, resentment, anger, regret, alienation and all the other manifestations of *pizur hanefesh* that invade the *kedushah* of *shalom bayis* and leave us feeling that we have no other choice.

◇ Angry from the Start

I worked with a couple, where the husband, Chaim, had a history of becoming enraged, particularly around the Shabbos table. His wife, Elana, was threatening to end the marriage. He was very distraught. When I asked him what he thought was behind his outbursts of anger, he said, "I love my family, but what can I do? My parents were angry people and it looks like I was just born that way, as well."

My response was to tell Chaim the story of the bird and the snake. I shared with him the following thought: "If you were that bird staring at the snake fifty feet below, then you would not have been endowed by Hashem with free will. You would be paralyzed to behave in any other way. However, you have been created with the potential and responsibility to be an *eved Hashem* for each moment of your existence. So how is it possible that Hashem would create you with the ingrained need to act in a manner contrary to His wishes?"

Each of us always possesses the ability to make choices, to become aware of our true wings and our ability to fly. No one — not even Chaim, who viewed himself as destined to be an angry man for the rest of his life — is ever deprived of the ability to transform himself.

Chaim began to focus on learning that he had the ability to achieve *menuchas hanefesh* and discovered more positive ways of behaving toward his family, both on Shabbos and during the week. A few weeks later, he returned to inform me that he had never thought it was possible for him to quiet his anger, but that he was finally learning that his *bechirah chafshis* had never been taken away from him. As a result, his marriage has become closer, quieter and more focused on those feelings that enable him and his wife to experience the gift of *shalom bayis*.

To achieve his transformation, there were three concepts that Chaim came to understand and accept. The first is that we are never trapped and do not lose our ability to transform ourselves. The second is to appreciate that Hashem desires that we discover our ability to experience our free will to be the loving individuals we have been created to be. The third principle is to learn how to gain access to our true wings and never be deprived of the gift of flight, even when we are hurtling down from the tree and falling helplessly into the waiting jaws of the serpent.

Discovering this *bechirah chafshis* is at the heart of our history as a people. Isn't this what Yosef *HaTzaddik* was discovering as he saw the image of his father while struggling to break free of Potiphar's wife? And perhaps this is what Aharon *HaKohen* discovered as he silently accepted Hashem's will upon learning of the death of his two sons on the day of his inauguration as *Kohen Gadol*. In the same manner, Chaim discovered that Hashem had given him the strength to quiet his anger, and, through this, learned to express that loving side of him.

◇ **Transforming Tears to Laughter**

While there is much to learn about acquiring the keys to transformation, many such events occur, even without our direct efforts and almost instantly. While our exploration of transformations will encompass more methodical and gradual approaches, I want to share two additional illustrations of how transformations can occur, as *Chazal* term it, *k'heref ayin* (in the blink of an eye).

> There was a couple, Martin and Sarah, whom I had known before they were married. When we met again during their *shanah rishonah*, they told me the following story:

While they cared for each other very deeply, Sarah and Martin were both experiencing a very difficult adjustment, marked by continuous tension and even rage. The couple began to feel hopeless and the marriage seemed doomed.

During one particular fight, Martin's anger shot out of control. In his rage, he ran into the bathroom and slammed the door, all the while continuing the shouting with accompanying expletives. Feeling that all was certainly lost, Sarah sat on the couch and began to cry. She started to pray and beg Hashem for something to happen that would turn their marriage around.

Suddenly she heard strange banging and scratching sounds emanating from the bathroom. *What's happening in there?* she wondered. Finally she called out, "Martin, what are you doing?"

The voice on the other side of the door screamed back, "I'm locked in! The door is broken. I can't open it."

The image tickled her funny bone. "You're stuck in the bathroom?" She began to giggle.

Martin heard her laughing. At first, it made him even angrier. Then suddenly the entire situation seemed absurd to him—even comical—and he began to chuckle as well. Within an instant, both were laughing hysterically on opposite sides of the bathroom door. By the time Martin and Sarah finally figured out how to free him from the bathroom, their relationship had changed. Something funny had somehow transformed all their hurt and fighting. Their differences now all seemed ludicrous and certainly not worth losing their marriage over.

It's not that laughter turned their relationship around—although it may very well have helped. Rather, it's that suddenly they had a new perspective on what had been perceived as a tragedy, and this new view may very well have saved their marriage from deteriorating to a point of no return.

Where did this ability to see the situation as comical come from? It came from that force within us that is always there to place life in the perspective from which Hashem wants us to view it. It's never far away, because we are always standing at the crossroads between *menuchas hanefesh* and *pizur hanefesh*, and because of this, Hashem endows each of us with the ability to transform ourselves and our marriage at every moment of our lives. In our work, however, we will not resort to locked bathroom doors for this change in perspective. Rather, we will attempt to understand and utilize the keys that *Chazal* have provided us to live within that healthier state of self.

◇ At the Last Moment

Another incident depicting how a marital transformation can occur in a flash is one that I read in the book *Dear Daughter*, by Rav Eliyahu Goldschmidt, the former *mashgiach* of Yeshiva Gedolah Zichron Moshe in South Fallsburg, New York. The book is a very remarkable account of a father's wise and loving guidance to his young daughter.

Among other personal vignettes filled with deep Torah insights, Rav Goldschmidt shared the story of a couple from South America who were in the midst of divorce proceedings. (It is interesting to note that in the United States, seventy percent of divorces are initiated by wives. Following this pattern, here, too, the wife was determined to go ahead.)

> The husband had resisted greatly but his wife insisted, and he was left with no choice but to proceed. The husband reluctantly agreed to meet with the lawyer to finalize the divorce arrangements. An appointment was arranged for 9:00 a.m.
>
> Early on the morning of the scheduled meeting, terrorists struck in the downtown area and caused many casualties. The wife, listening to the news bulletin on the radio, heard

the name of her husband being mentioned among the names of the injured and dead. She became very distraught knowing that she had pushed him to keep the meeting.

She suddenly realized, too, that the divorce process had taken on a life of its own. Her husband had been trying to persuade her to forgive and reconcile, but she had been swept away by her compelling need to end the marriage. Broken-hearted, she now understood that she had made a tragic error. She tearfully called the lawyer to inform him of the tragedy and tell him that her husband would not be attending the meeting.

The lawyer answered the phone, heard what she had to say, and then told her, "You must be mistaken. Your husband arrived a few minutes early and he is sitting in front of me right now." The wife realized that another man with the same name as her spouse had been the unfortunate bomb victim. "Please put my husband on the phone," she requested.

When her husband got on the line, she said, "I have made a terrible mistake. Will you please come home?"

I decided to share this story because it demonstrates the ever-present power of transformation, even as the powerful pulls of the divorce process are in motion. The potential for transformation can just as easily impact on a couple in the middle of a divorce as during any other stage of marriage. Transformation is an integral aspect of how Hashem has created us. It only ceases when we cease to exist.

◇ Parting Words from a *Gadol*

There are times when this transformation occurs in a moment as the deeper voice of insight and wisdom speaks to us with great clarity. The impact of this insight is that there is paradigmatic change in our understanding of what marriage truly is meant to be.

When Rav Shlomo Freifeld, *zt"l*, was in the final stages of his long illness and was unable to accept visitors, a young man we'll call Ari showed great persistence in attempting to gain a few precious minutes with the *rosh yeshivah*. In the end, he prevailed. Several years later, Ari was asked what had transpired during those moments spent with Rabbi Freifeld. He answered that just a few words from his *rosh yeshivah* changed his life.

Ari and Aviva had been married for a number of years, and life together had been unstable and tumultuous. Ari was looking for guidance to help him understand what Hashem wanted of him in this marriage.

The *rosh yeshivah* told Ari that the answer can be found in the *sheva berachos*. He directed the young man to consider the *berachah*, "Samayach tesamach rayim ha'ahuvim," the essence of which is that close and beloved friends need to continuously provide each other with experiences that enable them to feel loving and beloved. This *berachah* is not just meant for the night of the wedding, but is a guiding principle for every second a couple shares in this world.

At that moment, the young man was able to grasp that he could find fulfillment and *shalom bayis* by bringing *simchah* to his wife every minute of their lives together.

How can a man change the direction of his life so quickly? I believe much of this has to do with his readiness to hear the parting words of his *rebbi*. The word *berachah* is closely associated with *beraichah* (a pool of water). A *berachah* needs a vessel into which to be collected. This young man was not only fortunate enough to receive the blessing, but he went in to hear his *rebbi* as a *kli kibul*—a vessel that was able to accept and internalize the *tzaddik*'s wisdom and blessing.

Rav Shlomo's guidance entailed a great challenge. The husband was told that loving his wife was at the center of his existence. We have a *mitzvah, v"ahavta l'rayacha kamocha* — to love others as we love ourselves. This *mitzvah* is most intensely experienced within the husband-and-wife relationship. And while we may attempt to define our life experiences in many other ways, none approaches marriage.

> Stephen Covey, the author of *Seven Habits of Effective People*, tells of a prominent executive who spent his life climbing the ladder of success in the corporate world. But when he reached the very top of the ladder and could see over the high wall, he came to a frightening realization. He suddenly understood that his single-minded focus on success had caused him to neglect his marriage. And when it was too late, he comprehended with great despair that he had spent his life climbing the wrong ladder!

All these vignettes are testimony of our ability to transform our lives and our marriages. In my work with both singles and married couples, I witness and experience the power of transformation each time I sit with two people. It has become part of the spiritual logic according to which I view life.

◇ The Power of Transformation

What is the source and purpose of this power? Each moment of our lives, Hashem places us between two diametrically opposing forces — *menuchas hanefesh* and *pizur hanefesh*. One will bring us closer to our purpose in life, and the other will send us far away from anything that can enhance our life. In marriage, these two forces continuously contend with each other, trying to influence the manner in which we view our spouse. Frequently it is the negative state of mind that locks us into a perception that seems inescapable.

> A husband walks into his house after a long day, feeling tired and irritable. He looks around at the disarray in

his home and feels even more upset. He may decide to sit on his feelings, yet internally he is heating up. He becomes a silent, brooding man. All that is needed is a spark to ignite his pent-up emotions.

In this familiar scene, the husband is clearly justified in his own mind. He has a right to come home to an orderly house. His perception is that the brooding is understandable and perhaps even inevitable.

In the following situation, a wife feels justified regarding her feelings of resentment.

> After they were married, Shira learned that her husband, Yonatan, suffered from Crohn's Disease, an intestinal disorder that affected his functioning both at home and at work. She felt resentful about not having been informed earlier about his medical situation. In response, Yonatan assured her that it hadn't been "serious enough" to warrant disclosure; at the time, he had asked a *posek*. However, the condition flared up after marriage.
>
> Shira couldn't accept having been misled and was unable to quiet her feelings. "Had you told me and been honest, I would have had a choice. I only found out later when I no longer had a say. I feel that I was fooled. Every time you stay home from work or I have to prepare special meals because of your condition, I'm being told by your parents and everyone else that I should be taking care of you. Yes, I should be. But I also believe I had the right to know in advance that I would be making sacrifices for you."

In these scenarios, the husband who walked into a "mess" and the wife who was "fooled" are both struggling with troubled feelings and thoughts. In the second situation, the husband's intestinal difficulties may even be exacerbated by the tension in the marriage.

In every marriage, we are continuously dealing with our feelings, and sometimes it's very difficult to know whether they are justified or not. Yet, the source of the feelings is not the main issue. Once we have the troubled thought or feeling, we are in a state of *pizur hanefesh*. However, *menuchas hanefesh* and *shalom bayis* always require us to feel a deeper sense of balance and control over our troubled thoughts and feelings.

At no time in our lives are we ever that bird falling out of the tree. We always have a choice to free ourselves of *pizur hanefesh* and then be able to make the correct decision. The husband returning from work and feeling that "this is not the kind of home I dreamed I would be walking into," or the wife feeling saddled with the burden of caring for her husband, are both in *pizur hanefesh* and need to free themselves of the iron grip of these feelings. And until they do, they will be victimized by these feelings even more than by the conditions under which they are living. They both may have understandably difficult situations that need to be resolved. However, they will never be able to arrive at solutions and insights that enable them to lighten their burdens without first transforming their state of mind.

In each of the five dimensions we discussed earlier — thoughts, feelings and moods, physiology, behavior, and emotional closeness and intimacy — we are never locked into a place where we are compelled to remain in our *pizur hanefesh*. To the contrary, the Torah wants us to understand that each sign of our moving toward any state of mind that is associated with *pizur hanefesh* is actually a mandate for change and growth. And, therefore, each troubled thought or feeling offers an opening to respond in a manner that will actually being us closer to *menuchas hanefesh*.

◇ **Dovid *HaMelech* and Transformation**

This concept of transforming our state of mind from *pizur*

hanefesh to *menuchas hanefesh* is at the heart of how the *Alter* of Kelm describes the meaning of Dovid *HaMelech's* declaration of loyalty to Hashem in *Tehillim* 94:19: "*B'rov sarapai bekirbi, tanchumecha yeshaashu nafshi* — When my mind and heart are filled with many foreboding thoughts and feelings, Hashem's comforts cheer my soul and bring me peace of mind."

The message that Dovid *HaMelech* is conveying is that at no moment in our lives, whether in a marriage that seems to be failing or, *chas v'shalom*, when we are in the throes of a devastating illness, or in any other state of emotional or physical despair, are we alone and helpless. Hashem always gives us the power to transform our *sarapim* — our foreboding thoughts and feelings. He enables us to discover the keys that unlock His ever-present comfort that warms and cheers our souls. This is the gift of transformation, and it resides in our ability to recognize each sign of *pizur hanefesh* — the *sarapim*, as they are called — as an opportunity to transform the moment into closeness to our own *neshamah* and to Hashem. This is why, at every moment of our personal and married lives, we are continuously monitoring our state of mind and learning how to transform adversity into opportunity. Our very fulfillment and joy in life is a result of learning to continuously monitor our state of mind so we can experience life with all the potential that Hashem has placed within us.

Even when all seems lost, we are never the bird that is paralyzed; rather, we more closely resemble the wily fox at the well. When it seemed that he was closed in on all sides, caught between his own thirst and the hunger of the wolf, he was given an insight that rescued him. In the same way, we are able to transform our own adversity into *menuchas hanefesh* and *shalom bayis*.

149

DEFINING OUR EXPERIENCE OF LIFE

Our journey into understanding Hashem's gift of transformation begins with becoming more aware and appreciative of a phenomenon that has always been at the center of our life experience, but rarely have any of us given much thought to it. This is our experience of our "self." Each of us possesses it. We are always aware of its presence. Yet we give little, if any, thought to where it comes from and how it is always changing.

There is a question I pose to individuals and couples I work with: "Where does your experience of life come from?" The initial answer will usually be that we experience life through our thoughts, feelings and other senses. We automatically assume that whatever our thoughts and feelings are telling us is correct, and tend to accept this perception as the unquestionable reality. We tend to rely on these perceptions because our experience of self runs on autopilot. We just accept it. In the same way, we never give any thought to our ability to breathe and circulate the oxygen in our bodies, digest food and carry out all the other functions that keep us alive and thriving, we also accept the content of our thoughts, feelings and moods as our own and never really question their veracity.

I see a lot of this in my work with dating and engaged couples. A frequent statement I hear is, "But when I look at her, she really is too short. I never really minded it until we became engaged, and now I can't stop thinking about it." There are many variations on this "new perception" relating to height, weight, intelligence, *frumkeit* and *middos*. However, I have rarely found that any of these new perceptions are based on anything but the increased anxiety that comes along with commitment. From the perspective of the perceiver, the response is, "It must be true because that's how I see it." The message we give ourselves is clear. First is that "I am my perceptions," and second,

"My perceptions are true and must be trusted, even if I decide to break my engagement."

The reality is that our experience of life is not solely our own and it does not originate with us. Just like every other life function, our experience of self is a gift from Hashem. Whether we are experiencing *shalom bayis* and *menuchas hanefesh*, or whether we are experiencing marital discord and *pizur hanefesh*, it all comes from Hashem. Without Hashem, there is no self. Yet we unthinkingly assume that our selves exist almost independently of Hashem.

◇ Discovering an Awareness of Self in a Refrigerator

> I know of a *rosh yeshivah* who wanted to help his children understand that we don't "just exist." Everything in life is a gift. He shared with me that when his children were young, they were taught not to go to the refrigerator and take any food without first asking permission. "We never refused them," he explained. "They just needed to remember to ask." His reason was that a child needs to learn that nothing is a given in life. Everything we have is a precious gift for which we need to experience a sense of *hakaras hatov*.

The lesson seems simple. Everything we have in life — even our sense of self — has been given to us by Hashem, and by those whom Hashem has entrusted with our well-being. However, we rarely consider this novel thought, and it needs to be reinforced throughout our lives.

When a child is hungry, he says to himself, "I am hungry, and therefore I will eat." This translates into, "I am hungry and therefore entitled." In Yiddish, the saying is "*Es kumt mir* — It's coming to me."

Of course, our children need to feel secure in knowing that

they will always be cared for, loved and fed. However, this *rosh yeshivah* did not want his children to confuse their need with the feeling of entitlement that leads to taking. He wanted, instead, to convey to his children that they were entitled, yet were being given and were therefore receiving. Only this leads to a sense of gratitude for what is being given.

The *rosh yeshivah* was teaching his children that the gift of food can never be taken for granted by instinctively saying, "I'm hungry, so I am just eating what's rightfully mine." The attitude of the child who believes that the sandwich he is holding is his because "I was hungry and I took it" is very different from that of the child who believes that the food was given as a gift from his or her parents because "I was hungry and my parents understood this, and this is the true sign that they love me and care for me." How much more is this true in relation to Hashem, Who lovingly gives us the gift of our consciousness of self each moment of our lives?

It's the same with our awareness of our experience of life, whether positive or negative. The very first step toward *menuchas hanefesh* and *shalom bayis* is to understand that our experience of ourselves, which means our consciousness and awareness, along with all of our other physical functions and senses, are all ongoing gifts from Hashem. Along with these gifts comes the responsibility to be aware of how our experience of self and our "right to harbor feelings and moods" must always be measured in relation to what Hashem expects from us.

A husband may feel angry and frustrated with his wife at a given moment. However, his feelings are never to be taken as reality. He cannot say, "I feel angry because I have a reason to be angry." A wife who feels upset about her husband's inability to "give me the things I deserve" may experience herself as being deprived. However, like the angry husband, her feelings cannot be justified by her instinctive need to say, "I'm entitled to feel this way because that's the way he is." If they accept their feelings as reality, there can never be any change in the marriage.

It's true that the spouse may need to change. But the change must first begin with two questions that continuously determine our direction in life on a moment-to-moment basis. The first is, "Faced with these feelings, how can I discover my way to freedom from the oppressive nature of these feelings?" The second is, "If Hashem gives me my sense of self, what does He want me to experience that will enable me to understand the true essence and fulfillment of myself in this marriage?" Merely asking these questions is the first step to opening the door to real change and growth.

CHAPTER VI
The Principles of Transformation

The most important concept you will learn from this book is that we always have the freedom to access a state of mind that experiences *menuchas hanefesh*. Learning to access this dimension of ourselves is based on our awareness of principles that continuously enable us to transform ourselves from a state of *pizur hanefesh* to a state of *menuchas hanefesh*. When integrated into the ebb and flow of our lives, these principles serve as the foundation for maintaining and strengthening *shalom bayis* and affection in marriage and in all our meaningful relationships.

These principles can be summarized as follows:

1. **Chiddush**: *Chiddush* is renewal. It is the awareness that at every moment of our lives Hashem recreates us as a physical, emotional and spiritual being who is capable of growing and changing, regardless of how limited we are in our own view.

2. **Tzomet**: *Tzomet* means crossroads. Through understanding this principle, we become increasingly aware that at every moment Hashem places us at the crossroads to experience two towering forces within us, *menuchas hanefesh* and *pizur hanefesh*.

3. **Mishkan**: *Mishkan* means sanctuary. Through an appreciation of *Mishkan*, we gain greater clarity on how to cultivate a state of mind that brings us closer to a relationship rooted in a deeper appreciation of marital love, beauty and *kedushah*.

There is an additional concept that underlies all the above principles, which is called ...

Yegiah: *Yegiah* represents the value of our efforts to transform our state of mind. Hashem rewards these efforts with His loving gifts of insight and freedom.

Understanding and following these principles opens up the possibility of continuously transforming every aspect of our personal and shared lives.

Now we can take a closer look at these principles.

THE 1ST PRINCIPLE: *Chiddush*
We Are New Creations at Every Moment

◇ **Receiving Life with Every Breath**

The principle of *Chiddush* means we are aware that at every moment of our lives Hashem is recreating us. Recognizing this phenomenon that Hashem is continuously renewing our physical, experiential selves and spiritual selves opens new vistas in our perception of the possibilities inherent in every moment. *Chiddush* is being aware that while we may feel entrapped in a state of *pizur hanefesh*, in reality, we are in a continuous state of renewal with endless choices to enhance our growth and well-being. The concept of *Chiddush* is based on the phrase we recite twice each morning: *"Ha'mechadesh betuvo bechol yom tamid,"* which means that Hashem continuously renews us with love and goodness. Our praise of Hashem for granting us life at each moment is also expressed by *Dovid HaMelech* in Psalm 135, with the phrase, *"Kol haneshamah tehalail Kah."* While the literal translation is that every *neshamah* praises Hashem, *Chazal* interpret this to mean that with every *neshimah*, each breath we take, we are recreated by Hashem.

The Chassidic master, Reb Levi Yitzchak of Berditchev, *zt"l*, deepens our understanding of this prayer as he explains that our soul is always yearning to leave us and rejoin its Master in Heaven. With each breath we take, Hashem returns our soul to us. Therefore, as life is flowing away from us, Hashem is continuously breathing life back into us.

All this may sound very mystical and esoteric. However, when we appreciate the implications of *Chiddush*, we can begin to appreciate how being aware of this continuous state of renewal holds the keys for discovering the possibilities for growth and fulfillment in every moment. Through this principle, we can become acutely aware that Hashem provides each of us with life in a very personal and loving way. We each receive precisely what we require to exist throughout every moment. Through this gift, life reaches every cell of our being. We experience the gift of life in our ability to think, feel, breathe, move and perform every function that enables us to be ourselves. And all the while, we are also provided with another gift. It is the gift of self and soul that enables us to be aware of our moment-to-moment experience of life. This gift begins at birth and ends when we have finished our mission in life. Therefore, as we consider Hashem's love and caring for our existence at each moment, we can begin to appreciate the revolutionary impact this can have on how we view ourselves and our life partner.

◇ **A Dialogue About "Self"**

In a workshop that I frequently conduct on *menuchas hanefesh* and relationships, I attempt to teach participants how to become more aware that we each have a distinct and unique "self" that is rooted in the eternal. The way I begin teaching this concept is through a dialogue with a participant of the group.

The purpose of this dialogue is to create awareness that while our sense of self is always changing, reflecting the tapestry of our many thoughts and feelings, there is a deeper self that is constant and never changes. My goal is to enable participants to become more aware of this eternal dimension of self that is anchored in the One-ness and eternal quality of Hashem. The practical implication of this awareness is that the self that yearns for a new car, or that experiences anger and jealousy, is not the same dimension of self that experiences closeness to Hashem and to those we deeply care for. Our goal in life is to always strive to experience the deeper dimension of self.

I begin by saying that we are all aware that we possess a unique self that enables us to experience our moment-to-moment sensations of life. Yet how do we know that what we experience is really our unique self?

This is how the dialogue is conducted:

S.O.: What is your name?

Channah: Channah.

S.O.: Do you remember the first time you knew your name?

Channah: No. But it was probably at about the age of two or three.

S.O.: Do you associate your name with your "self"?

Channah: Yes.

S.O.: So you have known that you are Channah for about twenty-five years?

Channah: That makes sense.

S.O.: Was there ever a time when you did not know you

were Channah, or you didn't know you were yourself?

Channah: I always knew I was myself, perhaps except when I was sleeping.

S.O.: Where do you think you received your ability to know that you are really you, and your experiences represent who you are?

Channah: I imagine it came from my brain cells, synapses and many other functions of my intelligence and nervous system.

S.O.: Did you know that at your age, most of the cells you had in your childhood have since died and new ones have taken their place? And while your physical cells may have changed, you are still Channah?

Channah: I know that my cells die and are regenerated. But I never really thought about how my self continues, despite the death of the cells. That's very interesting. So tell me, where does my consciousness of self come from?

S.O.: You are aware that you are yourself because self has a dimension of Hashem's eternal being. It is beyond the physicality of cells and it gives us the power of awareness and consciousness.

When you daven *Shemoneh Esrei*, you say, "*Atah chonein l'adam da'as* — You [Hashem] give us the power to think and be aware." This includes your ability to know that you exist and experience your own life and the world around you. No other creature in the world has the power to think and be aware.

Do you know why I am placing such an emphasis on being aware of your consciousness of self?

Channah: No. Please tell me.

S.O.: The foundation of everything I am teaching you is based on being aware that Hashem gives us life at each moment, and Hashem gives us a deeper self at each moment. This deeper self, which is a part of our *neshamah*, always has the ability to discover the road to freedom and *menuchas hanefesh*, regardless of where we are and what we are experiencing.

Therefore, the "self" that feels trapped and insecure and hurt is not the "self" that Hashem wants you to experience as the true and unique reflection of your *neshamah*. And we become aware of this deeper self through *Chiddush*.

You see, Channah, our *Chiddush* and our deeper self always holds the keys to our transformation.

Channah: I always believed that Hashem gives me life, but never really thought about being recreated at each moment. I also need to be more aware of how my deeper experience of my self is a gift from Hashem.

◇ We Are Always in a State of Receiving Life

This first discovery is that living is not a passive or reactive process. We have choices between experiencing our lives from either deeper or more internal dimensions of our "self," or from a superficial dimension of our being. True living is being aware that our self is the result of our constant state of receiving through Hashem's flow of love. Just like the children who were taught the meaning of receiving by asking before they took food from the refrigerator, we, too, learn to be aware and appreciative of our state of receiving life from Hashem on a moment-to-moment basis. This awareness is the first step toward transforming our *pizur hanefesh* to *menuchas hanefesh*, and it transforms our relationship with those who share our lives.

◇ A Power Beyond Self

This means that even when I feel angry and hurt, the "I" who experiences this anger and hurt is still receiving its ability to experience these emotions from Hashem. However, the same Hashem Who gives me the ability to experience these emotions does not wish me to be stuck in them. The implication, especially in marriage, is that even as I may harbor these feelings, Hashem gives me the ability to feel them only because He wishes me to change them. Understanding this choice and learning to transform our negative perceptions is the essence of *avodas Hashem.*

The Freedom of Creation

The reality that I am being recreated at each moment informs me that I am always given the opportunity to rediscover my freedom from the strong pull of *pizur hanefesh.* We are never created to be imprisoned by our present negative perceptions. We may not yet understand how to find the key to freedom from our anxieties, anger, sadness or any other negative state of mind. However, the realization that we are being continuously created comes with the belief that along with our renewal, Hashem will also enable us to discover the gateway to our freedom.

Experiencing Time as a Loss of Control

Another aspect of this awareness is that of time. When I live in an awareness of *Chiddush,* I am experiencing life in Hashem's dimension of time, rather than being driven by my own compulsive sense of time.

In reality, we have no concept of Hashem's dimension of time, for He is beyond time and not bound by its finite limitations. We, on the other hand, will always have to answer to insistent demands of time. It's the nature of our mortality. However, some are more bound and imprisoned in time than others.

For example, some people always feel impatient and in a rush. They have no awareness of their choice in life to slow down. It's like their engines are running at full speed, but the gears are in neutral. They're not really going anywhere. The reality is that their lives are driven by tension, insecurity and the inability to feel quiet within. They are always in a rush because *pizur hanefesh* always distorts time. It causes them to feel impatient and jumpy.

Imagine waiting at a traffic signal for a red light to turn green, and there is a car next to you with its driver revving his engine impatiently. Suddenly the light changes — and he's off, leaving a trail of burning rubber in his wake. What was his rush and what will he do with the three seconds he saved before he needs to stop at the next light? The answer is that his behavior is being driven by *pizur hanefesh*. His concept of time is distorted because he possesses poor internal controls. His impatience is a reflection of inadequate self-control masquerading as success behind the wheel of a high performance car. Internally, he is just a little boy who has never learned to gain control of the forces that are relentlessly driving him. He cannot be aware of *Chiddush* because the engine of his drives is louder than the sounds of his deeper self. This deeper self can only emerge when we attempt to aspire toward *menuchas hanefesh*.

◇ How a *Gadol* Experiences Time

The minute we are aware of Hashem's renewal of our lives at each moment, we are enabled to feel greater internal control and become less driven by tension, impatience and internal anxiety. Rav Dovid Feinstein, *shlit"a*, spoke of how his father, Harav Moshe, *zt"l*, always had patience for anyone. One moment he would appear to be in a rush, but the next — if someone needed his attention — he was able to speak calmly and carefully and never give the impression that he was rushed or tense.

This ability to experience Hashem's time enables each of us to be a *savlan* — a tolerant and patient person. With this strength, we each can be a more caring and understanding spouse.

◇ *Hakaras Hatov*

The final awareness related to *mechadesh betuvo* is that since I am receiving life at each moment, Hashem expects me to be aware and grateful for this gift of life. *Chazal* call this *hakaras hatov*.

We demonstrate our *hakaras hatov* to Hashem by caring for those Hashem wishes us to care for. This relationship is personified between life partners.

◇ EXERCISES TO CULTIVATE OUR AWARENESS OF *CHIDDUSH*

To help you internalize this first principle — our awareness of receiving the moment-to-moment gift of life — I would like to suggest a few activities or exercises that you can integrate into your daily schedule.

1. The Awareness Walk

+ Take a walk on a quiet street while staying focused straight ahead.
+ Be aware of the trees, birds, clouds, sky and everything around you that is receiving the gift of life from Hashem.
+ Now focus on your own self receiving these gifts of life that enable you to think, feel, walk, hear, see, breathe and perform every other function that enables you to be a living being.
+ Remind yourself that at every moment Hashem is a loving Creator, continuously breathing life into you and every molecule in this universe.

2. Awareness of Receiving Life

+ Throughout your day, whether alone or with others, be aware that regardless of what you are experiencing

toward yourself or others, you are receiving life from
Hashem at this very moment.

+ Take this moment to express to Hashem that you are
grateful for the life He is breathing into you.

3. Your Awareness of Time

+ Learn to quiet the feeling of impatience or being rushed
by taking a minute to remember that Hashem is renewing your life at every moment.
+ Follow this awareness by a deep breath.
+ Observe how this quiets the inner drive that creates tension, intolerance and impatience.

THE 2ND PRINCIPLE: *Tzomet*
We Live at the Crossroads

The second principle is being aware that we are always standing
at the crossroads (Hebrew: *tzomet*) where we are given the freedom to choose between two states of being. In one direction, we
face a state of mind that reflects *menuchas hanefesh,* and in the
other direction we face toward *pizur hanefesh.* We need to know
how to exercise this freedom.

◇ **There Are No Accidents in Our Lives**

In the classic *sefer Chovos Halevavos,* the Gate of *Bitachon* defines
the meaning of *bitachon* as our ability to believe that no event
can occur in our lives that is not the direct result of Hashem's
intervention. *Chazal* tell us that no one can even lift a finger here
below without the consent of Heaven. As the *gemara* in *Berachos* (33b) teaches: "All that occurs is from the hands of Heaven,
except for the fear of Heaven." Nothing is ever "accidental" or
"by chance." At every moment of our lives, Hashem is placing

us at the crossroads. Our responsibility is to first define which direction of the crossroads brings us closer to Hashem and *shalom bayis* and which distances us.

Being aware of our lives at the crossroads means that we can be cognizant of shifts in our choices of how we perceive life at any given moment. At one moment, we can experience a sense of well-being and security, and the next moment, insecurity and emotional despair may overwhelm us. We may look at our husband or wife and feel a sense of gratitude and affection, and just hours later, feel disinterested and distant.

Where do these shifting thoughts, feelings and sensations come from? The reality is that they may be coming from many possible external or internal sources. Perhaps we can say they come from our daily pressures of work, our memories of past events from earlier life experiences, or challenges that we are facing in our marriage, parenting and every other significant area of our lives.

◇ A Story of Entrapment and Freedom

> I met a young woman, Sheryl, who had been married to Mark, a man with serious addictions. After three years of marriage, she told me that she had had enough and just couldn't bring herself to forgive him for the way he had destroyed their lives. Mark finally came to realize the extent of his addictions and committed himself to a rehabilitation program, while also undertaking other serious efforts to regain control over his life. All he asked was that his wife give him the opportunity to demonstrate his commitment to change.
>
> Understandably, Sheryl could not bring herself to change her feelings. Her sense of resentment and betrayal was as unshakable as an iron claw. "I knew that he was trying," she confided to me, "but I was so hurt. I just couldn't

let go of my resentment and mistrust of him. My feelings were so powerful that I literally couldn't let him get near me ever again."

From Sheryl's perspective, there was no other choice. We can understand how this young woman was seized by these feelings and was unable to experience the other side of herself that would enable her to feel trust in Mark. She felt she could never permit herself to be open to him ever again. Although the capacity for her to trust still lived within her, she was unable to access this strength. The reality is that we are always at the crossroads, regardless of what has occurred in our lives. Based on Mark's past behavior, Sheryl's initial feeling of certainty was correct. However, once he began to assume responsibility for his life and marriage, she needed to be able to have the choice — the *bechirah* — to see both sides and be able to evaluate her options. He was beginning to change and she was still stuck. The challenge is to understand that we are never locked in to a state of mind without choices. When we believe we have no options, we are giving in to the illusion that is inherent in *pizur hanefesh*.

Although initially Sheryl was certain she could never again bring herself to trust Mark, as he demonstrated his determination to recover, she discovered that she could learn to forgive him. As Mark learned to overcome the illness that had afflicted him, Sheryl learned that she had the internal strength to forgive. Over time, both learned there is always another side of our deeper selves waiting to emerge.

Bitachon is the awareness for Sheryl — and certainly for Mark — that their challenges are not strange and unknown to Hashem. The events in their lives, at each moment, have unfolded to bring them to this crossroads. Each has a different challenge. For Mark, it's the challenge of overcoming the illness of addiction. For Sheryl, it's the challenge of being open to the possibility that her husband has the desire and strength to be a husband and a father in the fullest sense.

At every moment, each of us stands at these crossroads between our two states of mind of *menuchas hanefesh* and *pizur hanefesh*. We are brought to this place by our upbringing, life experiences, biology and hard-wiring. And we are always challenged to emerge through a greater understanding of Hashem's will and our own latent strength to fulfill this will.

◇ Eating the Bread of Embarrassment

"Why do we have to be challenged throughout our lives?" This is a question many have asked me. The answer, as I have come to understand it, is that each of us is given a *neshamah* that accompanies us throughout our lives. Each morning, we thank Hashem for this gift. While our physical selves are mortal and finite, our souls are immortal and infinite. Eventually, after 120 years, our *neshamah* will leave our bodies and stand face-to-face with Hashem. At that time, Hashem will want to give us many rewards because of His love for each of us. However, we need to feel that we deserve this love.

Imagine that a friend asked you to accept an award for an organization that he was running, and you agreed. Now imagine how, at the award ceremony, he spoke of your dedication to his organization — but you knew that his accolades were not based on fact. You had done very little for this organization and felt truly embarrassed. Had you done something to deserve the award, you would have felt much easier about the praise.

Chazal tell us that it's the same way with our life challenges. Hashem has a deep love for each of us and wants to bestow this love on us. However, we need to feel that we deserve it; otherwise, it is what *Chazal* call "the bread of embarrassment." We need to know that we worked hard to deserve this love. And this is why we are always at the crossroads. We are accumulating the experiences to be able to say to Hashem, "I am aware of my own struggles to deserve Your love."

Therefore, each moment when we realize that we are at the crossroads, we come to understand that Hashem has actually placed us in this position. We are placed in this challenging moment so we can transform *pizur hanefesh* to *menuchas hanefesh* and gain an additional gem in our crown of pride and accomplishment that make our journey in this world worthwhile. These are events that occur in the here-and-now, but their impact resonates for all eternity.

THE 3ᴿᴰ PRINCIPLE: Mind as *Mishkan*

Let's do a brief review. There are three steps in the process I have been describing. The first is realizing that we are in a troubled state of mind that is threatening our *shalom bayis*. *Chiddush* opens our vistas and informs us that we are not imprisoned in our *pizur hanefesh*. The second step is our awareness that we are standing at the crossroads between the two states and that there are other, more productive ways to experience our relationship. The third step is to navigate our state of mind in a direction that can heal the wounds and bridge the gaps in our relationship.

To move toward this choice, we need to sensitize the internal compass that points us in the right direction. The direction we will be following is *Shechinah* — the presence of Hashem in our lives. By defining the states of mind with which the *Shechinah* can be compatible, we are also defining the states of mind that are compatible with *menuchas hanefesh* and *shalom bayis*. Since the *Shechinah* rests within the *Mishkan*, we can appreciate how the third step in this process is cultivating the value of Mind as *Mishkan*.

Before I describe the process of how we learn to cultivate this concept of Mind as *Mishkan*, I would like to describe a young man who came to see me.

> Yisrael was a young lawyer who had been brought up in a divorced home. He vividly remembered his parents as being in a continuous state of conflict. Along with their conflict, he remembered his own sense of hurt, anger and deprivation that pervaded his growing-up years.
>
> Now that he is married and a parent of three children, he has become aware that in his own marriage, he continues to harbor the same troubled state of mind. But his hurt and anger are now directed toward his wife.

Being aware that our choices are not limited to our present troubled state is certainly important. However, we need to know how to discover the options that Hashem offers us. Yisrael had become aware of his patterns of anger, yet was skeptical about his ability to overcome habituation to angry moods that he had been repeating since his childhood. He felt that someone like himself who was deprived and "emotionally blind" could have no concept of healthy emotions. He viewed himself as trapped in an emotional darkness, and believed he would never experience the light of healthy feelings toward his wife and family.

Yisrael had become aware that he was stuck in the same feelings of anger that had pervaded his childhood. Yet, to take the next step toward rescuing his marriage, he needed to believe he possessed an internal compass that could not only guide him *away* from his anger, but even more importantly, *toward* a healthier state of mind and relationship with his wife.

His sense of deprivation had caused Yisrael to feel that life had offered him no real opportunity to grow. Yet he learned that Hashem had not abandoned him, and had provided him with the internal strengths to overcome this perception of himself.

He achieved this through understanding the concept of Mind as *Mishkan*.

◇ My Reflections at the *Kosel*

As an introduction to how the concepts of *Mishkan* and *Shechinah* play such a crucial role in our internal compass, I would like to share some personal reflections and observations from my recent visit to the *Kosel HaMaaravi* (The Western Wall).

> As I approached the plaza and saw the mosque standing where the *Bais Hamikdash* once stood, I tore my shirt, thereby fulfilling this special *mitzvah* of mourning just as we have done at this site for over two thousand years.
>
> The July sun intensified the whiteness of the *Kosel*'s immense stones. Approaching the wall, I observed throngs of visitors drawn as if by a magnet to experience a spiritual presence that exists nowhere else in the world. It's difficult to articulate exactly what this phenomenon is. However, everyone who has been there will testify that "something extraordinary happens" at the *Kosel*.
>
> As I davened Minchah, I sensed I was standing closer to the living presence of *Hashem* – the *Shechinah* – than was possible perhaps any place else on earth. I experienced Hashem's nearness in the profound clarity of each word of prayer I uttered. The act of praying in this place, coupled with my prayers themselves, evoked within me a sense of the possibility of being a deeply spiritual – *ruchani* – individual. This is a feeling that is experienced by so many here.

In fact, I have many memories of the *Kosel*, but the one that stands out the most actually took place away from the site.

> A number of years ago, when I was traveling from Israel to America, I sat next to a software developer who

was busily writing programs on the plane. For the first few hours, no words were exchanged between us. After a while, he finally closed his computer and we spoke.

Jim hailed from California, where he lived in a beach house on the Pacific coast, and was now returning from his first visit to Israel. I asked him how he had enjoyed himself. "Well, I really enjoyed the night life in Tel Aviv!" he replied enthusiastically, obviously referring to everything that Hashem does not wish *Eretz Yisrael* to be. However, I understood that his superficial view of Israel was tied to his beach-house/bachelor lifestyle. Yet I also believed that somewhere within his memory of Israel was a deeper, more spiritual and meaningful impression.

I asked him if he had been to Yerushalayim. He courteously told me he had visited the Wall and the Old City. However, while his parents are Jewish, he explained, he had never had any religious education, so these sites meant little to him.

It struck me as strange that someone could visit Yerushalayim and the *Kosel* without a memorable moment to share. But as we continued our conversation, his attitude began to change. The more I asked him about his first impressions of the Wall and the Old City, the more his memories brought him back to the experience. He now seemed more willing — even eager — to share what had happened. It was almost as if he'd had a deeply moving experience at the Kosel that had been forgotten and was now being remembered. It's somewhat similar to a dream that we can't seem to remember, until an association is made and suddenly it reappears in our memory. In the same way he was now remembering with great excitement what had occurred within him.

It only took a few minutes before he began to describe a deeply moving memory of seeing the *Kosel* for the first time and approaching it with great reverence. He could remember getting close to the Wall and uttering prayers to a G-d that he had never felt existed before that moment. Then he shared with me what he had prayed for: He prayed to Hashem that he would be able to find a Jewish woman with whom to share his life.

I gazed at him in amazement. One minute, all he could remember was the Tel Aviv nightlife, and he had no recollection of Yerushalayim at all. The next moment, he divulged a personal experience that transcended his present life of living in a beach house, pursuing women and enjoying the nightlife of a foreign country. Somehow, just being at the *Kosel* evoked his deeper thoughts and aspirations about belonging to *Am Yisrael* and bringing a Jewish woman into his life.

Before that moment, he told me, he had never understood why he should marry a Jewish woman. Suddenly, and without any rational explanation, it made clear and profound sense to him. Clearly, "something" had called out to him and had touched his uneducated, yet receptive, Jewish soul like never before in his life.

I'm sorry to say that I did not have the ability to pursue a relationship with Jim. However, this and countless other personal experiences that we all have had cause us to ask, "From where does the *Kosel* receive its immense spiritual power?"

We all understand the answer. The *Kosel* stands at the Temple Mount — the center of the universe. It is on that specific place that Hashem has chosen to rest His *Shechinah*. When we are in its proximity, we can sense its Divine and holy beauty.

This is where Avraham *Avinu* brought his son Yitzchak to the *Akeidah* (the Binding); where Yaakov *Avinu* laid down his head and in his dream envisioned the presence of Hashem atop the ladder; and where that Dovid *HaMelech* purchased land for the site of the *Bais HaMikdash* that was eventually built by Dovid's son, Shlomo *HaMelech,* and then rebuilt under Herod. Today's *Kosel* represents the sparse remains of the Second Temple.

Moshe was commanded to make a holy place for Hashem, and He would dwell among His people. The vessels that were contained in the *Bais HaMikdash* were fashioned in the desert and were originally contained in the *Mishkan,* which Moshe *Rabbeinu* had constructed before *B'nei Yisrael* entered *Eretz Yisrael.* We read about this in the weekly Torah portion of *Parashas Terumah,* "*Ve'asu li mikdash veshachanti besocham* — Create for Me a sanctuary, and I will dwell among you."

The *Mishkan* was a fitting place for the *Shechinah* to rest, as its sacred beauty was unique in the entire world. It was filled with wondrously beautiful vessels crafted from precious metals. Its fabrics were colored using rare dyes. Intoxicating aromas of incense wafted through its space and beyond. The enchantment of the songs of the *Leviim* filled the air. This was the daily ebb and flow of spiritual life that was the *Mishkan.* All this was accompanied by the offering of sacrifices and the ever-burning light of the Menorah. There was no other place in the world fitting enough for us to experience the Presence of Hashem as the *Mishkan.*

◇ The Whisper of *Shechinah*

Clearly, our state of inspiration at the *Kosel* today is distant from even a faint whisper of what it was when the *Bais HaMikdash* was standing. Yet, even today, 3,500 years after the building of the *Mishkan* in the desert, just the sight of the stones and the throngs who come to soak in the *Kosel's ruchnius* is so deeply inspiring. The mere sight opens our hearts to realize that Hashem has placed this power of beauty and *kedushah* in our world that elevates our lives. Merely standing at the *Kosel* gives our lives clarity, focus and an awareness that is unavailable anywhere else on earth. Through the spiritual presence of the *Kosel,* we can experience a sense of connection to the precious and infinite gift of life that Hashem gives us all.

What I have come to understand when I am near the *Kosel* is that even this faint whisper of the *Shechinah* is transforming, and each experience of transformation brings us a small step closer to being the individual Hashem has wanted us to become ever since we opened our eyes to the world around us. At the *Kosel*, we are all equal. Standing near these holy stones, we no longer carry the illusion that we are defined by our possessions, the size of our house, the make of our car, the label on our clothing, or our place on the dais. Here, we realize life's true value when we permit the power of the *Shechinah* to permeate our consciousness. At this holy site, even a beach dweller without a moment of Jewish education can sense a yearning deep within himself for a life partner who will enable him to attach himself to this place forever.

Along with this understanding about life, we also become aware of our human vulnerability. We can appreciate the meaning of our relationships with the people who share our lives. We realize how deeply we need human love and caring. We understand that life's true treasures reside in our ability to receive and give love. This is why the crevices of the *Kosel* are filled with tiny notes of prayers for *shalom bayis*, health and finding *shidduchim*.

Taking leave of the *Kosel* is never without a deep sense of loss. I notice how many visitors walk backwards, maintaining visual contact as they express their wish to hold on to the connection. It's as if prolonging the sight will enable them to fully internalize its treasure into their everyday lives. It is here, at this wall, that each of us is able to experience some sense of the *Shechinah*. And because of it, we are able to experience our deeper and truer selves.

◇ The Way Hashem Wants Us to Live

I have shared these thoughts because they introduce us to the third principle, that of Mind as *Mishkan*. When are we truly ourselves? We are only ourselves when we are aware of Hashem's presence in our lives. This is how we were intended to live. The entirety of our lives is intended to be a *Mishkan* — a resting place for Hashem's presence, whether we are in Yerushalayim, New York, Toronto or Los Angeles. Anywhere we are, and at each stage in our moment-to-moment experience of life, Hashem has given us a mind and a *neshamah* to emulate the *middos* that approximate the beauty of the *Mishkan*. Our awareness of this potential within us is transforming, just as the *Kosel* is transforming.

Hashem has placed countless opportunities for the *Mishkan* and *Shechinah* to reside in our lives. Each of these opportunities enables us to experience the true depth of who we are.

First, there is the dimension of prayer. We recite the *Shemoneh Esrei* at least three times daily. Each time we *daven Shemoneh Esrei*, we enter the domain of the *Shechinah*. When we begin, we take three steps forward to prepare ourselves to enter its domain; when we end, we take leave of Hashem's Presence by stepping backwards. Perhaps this is why Rav Kook, *zt"l*, the late chief rabbi of Israel, said that whenever he davened *Shemoneh Esrei*, he always saw the *Kosel* in front of him.

Another area of our lives where the *Shechinah* is present is on Shabbos. In *shul* on Friday night, we greet the *Shechinah* when we sing *Lecha Dodi* ("Come, my friend, let us greet the Shabbos Queen"). Throughout the twenty-five hours of Shabbos, we cultivate this relationship to the *Shechinah* through our dress, eating, pace of life, family experiences, Torah learning, davening and achieving a state of *menuchah*. Through the Shabbos, we become a suitable place for Hashem to rest His Presence.

The *Shechinah* yearns to reside within our homes, through the ongoing experience of *shalom bayis* shared between a husband and wife. In this home, the love and caring that exists between a man and woman is where Hashem finds it suitable to permit His *Shechinah* to dwell.

There is the wonderful and well-known story about Rav Shlomo Zalman Auerbach, *zt"l*, who, while walking home, paused to straighten out his clothing and smooth his beard. When asked the purpose of his behavior, his response was that he was going home, where he would see his wife, and their meeting would be as if he was greeting the *Shechinah*. This same *gadol* stated publicly, at his wife's funeral, that it is customary to ask for forgiveness from the deceased for anything he may have done to be hurtful to her over the many years of their marriage. However, he was not aware of a single moment when he did not treat her with respect and kindness. This is the essence of a relationship where the *Shechinah* dwells.

All these are experiences of our lives that permit the *Shechinah* to reside near or within us. However, perhaps there is one dimension which encompasses all of these, and without it, the others are not possible. It is in our state of mind. Without a suitable state of mind, our connection to Hashem's Presence would not be possible.

◇ Where the *Shechinah* Rests

The *gemara* in *Shabbos* says that the *Shechinah* never rests in a place of sadness. It only rests in a place suffused with the joy of the ongoing *mitzvos* of our lives. This means that we need to be in a positive and secure state of mind for the *Shechinah* to reside within us. Using the familiar example of the glass of water, when the glass seems half full and we are grateful to Hashem for all of life's gifts, our mind is a resting place for the *Shechinah*. But when the glass seems half empty, even when the quantity is unchanged, we have lost our ability to be a resting place for the Shechinah.

It is not as if I really have a choice in the perception. When one state of mind brings me closer to who Hashem wants me to be and how He wants me to perceive the world, then I am actually being myself. When I enter a negative state of mind that distances me from Hashem and myself, I no longer serve as a vessel for His Presence.

This is why I call the third principle Mind as *Mishkan*. It is based on our awareness that we are all created to experience thoughts, feelings and an experience of life that enables us to achieve our own human potential as individuals and to share *shalom bayis*.

⬦ The Rambam and *Shechinah*

This concept of Mind as *Mishkan* took on even greater clarity as I read the thoughts of the *mashgiach* of Mir, Rav Yeruchem Levovitz, *zt"l*, in his *sefer Da'as Torah*, which deepens our appreciation of the meaning of the *Mishkan* in our lives. He cites the Rambam's view that all the vessels of the *Mishkan* were designed to serve as metaphors for each of us. For example, the spreading of wings of the angelic figures, the two golden *Keruvim*, above the *Aron HaKodesh* served to bring life-giving *kedushah* from the heavens into our world. The Rambam sees this spreading of the wings as a metaphor for the manner in which we breathe, where the opening and closing of the chest cavity brings life-giving air into our bodies. Just as the *Keruvim* used their wings to bring life into the world through their wings, so, too, do our lungs bring life-giving air into our bodies.

Another sacred vessel was the *Aron HaKodesh* — the Ark containing the Tablets of the Ten Commandments, as well as the Torah itself. The Rambam explains that the Tablets and the Torah are the heart of the Jewish people and were concealed within the Ark. This is a metaphor for the heart of man, which is concealed within the chest cavity.

The Menorah, which illuminated the *Mishkan*, represents wisdom and all human enlightenment, and contained seven branches. Here, too, the Rambam cites these seven branches as a metaphor for our five senses, our power of imagination and our speech.

In each of these and other comparisons, Rav Yeruchem shares his understanding of Rambam's vision of how Hashem commands us to create a *Mishkan* that He will dwell in. By creating the vessels that are a metaphor for each of us, Hashem is telling us that just as He desires to dwell in the *Mishkan*, He desires that we recognize that we are all the embodiment of the *Mishkan* and it is an embodiment of us. As we learn that we can think, feel, see and live as the *Mishkan*, we are being ourselves and fulfilling our purpose in life.

What is there about the *Mishkan* that causes it to be a suitable place for Hashem to reside? The *Mishkan* is where Hashem's love for us and all mankind is most evident. It is a place of peace and harmony. In the *Mishkan* and in the *Bais HaMikdash*, no metal tools were used to fashion the vessels contained within, because metal tools symbolized weapons of war, the antithesis of peace. The position of the *Keruvim* signified Hashem's love for us. When *Am Yisrael* was united as one, they faced each other lovingly. When there was conflict among Hashem's people, the *Keruvim* turned away from each other. The floor of the *Mishkan* was called *ritzpas ahavah*—the floor of love. The inner chambers of the *Mishkan* were filled with the beauty of song, the illumination of the Menorah, the aesthetic harmony of colors, textures and materials, and the sublime feelings and thoughts that permeated it.

◇ The *Mishkan* in Our Lives

The *Mishkan* is the paradigm of beauty, *kedushah*, closeness, pleasantness and clarity in human life. It represents the environment that brings us closer to our own natural beauty with which Hashem endowed us all, and our potential to share lives of love and closeness together. Our awareness of the *Mishkan* is our internal compass that directs and guides our deepest yearnings to be ourselves and share our lives in love and peace.

The significance of what the *mashgiach* and the Rambam are telling us is that throughout our lives, we are all accountable to remember that at each moment Hashem wants our state of mind to be an experience of exquisite and sublime beauty. Hashem desires that our thoughts and feelings and every aspect of our beings emulate the beauty of the *Mishkan*. It is only when we experience this state of mind that we are truly ourselves. Remembering the *Mishkan* as the paradigm for our state of mind means that we have a "gold standard" for defining how Hashem wishes us to experience life. In summary, being aware that Hashem created us to serve as a *Mishkan* enables us to fulfill the purpose of our existence.

This doesn't mean that our lives are free of stress and distress. It does mean that we are created with a mandate to discover how to experience life from within the *Mishkan* even when our lives are challenged. For example, our sense of gratitude and *menuchas hanefesh* can pervade our lives even under the most difficult trials. When Rav Shimon Schwab, *zt"l*, lost the power of his legs in his later years and was confined to a wheelchair, he was asked what enabled him to maintain his sense of hopefulness and belief. His answer was that he had so much to be grateful to Hashem for; how could he even consider feeling upset over what was missing in his life? In marriage, as well, when we fall into a trap of feeling upset with our spouse, we have forgotten all the countless ways that our lives are intertwined, that bring us a sense of stability and continuity.

There is an exercise I give couples called the Sharing Tree. It is composed of considering all the myriad of ways that our lives are connected at the roots. It has the power of reminding us to be aware of a sense of gratitude for all that we do and are for each other. This awareness of *hakaras hatov* is redolent with the aroma of the *Mishkan,* as are all other positive perceptions.

This third principle teaches us that regardless of what we are experiencing in life, Hashem desires that we cultivate a state of mind and quality of *shalom bayis* that enables us to be a resting place for His *Shechinah.* Not only has He fashioned this yearning within us as native to our minds and hearts, He has also filled our lives with countless impressions and experiences that point us in this direction. The mere mention of *Mishkan* evokes our internal longing for beauty, delicate refinement, *kedushah* and the most gentle of human emotions that bring our lives together in love and closeness.

The practical implication for this principle is that when we remember that Hashem created our minds to be a *Mishkan,* we can now evaluate how our state of mind compares with the concept of Mind as *Mishkan.* We are contrasting our present thoughts, feelings and forms of behavior with the beauty and *kedushah* of Mishkan, because this is the only experience of life that is a fitting place for the *Shechinah* to reside.

◇ **The Interior Decorator**

Our striving to discover that state of mind that is compatible with the *middos,* thoughts and feelings of *Mishkan* is analogous to an interior designer in search of the ideal colors and textures that will blend well with a design pattern. The designer will bring swatches of fabrics and samples of materials into a show-room to determine the overall visual and aesthetic harmony of all the objects when they are brought together. In the same way, we are constantly "matching up" our present state of mind with *Mishkan*, which is the state of mind in which Hashem wishes us to be. This means that the *middos* of being patient, loving, empathic, gentle, understanding, giving and humble all enable us to be appropriate environments for Hashem's Presence. This is what we are searching for.

Therefore, as we learn to monitor the shifting patterns of our state of mind, we learn to remind ourselves: "My responsibility in life is to remember that I have the ability to transform this thought, feeling or behavior from *pizur hanefesh* to *menuchas hanefesh* through remembering that Hashem has created my mind to be a *Mishkan*." This is the essence of the third principle. It uncovers a vast area of sublime human experience that we all have within us that points us in the direction of *Mishkan*, and enables us to be who we truly are. When we can remember this third principle, we are empowered to recognize and distance ourselves from negative and even toxic states of hurt, anger and resentment, and all the other states of mind that lock us in the quicksand of *pizur hanefesh*.

◇ **Defining the Desired Achievements of *Mishkan***

Once we have defined *Mishkan* as the direction of *menuchas hanefesh*, we can define what we can achieve as a result of our freedom. This could include aspirations such as, "Hashem wants my mind to be a *Mishkan* ... so I can be a better husband, father, etc. Articulating these desired achievements is a broad and promising vision of the future, as opposed to the myopia and paralysis of *pizur hanefesh* that we were caught up in before employing these principles.

◇ Reviewing the Three Principles and Their Meaning for Transformation

At the heart of all transformation is an unshakable sense of *emunah* that whatever the personal challenges that Hashem has placed in our lives, He has also given us the ability to continuously rediscover the pathways leading us toward *menuchas hanefesh* and *shalom bayis*. Among the many resources he has given us to achieve this, the three principles of *Chiddush, Tzomet* and *Mishkan* serve as our lighthouse, constantly guiding us back home to our deeper and truer selves. When we understand this, experiencing *pizur hanefesh* is almost as if we are driving on rumble strips that alert us when the car we are driving is veering off the highway. It's a warning to find the pathway to be reinspired and reconnected.

The implication of these three principles in our lives is that we have mastery over our own destiny through learning to continuously transform ourselves. As we learn to return to these principles and use them as our compass in life, we discover inner strength and wisdom that we otherwise never realize exists within us.

With this in mind, I'd like to review the principles and embellish their meaning for each of us in our personal and marital lives.

1. The 1st Principle is our awareness that Hashem creates us as new beings at every moment of our lives.

When we are experiencing a state of *pizur hanefesh* through our thoughts, feelings, physiology, behavior or relationship to our spouse, there is always a sense that not only is the negative perception true, but that it will never change. This first principle immediately rescues us from the entrapment of the negative perception. Once we are aware that we are receiving life at this very moment, we open our vistas of life and realize that we can free ourselves from the myopic, narrow and self-centered perception. We realize that there is a Hashem in the world; and even our very consciousness, which is presently ensnared in the iron grip of *pizur hanefesh*, is actually being given life by Hashem.

It's a remarkable thought to realize that while we may feel resentful toward or angry at our spouse, Hashem is giving us the power of consciousness to be in this negative state of mind. And in the same way that He gives us the power to be aware of our negative states, He also gives us the power to transform our state of pain into a positive state. In essence, with this principle, we become aware that there is a power even greater than our anger, hurt, impatience, addiction, resentment or any other form of *pizur hanefesh*. This is the power and domain of Hashem. We express our awareness that all change only comes through Hashem by expressing our desire to grow through articulating a *tefillah* that enables us to ask Hashem for His assistance in transforming our state of mind.

The *Chiddush Tefillah*:

This *tefillah* corresponds to the first of the three principles we have learned. We will learn each *tefillah* individually, but all three are recited together. You can express the *Chiddush* principle by saying:

> "Hashem, You create me every moment, and You don't want me to be in this state of *pizur hanefesh*.

2. The 2nd Principle is our awareness that at every moment we are standing at the crossroads.

This principle informs us that regardless of the intensity of our state of mind, our troubled experience is only one side of a crossroad, and a second side exists at this very moment. We may not know what it is, but we accept that it was Hashem Who placed us here. And it is Hashem Who desires that we discover a portal into the other state of mind that is *menuchas hanefesh* and *shalom bayis*.

The *Tzomet Tefillah*:

You can express the *Tzomet* principle by saying:

> "Hashem, You have placed me at the crossroads between my expression of *pizur hanefesh* and *menuchas hanefesh*, and You want me to learn to transform myself."

3. The 3rd Principle is that our mind was designed to be a *Mishkan*.

This third principle now provides us with a direction in life that we have internalized many times over in our lives. Now we can match our present state with internalized thoughts, memories, and feelings of the beauty and *kedushah* that is *Mishkan*. We don't even need to select a specific aspect of *Mishkan*. It can be very general and impressionistic. However, once we are able to articulate this all-encompassing definition of how Hashem would like us to experience our lives, we can define the many expressions of this positive state of mind. In essence, we have prepared ourselves to receive a transforming gift of wisdom and insight from Hashem.

We can now wait securely and patiently for that transforming state of mind that is compatible with how Hashem has created us. It may be experienced through a clearer and more positive thought, a better feeling, a quieting of symptoms and urges, or a feeling of being closer to our spouse. The possibilities for experiencing our capacity to experience *menuchas hanefesh* are endless, and they are available throughout our lives.

The *Mishkan Tefillah*:

You can express the *Mishkan* principle by saying:

> "Hashem, You want my mind to be a Mishkan because it will help me be a better husband, father, etc."

Finally: *Yegiah* – Transformations Are Discovering a Gift

There is a final dynamic that enables transformation to occur. I do not include *Yegiah* in the principles as it does not need to be articulated. It is our realization that like all else in life, transformation is a gift from Hashem. It is the reward for our belief that all our efforts *l'shaim Shamayim* (for the sake of Heaven) are what Hashem views as our own inner preparation to be deserving of the gift of transformation. Throughout our lives, whether we are looking for a *shidduch*, earning a living wage or finding a beautiful *esrog*, we are required to make the effort. Yet, we must always realize that the results come only from Hashem. Success for our efforts is the gift. All else is an illusion.

This concept is even true when we are attempting to free ourselves from powerful and negative thoughts, overwhelming and disabling feelings, physiological states of anxiety or physical distress, a behavioral addiction, or marital conflict. It is up to us to make the responsible effort, and it is only through Hashem's loving guidance that we can be aware of new insights that are the key to our well-being and *shalom bayis*.

◇ The Sfas Emes Defines *Yegiah*

This experience of discovering new insights into our emerging sense of empowerment is described so eloquently by the Sfas Emes, the Gerrer Rebbe, *zt"l*. The Rebbe uses the term of *yagata matzasa* ("if you try, you find")to define this process of discovery. In the Torah reading of *Terumah*, the Sfas Emes describes that Moshe *Rabbeinu* found that visualizing the *Menorah* was beyond his human capabilities. As a result of the depth of his desire to fulfill the commandments of Hashem, he was not only provided with a visual image of the *Menorah*, but Hashem actually created the *Menorah* Himself as a gift for Moshe and the *Mishkan*.

For us, this means that when we have invested our deepest possible human effort to achieve a lofty goal that exceeds our human limitations, Hashem rewards us with this *m'tziyah*, this find, as a gift for our efforts.

This is the concept of *yagata matzasa*. It is unlike anything we have come to understand in our acquired concept of how we achieve results in our lives. Whether our strivings are toward the building of the *Menorah* for the *Mishkan*, achieving freedom from a troubled state of mind, or transforming marital conflict into *shalom bayis*, the reality is that we are helpless to leave our limited dimension of self. It is only through our deepest and most noble yearnings that we are able to receive this gift directly from Hashem. This is why *Chazal* use the word *matzasa*, you found.

Mitziya means something that was found. We are "surprised" to find the wallet that suddenly appears in front of us lying in the street. A moment ago, it was not there. We had no previous relationship to it. Now it's there and it's ours. In the same way, Hashem suddenly sends us the *mitziya* of transforming thoughts, feelings, inner strengths and perceptions that continuously bring a husband and wife closer. These "discoveries" are loving gifts from Hashem.

CHAPTER VII

Acquiring the Tools of Transformation

◇ *"Mayim amukim eitzah b'laiv ish ..."*
— **The Treasure beneath the Surface**

There are countless discoveries in human history that have led to a new paradigm for understanding the world we live in. It could be the journeys of Columbus, or the calculations of Einstein. However, one of life's great discoveries is available to us continuously. It occurs when we realize that we are never that bird without the use of its wings. It is the discovery that regardless of our situation, we always have the ability to transcend the seeming limitations of the moment to escape the quicksand of *pizur hanefesh* and experience the clarity of *menuchas hanefesh*.

The potential to experience insight and inspiration is always present within us, even at those moments when we feel a sense of abject hopelessness and powerlessness. Our ability to receive these gifts from Hashem is never beyond our grasp. We need to know what enables us to have access to them. We may not always be aware of our choices, because the wisdom and clarity that comes with *menuchas hanefesh* resides deep within us. This treasure never sits on the surface. Like the water at the bottom of the well, waiting for the wily fox in our earlier story to figure out how to bring it to the surface, the insight was always there, waiting to be grasped and understood. Our task is to know how to access it.

Water is an apt metaphor for this wisdom. Shlomo *HaMelech* teaches in *Mishlei* 20:5: "*Mayim amukim eitzah b'laiv ish, ve'ish tevunah yidlenah* — Counsel in a man's heart is like deep water, but a man of understanding will draw it out." The Malbim, a noted nineteenth-century *talmid chacham* who wrote a commentary on the entire *Tanach*, explained the meaning of this verse. He wrote that there are deep waters within us containing great wisdom and insight. But to gain access to our own potential, we need to draw this wisdom from the depths of our mind, as if by a pail tied to a long rope. The wisdom that helps us emerge from our entrapment is always waiting within us to rise to the surface. We need to know how to gain access and free up, these treasures that Hashem always wants to give us.

When an insight suddenly illuminates our thoughts, it has the effect of a lightbulb being switched on in a dark room. Such an "aha!" moment can occur while dealing with a personal problem, pondering a decision, seeking to understand a difficult Torah concept or facing any of life's countless other daily challenges. The answer that had been so elusive earlier is suddenly right there, shimmering with crystal clarity.

> A couple I knew was under serious pressure because of a medical issue involving one of their children. The strain led to a severe clash between them. The husband felt that his wife, behaving in an overly emotional way, had said some hurtful things to him. She insisted she was right and maintained her position to proceed with the medical procedure despite his strong fears and hesitations.
>
> I suggested that she take some time and think through her position about the procedure. A few hours later, she realized that she was permitting her anxiety and stress

to influence her sound judgment. She called her husband
to apologize and get their relationship back on the right
track.

Once her "light" went on, her path was crystal clear. Until then,
she had been gripped by instinctive anxiety, which had distorted her better judgment. Deep within herself, she had a clearer
understanding, but it had been unavailable to her. The wisdom
was always there; she just needed the time to regain her sense of
clarity and gain access to her "deeper counsel."

◇ **Learning the Skills to Go Deeper**

Entering the state of *menuchas hanefesh* occurs through gain-
ing access to our *"mayim amukim,"* the deep waters of counsel
and wisdom. This is how Hashem has created us. This deeper
wisdom is a guiding voice from within that constantly attempts
to direct our lives toward the fulfillment of who we truly are.
For just as the *neshamah* regulates our immune system, which
maintains the delicate balance of our physiological well-being,
this same *neshamah* grasps the deeper truth inherent in each
moment of our lives and attempts to have its thoughtful and
wise counsel heard and understood.

Our ability to make wise decisions and gain insights is never
available to us on a superficial level and without efforts. The
guiding principles of many of the tools we will be learning are
based on understanding how to permit this deeper, wiser voice
of our *neshamah*, residing within us, to once again be heard.
Once we can recognize the guidance emanating from our *mayim amukim*, we can then become suitable vessels to receive the
gift of *menuchas hanefesh*.

With this in mind, the approaches and exercises in this section focus on acquiring the tools for transformation to gain
access to our *mayim amukim* and achieve the following goals:

1. Learn to let go of troubled thoughts and feelings that entrap us in *pizur hanefesh*.
2. Ease stress and anxiety that lead to marital conflict and personal insecurity.
3. Learn to tap into a deeper wisdom and insight that Hashem has placed within each of us.
4. Modify and bring under control *pizur hanefesh* forms of behavior that destroy *shalom bayis*, and replace them with behavior that brings two lives together.
5. Reawaken deeper emotional connections within marriage.

With these goals in mind, we can now proceed to learn the skills of transformation.

◇ Transforming Thoughts and Feelings

In marriage, it's so easy to slip into negative thoughts and feelings about a spouse. These can take root and remain embedded and unchallenged for years.

> A couple, married for more than a decade, came to see me. The husband began to complain about his wife's behavior. "It may not be kind of me to say this, but over the years of our marriage I have come to see my wife as a very selfish person," he declared, and then proceeded to pull out and read a list of his resentments and complaints. He had clearly spent hours compiling his list of complaints and "irrefutable" evidence of her "selfishness." There appeared to be no way I could challenge his perception. Yet when I spoke to his wife, I did not find her to be selfish or self-centered at all. In fact, my sense was that she was far more concerned about her husband's well-being than he was about hers.

This man had been carrying around his perception of his wife as a selfish and self-centered person for years and never questioned it. I have found such characterizations about a spouse to be quite common. These thoughts and feelings burrow into our consciousness and are repeated over and over, frequently becoming what I have called "emotional wallpaper." We just accept them without ever understanding how destructive and distorted they are. It is these same critical and negative perceptions that become the "accepted assumptions" of how we view our spouses. These unquestioned assumptions have the power to trigger and sustain conflicts. This is why I frequently hear statements like, "I know I'm angry, but if you understood what I have been putting up with all these years, you would appreciate that I have every right to be."

> A young couple, relative newlyweds, consulted me about conflicts they were having regarding their respective parents, money and a plethora of other issues. Within the first five minutes, I felt that the tension between them was so intense that I had to comment, "It seems to me that both of you feel you're justified in your mistrust of each other. Just being together with both of you makes me feel as if I'm standing between two rows of barbed wire. I wonder what it must be like to live together."
>
> Both spouses were surprised at my comment. They had become accustomed to living together on the "third rail" (the third rail in the New York City subway system is electrified). They were both living in an emotional prison camp they had come to define as "marriage."

Why do couples remain in these destructive and negative states of mind for a week, a year, a decade, or even a lifetime? Internally we know the truth about love, closeness and *shalom bayis*. It's in our DNA. We have been created to strive toward love in our marriage and family lives. But we have also been given a drive that pulls and pushes us toward repeating negative thoughts, feelings and behavior. This creates an entrapment from which it seems impossible to escape.

◇ The Ski Slope

Sometimes after years of repetition, the seemingly innocuous wallpaper of these negative feelings begins to show signs of buckling, and then suddenly bursts into a full-blown crisis. Once this begins to occur, it can escalate at lightning speed. We see this frequently on *erev* Shabbos, when, *Chazal* caution us, the seemingly quiet atmosphere in a home can erupt without warning into a dangerous argument — even as the candles are being lit. One moment the air is quiet and calm, and then someone says or does something that triggers an unexpected sequence of events that spirals downward in the blink of an eye.

This lightning-speed process of the downward spiral reminds me of a story shared by a close friend describing a scene he had witnessed on the Swiss Alps many years ago.

> A father was enjoying the adventure of watching his young son run down the snowy foothills of the Alps. The proud father placed his child on a gentle and seemingly safe slope and encouraged him to run down. The boy would start running, fall, and roll in the snow. The father and the son would then laugh and start all over again. The father repeated this playful game a number of times until the boy felt more confident as he ran down the snowy slope.
>
> The next time the boy started running, he was able to keep his balance. The snow and the hills were now his friends. He made his way down the slope again, this time with greater speed and glee. The boy was mastering the art of running down a snowy hill, and he and his father laughed triumphantly. But the father's laugh was suddenly cut short and replaced with shock, fear and panic: his son

had become so proficient that he was running downhill at a speed far greater than either had anticipated. At this rate, the child would pass the father in a few seconds and continue to build up speed as he headed toward a precipice perhaps two or three hundred feet below them! The man had failed to judge what would happen if his son learned to keep his balance while running at full speed. The father's laughter turned into an ear-piercing scream as he realized that with every passing nanosecond, his son's life was closer to slipping away.

The desperate father lunged head-first toward his son, tripping the child as he was about to pass by. His fingers barely touched the boy's legs, but it was just enough to upset the child's delicate balance and send him tumbling harmlessly off to the side. Father and son were both crying — each for very different reasons.

Here, a father and son were enjoying the moment surrounded by the breathtaking peaks of the Alps. An idyllic scene was suddenly transformed into a nightmare when the boy was helplessly pulled by a downward spiral toward a precipice. How long did it take for the father's laughter to turn into a scream of pain and torture? Did it take a second, or just a nanosecond?

I ask the question not because there is an answer, but because I want to create an awareness of how long it takes for a fight to break out between a couple. It occurs in an instant, even faster than a child running helplessly down a slope. With a couple, all we need is a gesture of the hand, a word, a reference to an event, and then suddenly not one, but two individuals are racing downhill toward the precipice. They push and pull and provoke each other to build up to breakneck speed, faster than the ear or eye can detect. And it's all because when negative thoughts and feelings emerge from *pizur hanefesh*, they take on a destructive power that accepts no limitations.

◇ What We Learn from Monkeys

Why is it so difficult for couples to let go and break away from these conflicts? The answer is that just as there are forces of nature propelling the child toward the precipice, there are also natural forces within a couple that drive and sustain a conflict that is never in anyone's best interests.

In his classic book on therapeutic communication, *The Language of Change*, Paul Watzlawick describes how members of a tribe in Africa capture a live monkey. They place a banana into a wicker basket, which is attached to a tree. The top of the basket is large enough to accommodate the open hand of a monkey, so it can place its hand in the basket to grab the banana. However, the opening is not large enough to permit the closed fist of the monkey to be pulled out of the basket while holding the banana. When the monkey grabs the banana, the hunter knows that no force on earth will make that monkey willingly let go of its prize. The helpless animal will now be trapped by its own determinedly closed fist, unable to let go for even a moment. Losing its freedom and probably its life is a steep price for a monkey to pay for holding on to a banana.

There are many individuals who simply can't let go. I have lost track of the number of times I have heard a husband or wife admit, "I knew I shouldn't have said that" or "I know it's killing our marriage, but I can't help myself." And along with these negative thoughts and feelings comes the inevitable perception that "it feels almost impossible to let go." In reality, the question I hope couples will ask is, "How can I let go of the banana?"

> I sat with Malkie and Lenny as they discussed their marriage. Lenny insisted, "You know there was never a time when I hurt you." Suddenly Malkie turned red. "And what about the hotel room in Palm Springs when you lost your temper and said terrible things to me?" Lenny was

incredulous. "That was almost ten years ago, and I asked you to forgive me. And you still can't forget it!"

◇ E.A.T.

How do we begin to let go of the banana? How do we learn that we have the strength and power to change? I have used the acronym "E.A.T." to describe three steps in the transformation process.

E is for Experience: We experience the negative thought, feeling, physiological sensation or the quality of our connection toward our spouse.

A is for Awareness: We become aware that our thoughts, feelings, physiology, behavior and relationship experience are in conflict with the state of mind that Hashem has intended to bring us closer to each other.

T is for Transformation: We are able to use this awareness to employ specific thoughts, perspectives and behaviors to transform our present state.

With this in mind, we can now take a close look at the tools that can be helpful toward transforming a person's state of mind and lifestyle in a way that is aligned and in synchronization with the *ratzon Hashem.*

TOOLS FOR TRANSFORMATION

TRANSFORMATION TOOL #1:
Using the Three Principles

The first and most important of all the tools you will learn in this program is to integrate the three principles of *Chiddush, Tzomet* and *Mishkan* into your moment-to-moment experience of life.

The first step is to be aware of the negative thoughts or feelings that are constantly flowing through your consciousness and realize that you have the ability to transform them. It's so crucial to understand that nothing justifies these feelings. Even if you feel your spouse is insensitive or worse, there is no effective action you can take to educate your partner unless you can quiet your troubled thoughts or feelings.

If your spouse tells you that you are behaving in a hurtful way, avoid reacting negatively and concluding that you are being misjudged. Instead, once again, the answer is to subdue your tendency to fight back, quiet down your thoughts and feelings, and listen carefully to what you are being told.

For example, I frequently hear a husband or wife say, "I don't know why you're shouting at me; please stop being so angry." And the response is, "I'm not shouting and I'm not angry." The anger and hurt creep in steadily and just sit there almost as a "friend," but they are a lot more poisonous.

◇ **Internalizing the Three Principles**

If you are harboring troubled thoughts and feelings toward your spouse, the first step is to realize that you do have the ability to quiet your state of mind and to listen more carefully by remembering the three principles.

When a husband walks into his home and senses a voice of criticism welling up inside, or when a wife looks at her husband and views him as a "failure," be aware that these thoughts and feelings are expressions of *pizur hanefesh* and will only intensify your own hurt and isolation, as well as the hurt and isolation of your spouse and family. Just because we experience them, they are not the undisputed "reality." We need to assess whether they are bringing us closer to the state of mind that Hashem has created us to experience — or further away.

Let's look at some of these possible thoughts and feelings:

+ Walking into your home, you see the place as untidy and noisy. You say to yourself, "I'm fed up with this mess."
+ You are in a public gathering and see someone else's spouse. You think, "*This* is the kind of spouse I deserve."
+ You are looking for your papers and can't find them. You feel angry at your spouse for always putting your things in places where you can't find them.
+ You feel unsatisfied with your physical intimacy and look at others as being more fulfilled. Perhaps you even harbor fantasies of being with another person.
+ You feel your spouse is a failure.
+ You find your spouse unattractive.
+ You feel your spouse is insensitive.
+ You think your spouse is unintelligent.

I can write a list that would fill volumes.

Even if a panel of blue-ribbon judges agrees with you, your state of mind only exacerbates and feeds the problem. While it may very well be that your spouse is challenged in a particular area, your state of mind locks you into *pizur hanefesh* and you can never help your spouse be open enough to hear you and learn how to grow in this area. After all, what other reason is there for you to be angry or upset if it isn't to help your spouse change? And if your anger or hurt is maintaining the status quo for years and making things worse, isn't it time to try and improve the relationship?

The first step is to realize that regardless of the validity of your feelings, your thoughts and feelings are negative and troubled. Your state of mind is steeped in the quicksand of *pizur hanefesh*. There is no positive change you can make from the perspective of your negative state of mind. Your first goal is to rebalance yourself and rediscover your *menuchas hanefesh*. Deciding that this is your direction is the most important decision you can make. Once you make it, you will discover solutions to the perceived problem. Once you understand that your primary problem is with your state of mind, you can begin to use the principles of *Chiddush, Tzomet* and *Mishkan* to be open to meaningful solutions.

To prepare you for using this tool, I suggest you spend a few moments learning to internalize these three principles by focusing on four concepts and repeating the appropriate *tefillah* for each principle:

1. Chiddush

First, be aware and accepting of the reality that your very existence is the result of being given life every moment by a loving and nurturing power that emanates from Hashem. This life-giving energy imbues every cell of your body with the power to think, feel, behave and perform every physical function required to exist, thrive and be free to fulfill your potential.

2. Tzomet

The next step is to realize that you have been placed at these crossroads by Hashem. While you are presently experiencing *pizur hanefesh*, where your thoughts and feelings are troubled, there is also another dimension to your self that can be experienced as *menuchas hanefesh* and *shalom bayis*. Hashem wants you to transform yourself.

3. Mishkan

The third step is to be aware that the only way you can select which direction Hashem wishes you to take in the crossroads is by learning to access a state of mind that is similar to the beauty and clarity of the *Mishkan*. Hashem desires that your state of mind be a resting place for His Presence — the Shechinah.

◇ *Yegiah*

Finally, the last step is to realize that once you have invested your best efforts, your *yegiah,* Hashem will provide you with the insight that you deserve and require — the *metziah.* For all outcomes are discovering Hashem's ongoing love and caring for you.

After following these steps, you can begin to be aware that your state of mind discovers new possibilities and pathways to transformation. They emerge as insights, decisions to take a needed time-out, the ability to reframe a perception in a more positive light, or feeling less stressed and more tolerant and patient. These three principles guide us to be more attuned to living in that state that Hashem desires us to experience. As we create appropriate states of mind that invite the *Shechinah* into our lives and homes, we also experience the revitalization of our *shalom bayis.* Whenever your thoughts and feelings bring you to a negative place, using these principles will enable you to discover your *mayim amukim,* those deeper insights and feelings that enable you to quiet your mind and enable new possibilities to be experienced in your marriage.

◇ The *Tefillos for Transformation*

Now that we have covered the principles of transformation, we can put the three *tefillos* together in the proper sequence.

The *Chiddush* Tefillah

"Hashem, You create me every moment, and You don't want me to be in this state of *pizur hanefesh.*

The *Tzomet* Tefillah:

"Hashem, You have placed me at the crossroads between my expression of *pizur hanefesh* and *menuchas hanefesh,* and You want me to learn to transform myself."

The *Mishkan Tefillah*:

"Hashem, You want my mind to be a *Mishkan*, because it will help me be a better husband, father, etc."

Mr. and Mrs. S. had been married for more than ten years. From the perspective of their community, they had an ideal marriage and family. However, the couple had been harboring feelings of simmering anger and resentment for many years. Mr. S. saw his wife as unkempt at home and unsupportive of his business efforts, while Mrs. S. had always viewed her husband as financially irresponsible and emotionally distant and uncaring. Their marriage ran in cycles, where they would "tolerate" each other for a few months, and then one incident would trigger a major conflict that would threaten their home.

The latest round of conflicts had resulted in feelings of personal damage that were now seriously threatening the marriage. Both realized that it had progressed beyond their ability to control the conflict and pull back. They were also aware of how important they were to each other and their four children.

Learning to use the principles in their interaction created an immediate shift away from the silence and anger and enabled them to feel a greater sense of cooperation. Mrs. S. shared her perceptions with me. "It felt like I had a choice," she explained. "I didn't have to react in hurt and anger. It freed me up to be who I really am."

When you and your spouse learn to use these principles, it is an empowering awareness. Suddenly you are no longer pulled into the vortex of a fight, or driven by your hurt and sense of justified anger. A small light seems to go on, and you have the ability to say, "There's a way out of this trap. I can keep myself free of the dangerous entanglement." It's a reassuring awareness to feel that you're off the ski slope.

◇ A Suggestion for Integrating the Principles into Your Life

For one week, repeat three times a day the three Principles and their corresponding *tefillos*. You can select specific times or places. By repeating the principles, you will enhance your awareness of them so they can be effectively used when you experience a troubled state of mind caused by *pizur hanefesh*.

TRANSFORMATION TOOL #2: Living in the Flow of Life

◇ Reynolds Channel

Near my home in the Rockaways, along the Atlantic coast, there is an inlet from the bay called Reynolds Channel where a number of small boats are docked. There are times when I walk by and the water level is so low that the boats are actually sunk in the mud near the shore. Then, when I return in the evening, or whenever the tide is in, the boats are bobbing in many feet of water. One day, I realized that had I only been there when the water level was low and never seen them bobbing during high tide, my perspective would be that these boats are always stuck in the mud. I would naturally think that they were abandoned, or I would wonder why anyone would want to dock his boat in the mud. However, once I realize that the boats rise and sink with the natural rhythms of the tide, my perspective is very different.

I call this Hashem's flow of life, and there are countless expressions of this flow of life in the world around us and within us. It exists in the small channel outside my home; it also exists in the revolution of night and day, in the changing of the seasons, within our own bodies, and even within the flows in our own thoughts and feelings.

◇ *Ba'erev Yalin Bechi …*

When we appreciate how Hashem's flow of life fills our world, it gives us a perspective that quiets our moments of insecurity and helplessness. Each morning we recite the phrase of Dovid HaMelech's hope for the future (*Tehillim* 30:6): *"Ba'erev yalin bechi, v'laboker rinah* — In the evening I lie in tears, but in the morning I will hear the song of joy." It is a belief that life is an expression of Hashem's flow of life. Just as the tide changes, even when we go to sleep at night feeling helpless, Hashem will enable us to wake up with a renewed sense of hope and strength.

This song of hope is not just for the hours of darkness. At any moment we may feel the gloom of night descend. Yet, we have the ability to realize that Hashem is preparing the song of morning for us. When we realize this, even when the boats are in the mud and we experience the pain and gloom of the moment, we have the ability to wait for the tide to turn and the morning to come. When we maintain this perspective, darkness never seems permanent. Perhaps this is what the *Tanna*, Nachum Ish Gamzu, meant when he said of all events in our lives, *"Gam zu l'tovah* — this, too, is for the good."

This awareness of Hashem's flow of life enables us to perceive life from a more elevated perspective. It's as if we are seeing life from 30,000 feet up rather than at eye level. We look at the bigger picture. We understand that our hurt feelings at the moment will pass, given the opportunity. Our thoughts of criticism will yield to healthier thoughts that bring us closer together.

◇ *Kiddush Levanah*

I was reminded of this one *motza'ei* Shabbos as I stood outside of *shul* and waited for the clouds to clear so we could bless the new moon by reciting *Kiddush Levanah*. Some men wanted to leave. However, I decided to wait. Then the moon, as if on cue, peeked out from behind the night cloud cover. This, too, is part of Hashem's flow of life. Sometimes we need to be patient, to wait and permit Hashem's flow of life to help the moon emerge.

Becoming aware that we are living within Hashem's flow of life brings on a deeper sense of security and inner stability. It is an awareness that we can learn to cultivate and internalize into our lives. Here are a few personal thoughts regarding how I have come to bring this awareness into my own life.

◇ Life Flowing through Our Beings

There are times when I take a moment, listen to myself breathe, and imagine the air entering my lungs and flowing through my bloodstream to find its way to every cell of my being. I realize that regardless of what is occurring in my life, there is a continuous inner river of life bringing nourishment and sustenance to every cell of my being. This is part of Hashem's flow of life.

I can walk on a tree-lined street and see clouds in gentle motion, birds in elegant flight, and flowers and trees in bloom. I can smell delicate aromas and hear the sounds of nature, even the voices of people in my environment. This, too, is Hashem's flow of life.

What do all these phenomena of life mean to us? Hashem has placed the flow and rhythms of life within us and all around us. It's in the animated world of nature that envelops us; in the air, trees, clouds, rain, sun and live creatures that populate our world. This flow of life brings us the energy to have healthy, loving and life-giving thoughts, feelings, and an experience of our selves.

Our appreciation of this flow of life that Hashem continuously causes to pulse through the universe has crucial implications for our thoughts and feelings. We learn to appreciate that a thought and a feeling never exist independent of countless other functions that are occurring simultaneously. For example, it's very fascinating to realize that Man is the only being in the universe who can think and talk. Each day we recite, "*Ata chonein l'adam da'as*" in the *Shemoneh Esrei*. It means that Hashem lovingly bestows the power of thought within us.

Yet, these thoughts are not an isolated phenomenon. They exist in a larger system as well. They emerge into our consciousness through the cells of our mind that Hashem nurtures at each moment. These cells are fed through the circulatory system that is an inner river of life constantly maintaining them. The system is driven by a beating heart and balanced by the delicate biochemical environment of our physical beings.

In the totality of this delicately balanced universe of self, we are aware of our thoughts and feelings. And even when we believe we have "nothing on our minds," our minds are actually never at rest. Throughout each moment of our lives, our minds are filled with a veritable stream of both positive and negative thoughts and feelings. Some have the potential to bring us closer to *menuchas hanefesh*, and some will drive us further away.

◇ Don't Feed the Bully

Frequently, when we have a negative thought, our tendency is to view it as the enemy and fight it off. Many find that this approach merely "feeds the bully," and intensifies the thought or feeling. However, when we realize that even our thoughts and feelings are part of Hashem's flow of life, we no longer feel the need to do battle with them; we have the real choice of learning to quietly "let them pass." *Chazal* say that when we are worried about a future event that we can't influence, our best approach is to quiet the worry by realizing, "*dai tzarah beshayta.*" It's enough to worry about it when it happens.

By saying this, we realize that there is an ebb and flow to

our consciousness, which is part of the rhythm of Hashem's flow of life. Many of these thoughts and feelings will frequently "self-correct" when we realize that we have the ability to drop them. This awareness is the same as knowing that as I pass by Reynolds Channel and see the boats stuck in the mud, I know at that moment that with a bit of patience I'll see the boats bobbing freely when the water returns. When I am feeling down and hopeless, or have a negative thought about my spouse, then the awareness of Dovid *HaMelech's* song of hope — that at night there may be tears, but there is hope that the morning will bring song — enables me to let go of the iron grip of the mood or thought. We need to get beyond that impulse that stays rigidly focused on the negative; otherwise, we compound the problem.

◇ ### *Sur Mei'ra, Va'aseh Tov*

Rav Nachman Bulman, *zt"l*, from whom I learned many precious lessons of Torah and life, shared with me the need to move beyond negative thoughts to discover the positive. Dovid *HaMelech* expresses in *Tehillim*, "*Sur mei'ra, va'aseh tov* — Move away from evil and commit yourself to do good." Rabbi Bulman explained to me that there are many who are obsessed with the *sur mei'ra* (leaving evil) side of the phrase. The problem is that they repeat it over and over until they become like a broken record and make a lifestyle out of it. They never really get to the marrow of life's precious experiences that exist in the second phrase of the verse: "*aseh tov.*" For Rav Bulman, the task at hand was to realize that the negative side requires us to leave it quickly — *sur mei'ra* — and then, just as quickly, jump to the positive "*aseh tov.*"

On a practical level, this means that we frequently become entrapped in how we feel about negative thoughts and feelings, and this makes us feel even worse.

A young woman had been married for almost a year, and the marriage had been rocky from the very beginning. First she described how she was uncertain about whether she had made the right decision about marrying her husband. Then she described how guilty she felt about her uncertainties. "I feel like such a bad person when I say these things." My response was, "Which is worse? Is it the initial doubt you had, or your feelings of being guilty over the doubt?" She thought for a moment and answered, "I guess I can live with the doubt and see how things progress. It's the guilt for feeling the doubt that makes me feel even worse."

For this young woman, the guilt itself became a source of even greater hurt when she said to herself, "I feel so terrible about feeling guilty." The problem was compunded by her "feeding the bully."

◇ Digging Deeper into the Ditch

Sometimes people act in a way I refer to as "digging deeper into the ditch." Picture the following scenario:

"Hey, what are you doing with that shovel?"

"I'm in a ditch, so I'm shoveling myself out."

"Well, how deep was the ditch when you first got in?"

"It was up to my knees."

"But now you've shoveled yourself down to your hips. Looks like you're just getting in deeper."

"So what do I do?"

"Well, first I suggest you stop digging yourself in even deeper."

◇ Hashem Gives Life to Our Difficulties

One way to stop digging ourselves deeper into the black hole is to remember that even our negative thoughts are part of Hashem's flow of life. We don't succeed by fighting them. We succeed by understanding that they are part of a larger picture, which is always shifting. Eventually it always shifts in the right direction because Hashem is always guiding our world to focus us in the right direction. I can learn to say that there are many other thoughts and feelings that are far more positive within me that I am presently not aware of. I can learn to let go of these negative thoughts and feelings. As I learn to drop these thoughts, I also learn to trust that far more comfortable and productive thoughts will bob to the surface. Even the most painful feelings of night will give way to morning song and moonbeams.

◇ Milton Erickson's Morning Light

There is a great deal I would like to share about Milton Erickson, MD, who died in 1982. Erickson was a larger-than-life figure who reshaped our conception of how people can change, and I want to share a story that Erickson told about himself that is very germane to our discussion of Hashem's flow of life.

Erickson was brought up as part of a large family in the Minnesota plains. As a teenager, he was paralyzed by polio. At the initial stages of the disease, his condition was extremely critical. The attending physician told his mother, "Mrs. Erickson, it seems that Milton will not live through the night." His mother began crying uncontrollably. The young Erickson was very upset to see his mother crying. He sensed the overwhelming gloom that pervaded the cabin. Although his use of his limbs was very limited, his mind was still very crisp and sharp. Before he closed his eyes and slept for what was believed to be his "last night of life," he motioned insistently to his mother to move the dresser away from the window.

Contrary to the doctor's prediction, the next morning he awoke. Erickson went on to achieve a lifetime of unparalleled accomplishments in his field of psychiatry and clinical hypnosis.

Some time later, when he was able to communicate, he was asked about his insistence about moving the dresser. His response was, "They thought I was going to die and were very depressed. However, I wasn't about to buy into that gloom. I knew I would live to see the sun rise in the morning. But the dresser was blocking the window, and I wanted to make sure that I would be able to see that sun the moment it started to rise."

◇ ## A *Berachah* from Rav Aharon, *zt"l*

An event that occurred in my own family is seared indelibly into my mind. In 1960, my younger sister was taken to the emergency room with spinal meningitis. The physicians told my mother not to expect her to live through the night. We were four children and my mother; my father, *a"h*, had died six years earlier. We heard the doctor's report and were all in a state of shock. My brother-in-law, Rabbi Shmuel Kaufman, contacted the *gadol hador*, Rav Aaron Kotler, *zt"l*, and informed him of the impending tragedy. Rav Aaron slammed his fist on the table and stated with unswerving certainty, "*Sie vet nisht shtarben* — She will not die." And in the morning, after a night of *Tehillim* and *tefillah*, I entered her room and she was indeed still alive. Here, too, we see Dovid *HaMelech*'s prophetic words: "*Ba'erev yalin bechi, v'laboker rinah.*"

We understand the difference between the *emunah* of a *gadol* such as Rav Aaron, *zt"l*, and the hope and determination of a young boy stricken by polio on the plains of Minnesota. However, the power to believe and trust in the goodness of Hashem's flow of life is inbred and instinctive, even when the moment seems dire or even hopeless. So when a husband or wife feels critical of a spouse or a marriage, or even about the quality of his/her own experience of self, the first instinct may be to believe the criticism as the unquestionable truth. That is the nature of *pizur hanefesh*. However, a wiser approach is to be able to take a step back and say, "I may be experiencing negative thoughts or feelings, but I have many different thoughts and feelings within me that are all a part of Hashem's flow of life. Therefore, I can drop this negative state of mind and be open to more positive states that I am not yet aware of."

Our awareness that even the troubled thoughts or feelings are connected to Hashem's flow of life creates an immediate respite from the compulsion to fight or flee. Perspective is a far better tool than combat or retreat. Even more important, the respite and freedom creates an opening for us to receive the wisdom of our own *neshamos* as we are now capable of focusing on our *mayim amukim*. The ability to quiet our negative thoughts and feelings now enables us to receive new and healthy perceptions from the inspiration that Hashem has placed deep within each of us, just below the surface. By being aware of the countless manifestations of this flow of life, we are opening ourselves up to be able to have access to other thoughts and possibilities.

Transforming Physiology — Our Body's Pathways

The primary tools we have learned are helpful for transforming the thoughts and feelings that impede *shalom bayis*. However, when it comes to transforming physiological patterns of *pizur hanefesh* and distress, I have frequently found that we require more sensory and behavioral approaches. This is because once the body has developed its own neural pathways of experiencing insecurity and discomfort, these patterns are triggered by anticipation, associations and habit.

> A young wife came to see me about her marriage. As she described her relationship with her husband, she shared that she frequently feels herself becoming physically tense just before she has any direct contact with him. "Just knowing that we're going to be in each other's presence in the

next few moments causes me to feel a sense of physical tightness and anxiety."

Whether the cause of anxiety is real or anticipatory, the effects are frequently measurable.

> I worked with a couple where the husband would develop severe stomach cramps after each conflict. At night he would awaken in severe pain. He was convinced that this was a sign that they could not continue in the marriage. *Baruch Hashem*, he was able to develop skills in quieting and managing his physiological reactions, as well as communication skills to bring him and his wife closer together.

In marriage, as I described in the last chapter, the physiological manifestations of *pizur hanefesh* are staggering. They include headaches, backaches, tightening of the jaw, panic attacks, high blood pressure, hyperventilation, stomach problems and many other similar physiological expressions of our negative state of mind and body that we call *pizur hanefesh*. Frequently I am asked whether any of these are purely physical. The answer is that they certainly can be, and it's always prudent to consult with a physician before any other diagnosis can be applied. However, when a physician feels the source of the symptom may have an emotional element, it's wise to apply some of the approaches that have the potential to quiet down the symptoms that may very well be rooted in our *pizur hanefesh* state of mind.

> Chaim had recently been married. While he had always experienced some degree of anxiety in the past, along with the unexpected pressures of marriage his symptoms grew in their intensity. Even beyond the physical tension, he began experiencing fatigue and headaches. He had been to both traditional and homeopathic medical

practitioners with poor results. However, as he learned to apply approaches that enabled him to transform his *pizur hanefesh* to *menuchas hanefesh*, Chaim came to appreciate that he had far more control over his symptoms than he had ever imagined.

In *Devarim* 4:15, the Torah commands us to watch over our health: *"V'nishmartem me'od l'nafshoseichem* — Be very careful with your soul. This *mitzvah* is more than just being aware of our vital life signs. It extends to developing a lifestyle that connects our positive emotional and cognitive well-being to a healthy physical experience of life. It means being aware of how these factors contribute to our physical functioning, and learning to apply effective approaches that have a positive influence on how our body behaves.

◇ **Overcoming Paralysis**

As we look at this interface between psyche and soma, or mind and body, I am invariably drawn to the groundbreaking work of Milton Erickson, MD, whom I had previously mentioned. Like many others who suffered from polio, Erickson was unable to move a muscle. His mother would place her motionless adolescent son on a chair in the middle of the cabin, where he would sit all day. While he could not move, his mind was crisp and clear. So he simply observed life moving all around him.

During this period, his mother gave birth to a girl. From his chair, young Milton observed how his infant sister learned to use every muscle in her body. She used her hands and feet to roll over and eventually crawl, her fingers to grasp and her knees to balance herself as she prepared to walk. From his observations he came to understand that it was the mind's ability to focus on muscle groups that enabled each of these skills to be learned. Sitting motionless in his chair, he wondered whether he, like his infant sister, could connect his thoughts to his muscles and regain the use of his body that the disease had stolen from him.

One day, the family was shocked to see that Milton had fallen off his chair. Everyone knew that since he was paralyzed, he must have been pushed. However, for him it meant that somehow his thoughts had caused his muscles to move his body. It was the beginning of a new life. Within a year and a half after that event, he mastered the ability to regain control over almost all his muscles. At the age of nineteen, he went on a solo canoe trip of fifteen hundred miles.

Erickson then went on to use his unique understanding of how the mind controls the body to become a psychiatrist and the world's foremost clinical hypnotherapist. His achievements were monumental. His accomplishments have always provided me with a sense of inspiration for our innate capacity to overcome the limitations of our physiological responses.

◇ Leibel's Speech Impairment

A *chassidish* young man, Leibel, came to see me about a severe stuttering problem that had prevented him from dating. He was the only one left in his *shiur* who was neither married nor a *chassan*, and was very depressed about his situation. Since his stuttering was so evident, he never had the opportunity to even meet a young woman. Leibel's family had spent many thousands of dollars for treatment over the years, without any appreciable effect.

As part of understanding *menuchas hanefesh* and change, Leibel learned a meditative and focusing exercise: the Pulse of Life. After practicing the meditation for a week, he felt capable of having his first meeting, or *"besho"* as it is called in Yiddish. He met with the young lady for the required time and was able to maintain sufficient mastery over his stuttering for the girl and her family to feel confident that this was no longer an issue of concern.

All this occurred without my knowledge. As I was driving home from a meeting, I received a call from him.

"This is Leibel."

"Hello, Leibel. I'm glad to hear from you. I was expecting to hear from you two days ago. Have you been doing the exercise?"

"Yes, I did the exercise many times, and I had a *besho*."

I was surprised. "That's great. And what happened?"

"*Mazal tov,*" was his answer. "I had the *besho*, and now I'm a *chassan*."

This story may seem to be somewhat bizarre. However, consider that Leibel and others suffering from this impairment can usually sing, *daven* and even read out loud without stuttering, providing it's not in a one-to-one situation. The ability is there to speak fluently and unimpeded. Leibel had learned that he could gain mastery over his vocal organs to control his speech in the social context as well.

My position is to demonstrate that Hashem gives us the ability to gain mastery over and transform our physiological functioning. This is not a new concept. There are many well-respected approaches that use the mind/body connection to improve health and well-being. Dr. John Sarno's methodologies have gained worldwide recognition for reducing back pain by overcoming stress.

◇ Rav Gustman's Root Canal

For our own work, I prefer to consider our own *gedolim* to appreciate the possibilities of how the mind can overcome the limitations of the body.

I know a dentist in Israel, Dr. Josh Daniels, who performed a root canal on Harav Yisrael Ze'ev Gustman, *zt"l*, one of the *gedolim* of the previous generation. The root canal procedure is particularly painful and always requires an anesthetic. (There was a best-selling book and movie in the sixties, *Marathon Man*, in which root canal was used as a form of torture.) Harav Gustman, however, told Dr. Daniels that there was no need for any anesthetic. He would simply review his Torah learning during the procedure.

I recently met Dr. Daniels at a wedding in Israel and he shared that while the *rosh yeshivah* insisted that he not use any anesthetic, Dr. Daniels continuously apologized and asked for his forgiveness. The *rosh yeshivah* reassured him that he was in no distress and thanked him. All the while, Rav Gustman sat quietly, undergoing the procedure and reviewing his Torah learning.

◇ The *Rebbe's Tefillin*

There are many similar stories, such as the one in which the Modzitzer Rebbe, *zt"l*, composed a beautiful and well-known *niggun* during a surgical procedure.

There is also the well-known episode about the Tchebiner Rav, *zt"l*, who was required to stay awake during neurosurgery. The dilemma was that without anesthesia, neither he nor anyone else could withstand the pain. But with anesthesia, he would succumb to sleep. His response to the problem was to put on a pair of *tefillin* during the surgery. Since there is a *halachah* not to sleep while wearing *tefillin*, he was certain that he would not fall asleep as long as he wore his *tefillin*. To the astonishment of the surgeon, the anesthesia was administered and he remained alert throughout the surgery.

◇ Transforming Physiology

My intention is not to focus on dealing with any specific physical discomfort or how to undergo a root canal without anesthesia, or neurosurgery with it. It is to guide individuals and couples toward overcoming the influence that adverse physiological symptoms can have on a marriage and *shalom bayis.*

> A husband who had been married for more than thirty years, came to see me. "My wife and I have an okay marriage. We have problems, but so does everyone else. My biggest problem is that she is a tense person and makes me very nervous. I have a history of tension headaches, and I also grind my teeth at night. I'm sure she's just making it worse for me."
>
> In another situation, a wife shared with me, "I just don't know what I can do. I think about our marriage and all its problems, and I feel that we can never make things better. It's been too difficult for too long. I feel fatigued and emotionally overwhelmed."

In these scenarios, there may very well be a plethora of contributing problems, some of which may never be fully resolved. However, the presence of a physiological symptom exacerbates and deepens all the other issues. Whenever we feel we are losing control of our physical functioning because of our partner, it depletes us of our strength and desire to make things better. This is why I will usually attempt to help the individual learn to transform the symptom. Even if nothing else is accomplished, if we are successful in quieting the symptom by learning to bring it under greater control, this in itself makes for a profound difference in our sense of personal empowerment. Beyond the correction of the physiological problem, I also attempt to enhance a couple's quality of life through exercise and strategic activities that contribute to a greater sense of *menuchas hanefesh* in the physical dimension.

◇ The Garden Hose

Physiological symptoms that are related to personal and marital stress are analogous to a garden hose. If the "hose" is unblocked, then the flow of physical and emotional energies within us flows naturally. However, if the "hose" is knotted or constricted, the flow of "water" will be inhibited until something gives. Suddenly there may be a surge of emotions, or the pressure will continue to build up and create small fissures that enlarge until the walls of the "hose" are like a sieve, with "water" squirting out from everywhere. In other situations, the blockage may be hermetically sealed, leading to the effects of profound emotional repression.

We can see the effects of these phenomena through high blood pressure, hyperventilation, rapid heartbeat, teeth grinding, stomach disorders and many other similar symptoms. One man told me that while he was on his way to a job he dreaded, his nose suddenly started bleeding. Clearly, the pressure in his blood vessels built up as a result of his emotions, until the delicate capillaries of his nose gave way and became an exit for the pressure.

◇ *Kotzer Ruach* in Mitzrayim

In our own history, we can see this phenomenon. When *Am Yisrael* was enslaved in *Mitzrayim*, we are told that they suffered from "*kotzer ruach*," which means shortness of breath. It is only when Hashem relieved the pressures of servitude that they were once again able to take a full and deep breath, pray and express themselves fully to Hashem.

◇ Exercises in Transformation

To transform physiological symptoms that I have found to be widespread in marriage, there are three approaches I prefer to teach couples. These are:
  1. The Power of Focused Walking
  2. Centering
  3. The Pulse of Life

TRANSFORMATION TOOL # 3:
The Power of Focused Walking

◇ Rachel's Walk

> It is a mild autumn day when Rachel begins her walk. She has chosen a quiet street near her home in a New York suburb. The street is lined with trees and has relatively little traffic. Just as important, it is unlikely that she will meet anyone she knows who may interrupt her exercise in Focused Walking.
>
> Rachel walks at a comfortable pace and appears to be looking straight ahead. The walk lasts for about fifteen minutes. We assume that she has used the opportunity to get some fresh air and exercise. While this is certainly true, something far more important is occurring. During this Focused Walk, Rachel is exploring the causes of her fatigue. Recently she had experienced periods of being tired. Medical tests revealed no clear diagnosis. My sense was that it was related to her marital stress. With this in mind, she agreed to do the exercise. Over time, Rachel learned she could overcome symptoms of fatigue and depression that were affecting her role as a wife and mother.

This section will explore the importance of Focused Walking as an essential tool to help you regain the delicate balance between your mind and your body, so vital in overcoming the physiological symptoms of *pizur hanefesh*.

◇ The Benefits of Walking

There is no need for me to advocate the health benefits of walking. That would be similar to promoting breathing. I am an avid walker, and I recommend it for others. When Rabbi Avigdor Miller, *zt"l*, was given a ride home from a wedding, he insisted that he be left off about two miles from his house. The *bachurim* in the car would not hear of it and insisted that he be driven home. He patiently explained that if he would be taken all the way home, he would simply walk a mile back in the direction they just came from and then return another mile. He had not yet had the opportunity to walk that day, and this was his opportunity.

Simply stated, there is probably no better and healthier exercise than walking. Yet, I am advocating walking both as a physical and daily transformational activity, which enables the body and mind to achieve a synchronization of awareness, insight, and physical well-being.

Physiological symptoms of *pizur hanefesh* are a sign of an imbalance between our thoughts and feelings as they impact on our physiology. Headaches, fatigue, palpitations, anxiety, panic attacks and the host of other symptoms may certainly have their roots in our hard-wiring. I know of one young man who has suffered from countless somatic disorders. "That's just the way I'm wired," he informs me. Moshe feels he developed colitis through pressures at home and at work. A young wife, Malkie, felt that her migraines got worse as a result of family pressures. In all these situations, there is a need to examine the physical aspect of the symptoms. However, once this has been responsibly explored, we can take a closer look at how we can recalibrate the delicate mind/body balance.

Focused Walking is an approach I have taught many couples and individuals to help them discover how their troubled thoughts and feelings may be contributing to their physical symptoms that undermine their relationships.

There are countless benefits for integrating Focused Walking into your life. A brief list includes:

- Overcoming physiological symptoms of stress
- Problem-solving and resolution
- Exploring and clarifying thoughts and feelings
- Regaining access to our more human and caring emotions

+ Experiencing emotional catharsis
+ Calming hurt, anger and frustration

◇ **The Dynamics of Focused Walking**

At the beginning of this chapter on transformation, I discussed the principle of *mayim amukim*, the deep wisdom that is within each of us, waiting to ascend to the surface of our consciousness. This wisdom is at the heart of our intellectual, emotional and physical rebalancing. It is a powerful insight that frees us from the compelling and repetitive patterns of *pizur hanefesh*, which are the causes of our physiological symptoms. These symptoms are the body's blind and chaotic way of trying to regain balance, and they never work. Hashem places this deeper wisdom within each of us to delicately assist in the regulation of our functioning, whether it's our body temperature, blood pressure, blood sugar, immune system, or the myriad of interrelated systems that enable us to fulfill our life tasks.

Pizur hanefesh keeps us distracted and emotionally "unintelligent," causing us to be imbalanced in a way that leads to physiological symptoms. Focused Walking, however, enables us to reach deep into the well of our own selves and gain access to our "*mayim amukim*," our deep waters of wisdom and insight. It's as if we are sending a pail deep down within the well of our selves to draw up waters of clarity. This clarity has a way of correcting the imbalance and helping us overcome our symptoms.

Why do we use walking? Through the synergy of forward movement, while focusing on a specific goal and using a visual focus, we gain access to insights that have eluded our consciousness. Focused Walking is effective because through the experience, our minds are able to receive insights and clarity that emerge from our *mayim amukim*. Armed with this wisdom, we gain new options for spiritually and emotionally healthy living that enable us to find better solutions to our challenges rather than repeat dysfunctional physical symptoms.

The concept of Focused Walking is based on how the *Alter* of Kelm, *zt"l*, encouraged Focused Thinking to reveal hidden treasures in our thoughts. In Focused Thinking he would suggest that a student close his eyes for a three-to-five-minute period and focus on one specific issue without opening his eyes. Many *talmidim* of Kelm practiced this every day as a way of strengthening their power of focus. The difference is that in this Focused Walking exercise you are literally "on the go."

◇ How to Create Your Own Focused Walking Exercise

The principle behind Focused Walking is that we use our visual focus on an external object, usually a tree, to learn how to resist distractions, which are the essence of *pizur hanefesh*. Overcoming the tendency to be distracted enables us to gain access to our deeper sense of wisdom. Through learning to maintain our visual focus, we create a deeper inner clarity on an issue we are thinking about.

As you begin the walk, you will notice how easy and compelling the need to be distracted is. This is the pattern of *pizur hanefesh*. Once you become aware that the distractions are caused by *pizur hanefesh*, you will learn that you have the ability to resist them. The moment you learn that you have this strength is when your thoughts and insights from the *mayim amukim* begin bubbling to the surface of your consciousness. Therefore, the challenge is to use the walk to continuously maintain a visual focus while concentrating on a specific question or thought.

The procedure for the Focused Walk is as follows:

1. Decide on a Focus

Select a question or issue that will be the focus of your walk. The goal could be one of the following:

Talking to my Physiological Symptom

+ What does my physiological symptom (fatigue, headache, etc.) say to me about my lifestyle, my relationship with my spouse, etc.?

Clarifying our Relationship

+ I can remember a moment when I felt connected to my spouse.

+ I can remember a moment when I felt a sense of gratitude toward my spouse.

Problem Solving

+ How can I learn to discuss the issue of money, children, vacation, schools, family customs, etc., with my spouse?

2. Select the Place to Walk

Choose a tree-lined street, a park, or anywhere you can walk with a minimum of traffic, people, and distractions.

3. Get Focused

Start walking, and as you walk, look straight ahead or preferably at a tree. Maintain your focus straight ahead or on the tree, and silently repeat your focus for the walk. For example, "What are the factors that may be contributing to my headache?"

4. Get Ready for Distractions

Permit your mind to be aware of any thoughts or images that it may perceive. Yet, you should also be aware of how you will be distracted from your visual focus. When you are pulled away, return your visual focus straight ahead or to the tree, and repeat your focus: "What are the factors that may be contributing to my headache?" You will notice that after about five or more distractions, you will realize that being distracted is the result of *pizur hanefesh*. At that moment, you will resist the pull.

5. Monitoring Your *"Mayim Amukim"* Thoughts

Once you have resisted distraction and can maintain your visual focus, you will discover that your thoughts become clearer. Unexpected flashes of impressions, insights and memories will bubble to the surface. Your ability to resist your *pizur hanefesh* tendency to be distracted enables you to reach *mayim amukim* insights that emerge from the bottom of the well. You will discover that once you have a single memory or insight, the next insight will be almost instantaneous. Once you are in this focused zone that we call *menuchas hanefesh*, you can walk for as long as you wish to continue to deepen your understanding of the many intricate and delicate connections that create your physiological symptom. With each insight, you are coming closer to a sense of mastery that reestablishes the balance between *neshamah* and body, which enables you to once again be in control of your physical functioning.

In my work with couples I frequently suggest that they each take a daily focused walk. They repeatedly share that they use these walks to gain valuable insights into their own behavior, transform moods, and also develop approaches to resolve marital issues that are a part of life's unfolding challenges.

TRANSFORMATION TOOL # 4: Centering

Charles returns from work at about 6:30 in the evening. Over the past few months as he walks through the door of his home, he has been feeling a rush of anxiety over the tension he expects will be in the air. In the past, the pattern was to come home, hear the shrill voices of children, sense his wife's "I've had it with them," and immediately become part of the battle. This would inevitably lead to an argument between the couple. Regardless of how determined he was to "maintain his cool," Charles would be swept into the atmosphere of tension and anxiety.

However, tonight, as Charles entered, he experienced a physical sense of reassurance. He observed the stress and tension, yet was able to maintain his sense of objectivity and decide on how to best help his wife and children during those critical moments right after he returned home. The result was that for the first time in his memory, he was able to be a positive influence in helping the family quiet down, thereby restoring a sense of security and safety in their home. What was different in this scenario was that Charles had learned to use the skill of Centering, which I will now describe.

The concept of Centering was developed in workshops I led for singles. During those sessions, I became aware that the stress factor in dating was severely intensified by the emotional and cognitive overload that dating couples experienced as they were exposed to the many differences between themselves and their dating partners. When you are attempting to learn about a relative stranger's life, observing *middos*, or assessing physical attributes, mannerisms, financial security, level of *Yiddishkeit*, and so many other factors, the result is frequently a heightened state of discomfort, uncertainty and even physical anxiety. I began to understand that this contributed to the lack of success between dating partners. I learned to view this overload as the quintessential expression of *pizur hanefesh*. There seemed to be a "loss of self" when dating partners were flooded by the sheer quantity and quality of stimuli they were experiencing as they considered each other's differences and uniqueness.

In my attempt to help the singles in these programs maintain their own sense of self, I came to appreciate the deeper meaning and implications of a concept I had earlier alluded to. Rav Yerucham Levovitz, *zt"l*, taught that within us there is a *neshamah*, as soft and gentle as silk. It is an inner entity that Hashem places in us each day. We thank Hashem for our *neshamah* each morning as we recite, "*Modeh ani lefanecha ...*" This *neshamah* is the guiding force to our inner sense of well-being, balance and *menuchas hanefesh*. When we are in an overload mode, and feel tension and anxiety, we not only lose our sense of our self, but we also become cut off from this silken *neshamah* that resides quietly and peacefully within us. The *neshamah* is the reason we are so sensitive to the nuances of words and feelings. When we are cut off from our *neshamah*, we tend to define ourselves by the tense and jarring quality we experience in our state of hyper-stimulation and overload.

The challenge that we faced in these workshops for singles was how to enable each individual to maintain a clearer and calmer sense of self during the demanding relationship-building process. Or, stated another way, how could we enable each individual to remember that regardless of the emotional overload of dating, he could still maintain his sense of intactness and inner balance? Even more important was for the individual to learn to remember that within him was a soft and silken *neshamah*. What would be an appropriate reminder or "anchor" that would enable him to remember who he really was inside?

This challenge led me to consider an observation I have repeatedly made over the years in my work with couples. When individuals are tense and anxious, many exhibit a tendency to express this tension in their hands through emphatic movements and gesticulations. It is as if the movement of the hands creates a more decisive exclamation than the words themselves. When they are calmer, they tend to keep their hands closer together, with far less emphatic and tense movement. I came to view these movements as a barometer of internal agitation or calm. In essence, I discovered that the greater the agitation, the busier the hand movements.

Chazal have always recognized the concept of busy hands, referred to "*yadayim askanios.*" Because *Chazal* recognize that our hands are always busy and continuously touching things, they incorporated the ritual of washing our hands when we awaken in the morning, when we *daven*, or upon entering a *shul*. I was told that Reb Yerucham Levovitz, *zt"l*, had said that there was really no reason for him to wash his hands in the morning, as he was always aware of what his hands were touching, even in his sleep. Nevertheless, he washed his hands.

In Jewish life, the concept of *yadayim askanios* is viewed in a negative manner. When we are davening to Hashem, *Chazal* recommend that we gently hold our hands together, quietly and calmly over our hearts, to emphasize our deep and calm sense of devotion.

As the group members and I explored this phenomenon of tense hand movements, I came to suggest that the participants learn to gently hold their hands together or even have their fingers delicately touch when they experience this sense of emotional overload in dating. In this way, they would be reminding themselves that just as their hands are soft and gentle, there is a soft and gentle *neshamah* in each person, in themselves and in the people they are dating. In this way, I felt it would be possible to enable singles to be in greater touch with their "selves" and be aware of their own *neshamah* during these important moments. I called it Centering, as it enabled them to return to the center of self.

The results were immediate and extremely positive. One young woman sent me an e-mail that read, "We were at the restaurant together and I was very disappointed and impatient, and wanted to leave. Then I decided that this was the time to get centered. Once I did, I was able to feel calmer, more relaxed and focused." I also began to hear that group participants were using centering in their professional work, with friends and family and even in their own *tefillos*. This was when I began to teach the method of Centering to married couples, particularly to those who experienced high degrees of physiological stress. The results have been very effective in enabling these couples to feel calmer and more in control of themselves, particularly as they interact around challenging issues.

Yet, as I learned more about Centering, I came to understand a more important dimension of its benefit. Initially I had understood its value in calming the anxiety related to emotional overload. Later I came to appreciate its deeper value as a way of cultivating an inner dialogue with our deeper selves and our *neshamos*.

Learning to gently touch our hands, palms and fingers becomes a method of deepening our sensitivity to who we are within. It's not just reminding ourselves of our silken *neshamos* in times of stress that is helpful; it is even more important to cultivate this gentle touch as a violinist learns to touch the delicate strings of the instrument. In this way, Centering becomes an effective skill in helping individuals continuously feel in touch with a quieter, gentler self on a tactile and sensory level. It becomes a tactile and sensory portal to our inner world of gentle *ruchnius*.

Once we have cultivated this gentler tactile experience of who we are, we can reassure ourselves that we are never our unsafe impulses, nor our anxiety. We are never really the "third rail." Once we can feel safe with our self, we can help others around us feel just as safe as we do. Once we trust ourselves, we can enable those we care for to feel trust and security, as well. This is essentially what Charles had learned as he entered his home. And this is what I have taught many other couples — a stratagem that has enabled them to maintain this deeper relationship with their inner selves as a way of quieting the physiological effects of tension and anxiety.

◇ Learning the Art of Centering

You can easily learn to center yourself in a few moments by following these steps:

Bring the tips of your ten fingers together. Permit them to touch gently. Then close your eyes and feel the delicate nature of your finger tips.

Now gently rub your palms and permit your fingertips to run over your palms and the back of your hands. Feel the soft and gentle touch of your skin.

Place your fingers within each other so they are interlaced, while keeping the touch as soft as ten feathers.

Place your hands on your abdomen, so you can feel the steady rhythm of your breathing.

Finally, close your eyes and spend a few moments exploring the gentleness of touch.

When you have completed this initial exercise, you can use Centering in a dialogue.

Approach your spouse or someone you know and center your hands in any way that feels comfortable. You may wish to have your fingertips touch, or your fingers touch the back of your hands or palms. You may create a slow motion or just keep your hands still. And, as I suggested before, you may also find that placing your hands on your abdomen enables you to feel even more centered.

As you speak, be aware of how the experience of Centering enables you to feel calmer, more relaxed and focused. You are able to listen better, respond more thoughtfully, and even be aware of emotions that were not previously available. Most importantly, it enables you to feel more secure and centered within yourself, and this is conveyed to your spouse or whomever you are communicating with.

You will discover that using Centering in this manner enables you to experience a circuit of comfort that is created as your hands and fingers make contact. This sends a very tactile and sensory message to your whole body that you are safe and secure, and reminds you that within, there is a very gentle *neshamah* that brings life to your every moment.

I suggest you begin to explore the many benefits of Centering as you speak to your spouse, children, colleagues and family members. It will enable a more secure dimension of your physiological self to emerge.

TRANSFORMATION TOOL # 5:
The Pulse of Life

The two previous transformation tools we have learned, Focused Walking and Centering are used to help with non-specific physiological symptoms and to gain greater clarity of your deeper thoughts and feelings. This third tool, the Pulse of Life, is used to transform specific symptoms. The Pulse of Life is experienced as a personal encounter between one's own body and *neshamah*. I will describe the experience and its dynamics; but due to the limitations of the written word, I hope to make the program available on a separate audio CD.

I have explained how our thoughts and emotions impact on our physiological functioning. We can experience its effect on our circulatory, digestive, nervous and glandular systems as our emotional imbalance and insecurity is expressed through our bodies. In effect, when we sense distress, our body acts on its own to attempt to correct what it views as a problem. The difficulty is that it acts in its own limited, unguided manner, and the results are always problematic.

Perhaps we can even use the metaphor of someone receiving a kidney transplant. After the transplant, the body's immune system starts to recognize the life-giving organ as an "intruder" and sets off an elaborate system to defend itself. If I were having such a procedure and my immune system was to act negatively, I would want to say, "Listen, immune system, I need this new organ to survive. Back off. You are working for me. And right now, you are not acting on my behalf." Without proper medication, my body's immune system would reject the organ, causing disastrous results. This, in effect, is what happens when our body compensates for signals of distress. It acts blindly and instinctively to attend to the emergency and creates a whole new set of difficulties.

The Pulse of Life is a guided imagery experience that uses our awareness of our pulse beat to regain control over our body's misguided functioning. It uses the synergy of relaxation, a higher vision of life, and the beat of our pulse to create a mind/body dialogue. The effect of this dialogue enables the compelling drives of our physical functioning to surrender to the higher wisdom of our mind and soul. By learning to focus on your pulse beat and understand how it affects your physical functioning, you learn to create a new language of inner peace in your thoughts, feelings and physiology.

◇ The Pulse of Life Meditative Exercise

While it is always best to be personally guided through this exercise, I will provide the basic elements that I teach couples. These contain thirteen steps and should take from seven to ten minutes. Of course, you can take as much time as you wish.

1. Select a relaxing and quiet place to sit or lie down, where you will not be disturbed for about ten minutes.
2. Locate your pulse on your wrist, neck or temple. Then,

close your eyes and count five beats of your pulse, followed by a full breath.

3. Repeat the count of five pulse beats followed by a full breath four more times.

4. Imagine a white light on top of your forehead (approximately where a man wears his *tefillin*).

5. Imagine this white light is your *neshamah* and it represents the essence of all the spiritual and meaningful aspirations you strive for in life. This can include *shalom bayis*, Torah, *nachas* from your children, personal happiness or any other meaningful life goal.

6. Realize that the white light is a sign that Hashem is always giving you life, always protecting and loving you, and that you are never alone or forgotten.

7. Feel your pulse once again and be aware that the beat of your pulse is the sound of an inner river of life flowing throughout your body.

8. Be aware that your pulse also carries feelings of tension and anxiety that you would like to quiet down.

9. Imagine that your pulse can speak to the white light, and says, "You, white light, have so much *chachmah* (wisdom). Please teach me to quiet my fears and anxieties."

10. Imagine that your pulse says, "I surrender myself to your wisdom."

11. Imagine a mountain in the distance covered with ice and snow. As the sun rises, the snow and ice melt and trickle down the mountainside.

12. Imagine your own pulse and your anxieties becoming softer and gentler and melting, just as the ice and snow are melting.

13. Lastly, imagine the white light descending into your mind and slowly bringing its warmth to every part of your body. Start by feeling the warmth of the white

light in your head, moving down your neck, arms and hands, continuing down your chest and stomach, and finally going down your thighs, legs, knees and ankles.

CHAPTER VIII

The EMBERS Program:
Cultivating Love and *Chessed* in the Marital Relationship

◇ The Nucleus of Our Lives

The last two of the five dimensions that comprise our experience of self are behavior and marital love. These are distinct from the first three dimensions of thoughts, feelings and physiology, as they represent how we interact with our spouse: Are we creating a shared experience of closeness, or distance and alienation? For example, when a husband starts spending more time at the office and away from the family, the effect on the marriage is very damaging. When a wife feels the need to develop relationships that interfere with her closeness to her husband, here, too, there is a palpable impact on the marriage. From the perspective of *Chazal*, our values are immutable. The home has always been the center of our lives and the marriage is the center of our home. Everything we do needs to be viewed in terms of its impact on the nucleus of the life we share with our spouse.

The greatest challenge for married couples who slip into dysfunctional patterns of behavior and an ongoing sense of mutual alienation and antipathy is the accompanying feeling that "nothing can ever change." It's an illusion that can imprison couples for years, and even decades. However, from my experience, with few exceptions, it is hardly ever true. In this chapter, we will learn the EMBERS program for bridging these seemingly "unbridgeable" gaps in marriage and explore creative strategies that transform the dimension of marital love.

◇ "My Behavior Is in My Genes"

Simcha and his wife, Chava, came to see me about Simcha's inability to stay away from the office. After becoming a CPA, he was hired by a small accounting firm headed by Orthodox partners. The firm's senior management encouraged their staff to leave early on Friday and maintain a healthy balance between work and home.

However, Simcha was eager to work hard and spent long hours in the office. He consistently arrived home just minutes before Shabbos and was always telling Chava that his work was never finished. His attitude toward his career was causing serious conflicts between the young couple.

Chava was adamant. "I've been playing second fiddle to his job for more than five years. He's the first to get there and the last to leave, and he can never get away for us to spend any time together. I can't stay married if this is all he can give me."

Simcha was apologetic. "I know I have a problem. But this is who I am, and I don't think I can ever change. I guess I learned it from my father. He would leave early in the morning and return home late at night. He just couldn't stop working. Maybe it's in my genes."

In a way, Simcha's erroneous perception that it's "in his genes" is quite understandable. When we learn to continuously repeat a pattern of behavior rooted in *pizur hanefesh*, this behavior becomes very difficult to bring under control. There is an insistent, powerful and seemingly unstoppable force driving the repetitive action, which takes on a life of its own.

My wife and I once attended a professional conference on the Jersey shore. In the evening we took a short ride to Atlantic City. I had never been in a gambling casino and was curious to witness one first-hand.

We entered a massive hall filled with countless slot machines. There were perhaps thirty people in the room. All were hunched over the slots, their hands automatically inserting the coins and pulling the lever as they watched the wheel spin. It was a mindless, almost lifeless repetition, without thought or soul. I was reminded of a story I had once read by the author Jack London, about a man in the Klondike freezing to death. He kept himself alive by running around a frozen lake. Even when he was losing consciousness and close to death, the thrust of his forward movement kept him running. He was essentially a dead body given movement by the sheer instinct of repeating the motion of his legs.

I walked out of the casino shaken to the core. I had witnessed the phenomenon of how living and breathing human beings can become emotionally and spiritually dead while automatically shelling out money.

I later learned how the industry had designed slot machines so that gamblers feel compelled to continue playing in this thoughtless way. I hoped that professional psychologists were not part of the nefarious design team.

In my mind, the thoughtless gamblers are similar to Simcha. Neither he nor they feel they have the desire or the ability to control their dysfunctional behavior.

I spoke to a young man who was dating a girl. The girl discovered that he "enjoyed going to Atlantic City once in a while." She was upset enough to want to stop dating him. When I discussed it with him, his response was, "What's the problem? I spend a lot of time learning. So what if I have a little enjoyment once in while?"

◇ **The Frog Kickers**

In all these situations, we are dealing with the same phenomenon. Addictions — whether to work, gambling or any other behavior — are expressions of *pizur hanefesh*. What these forms of behavior all have in common is a lack of any redeeming emotional, spiritual or marital value. They are always the result of our not having learned to master our impulses, coupled with the need to mindlessly repeat learned patterns of behavior. I have a name for this population that claims to be unable or unwilling to overcome these impulses. I call them the "frog kickers."

To understand what I mean, let's go back to our history as slaves in Egypt. The second of the ten plagues was the plague of frogs. Yet, a careful reading of the description of the frog invasion reveals that only one frog was initially sent. It was only when an Egyptian hit or kicked that single frog that it multiplied. Then, with each subsequent striking of a frog, the frog population grew geometrically, until there were millions of them. The Brisker Rav, *zt"l*, asked, "What if the Egyptians had not hit that first single frog? Then there would only have been a single, lone frog in all of Egypt. This is certainly not a plague!" The answer he gives is that Hashem knew the personality of the Egyptians. He knew they couldn't control their rage, even if they understood that the frogs would only multiply when they were struck.

My principle of repetitive behavior is simple. A frog kicker feels he can't control himself. He or she can be an outraged Egyptian, a gambler, a smoker, a workaholic or a shop-aholic. They are all driven by forces that create the illusion that their behavior is beyond their control.

Yet, we now understand that Hashem always gives us free will. The truth is that Simcha can always leave work earlier, the gamblers can leave the hall with their money, and the young yeshivah student can find a better way to relax. As I have said repeatedly, we are never the bird falling helplessly into the mouth of the predator.

An excellent example I can give of the power of transformation that lies within us is based on my own experience as a former smoker. While I now understand that I acquired my addiction through my gullibility and confusion, there was one aspect of my smoking that always fascinated me. On Shabbos, my urge to smoke disappeared. This was very strange, as I know cigarettes create a nicotine addiction. Yet somehow the power of Shabbos quieted that gnawing and perpetual need for the next cigarette.

This power of Shabbos to subdue a strong addictive urge has always demonstrated to me how the spiritual dimension of our being will inevitably prove to be stronger than our physical urges. Unquestionably, this is the strength behind the twelve-step programs that have proven to be the only effective approach to treating severe addictions such as substance abuse, porn, gambling and sex.

◇ EMBERS as a Guide Toward *Shalom Bayis*

Our behavior and sustained feelings of marital closeness that create *shalom bayis* are always the result of our control over our impulses. Instead of mindless and repetitive patterns that separate us, the relationship grows through an emotional environment that is continuously created through a conscious use of our language, our actions, our shared moments of pleasure, and the countless expressions of spirituality in our married lives. In marriage, happiness and fulfillment are never accidental. In essence, at each moment we are either creating sparks to unite us as a couple and thereby inviting the *Shechinah* into our home and marriage, or we are creating hurt, alienation and disappointment, which fragments and weakens our marriage.

This is the real choice that marriage places in front of us.

This section will identify six areas of married life that impact on the behavioral, spiritual and emotional climate which enable couples to experience *shalom bayis* between them. I call these areas of married life EMBERS for two reasons. First, because as an acronym, "EMBERS" enables me to relate to issues that I have found to be crucial elements of each marriage. And second, because it conjures up the image of living embers within each of us that are longing for connections to be rekindled within our marriage and in our relationship to Hashem.

This final section, therefore, deals with the integration of six areas of marital life that promote the behavioral and emotional climate leading to *shalom bayis*. Together they create the acronym EMBERS. They include:

1. **E**xpressions
2. **M**oods
3. **B**ehavior
4. **E**njoyment
5. *Ruchnius* (Spirituality)
6. **S**ensitivity

These are the latent yearnings, strengths and feelings that are always waiting longingly to be discovered and experienced between partners in a marriage. When we lead lives that fail to rekindle these embers, the result is not neutral. Instead, we are experiencing a penetrating emptiness and inner pain that reflects the lost opportunities of our lives.

EMBERS represents a rich and full palette of colors and experiences in married life that enables a couple to continuously bind their lives together. When these six elements are in synchronization, they create tones as rich and delicate as the strings of a Stradivarius violin. Each element of these EMBERS brings a married couple closer and more aware of their potential for deeper and more meaningful human emotions that Hashem has implanted in all of us. These are the shared emotions that marriage has always been destined to fulfill.

With this in mind, we can now take a closer look at the EMBERS that enables couples to enhance their experience of *shalom bayis* through the ways they behave toward each other and through the quality of love and closeness they can experience in their marriage.

1. EXPRESSIONS

The EMBERS Principle: *Expressions that emerge from menuchas hanefesh bring a married couple together in a shared bond of love and trust. Expressions that emanate from pizur hanefesh destroy the marital bond of love and closeness.*

One of the most memorable phrases that I remember from my initial training in marital therapy back in the 1970s is "You cannot *not* communicate." In marriage, we are always communicating, whether we are verbal or silent. The embers that lead to *shalom bayis* only grow from positive expressions that bring two lives together. I have rarely found that the expression of negative feelings and thoughts play any productive role in helping couples feel closer.

Many therapists do believe that encouraging a couple to vent their hurts and negative feelings is productive. Yet, I have met with countless couples who have told me just the opposite. "When we went in to discuss our marriage, it seemed like a challenge. But when we were encouraged to dig deeper and deeper into the negative stuff, we were left feeling hopeless." This is because Hashem has created us in a manner that enables us to grow from positive expressions much more readily than negative expressions, which tend to be destructive.

Many feel that it is unhealthy to "stifle" our emotions. Yet, in Torah life, we are guided to avoid negative expressions and share the positive. As a personal example of this emphasis on which expressions we should share, there is one incident that stands out vividly in my life.

> The *halachos* of Shabbos require us to refrain from any outward expressions of grief or sorrow. This is because Shabbos is a time when the *Shechinah* is present in our home.
>
> How well I remember when my father, a"h, tragically died on a Shabbos morning when I was ten years old. My grandmother, a woman of great courage and personal strength, had just lost her precious son, a true *talmid chacham* who suddenly passed away at the young age of forty-six. Yet, throughout that entire Shabbos, she did not utter a single note of grief or pain. But as soon as Shabbos was over, she let out a cry of agony that still reverberates in my mind more than a half century later.

The reality is that our expressions are at the heart of our Torah lives and our married lives, and we are always communicating.

> A husband shared his helplessness with me. "It's true, I'm not happy with her behavior. But I keep my mouth closed and say nothing." To which his wife responded, "I appreciate that you work hard at not criticizing me. But do you know what it's like to have someone glaring at you silently for hours at a time? I know you're seething inside. I can feel it. You might as well be screaming at me."

Perhaps this is why *Chazal* tell us that a sour face is like a *"bor b'reshus harabim,"* which means that a bad mood is like a ditch in a public domain. Everyone nearby is affected, and people invariably fall into it.

In marriage, our expressions, whether verbal or silent, have the power to build bridges of love and closeness toward *shalom bayis,* or they have the ability to destroy our homes and lives. Perhaps this is close to the meaning of *Shlomo HaMelech's* words in *Mishlei* (12:18), *"Yaish boteh kamadkeros charev, u'leshon chachamim marpeh* — There is one who speaks like the stabbings of a sword, while the language of the wise heals."

Very recently, I sat with a couple whose marriage was in serious danger of ending. At the time of our meeting, they were separated and had been referred to me by a mutual friend as a "last resort."

For the two years of their marriage, Benjy had been upset with his wife, Sima, for not being the wife he had hoped she would be. Throughout their short marriage, Benjy shared his disappointment with Sima in many ways. Even when he tried to "hold it inside," Sima could sense his unhappiness in many ways. After a series of unsuccessful attempts at marital therapy, Sima finally broke down. One day she announced to Benjy, "I tried everything and failed. You have never cared for me or loved me. I want a divorce."

Finally, as the divorce now seemed imminent, he began to press her to consider reconciliation.

"For the past two years, you never said anything nice or complimentary to me," she responded. "Whatever I wore, whatever I did, whatever I tried was never good enough and you made me feel it. Your words, your actions – even your silence – were all more hurtful to me than I can ever let you know. I can't let myself reconsider."

Sima decided to move in with her parents. Benjy was initially relieved. The marriage he had always felt was a "mistake" was finally drawing to a close. However, as the days and weeks passed by, he began to realize that he was missing Sima. The prospect of divorce was suddenly more foreboding.

Benjy realized that a process was in motion that he might not be able to stop. He attempted to change her mind about going to the *bais din*, but to no avail. He shopped for therapist after therapist, rabbi after rabbi. But nothing worked. It was clear that the damage he had been causing—word by word, gesture by gesture—had taken its full effect. For Sima, there was no turning back. She had already begun her own internal process of separating herself from the marriage.

The wish Benjy had been harboring for the two years of their marriage was now coming true, but he was not greeting it with the relief he had anticipated.

While he had begun to recognize the damage he had caused, Benjy never really came to understand how his anger and resentment had left scars that Sima was no longer able to bear. I saw the couple only once, and then proceeded to meet alone with Benjy for a few more visits. Sima had already hired a lawyer and was making arrangements for the *bais din*. Benjy's marriage was ending because he had not appreciated the power of his expressions, to either heal or destroy. He made a number of futile attempts to have Sima reconsider her decision, but she refused. I never heard from either one of them again.

In marriage, we are exquisitely attuned to the countless ways we and our spouses express ourselves; through our words, the tones of our voice and our facial expressions, and in all the ways we communicate in our shared lives. Because of the profound need for closeness and caring that Hashem has placed within our very beings, we can sense the slightest nuance of love and caring, and, of course, any feelings of hurt, anger, rejection and alienation. Therefore, the ability to maintain *shalom bayis* in a marriage means that we learn to express ourselves in ways that help us turn each moment into a shared experience of trust and security. The only acceptable expressions between husband and wife are those that enable each to feel emotionally cared for, loved, secure and respected.

We live in a society that urges us to be "honest" and to speak from "the gut." Many a couple has come to see me and shared the destructive experience of seeing therapists who urged, "Don't be afraid to be honest. Say what you are feeling. Get it off your chest."

Moshe and Hindy had been to see me a couple of times and I was just getting to know them. After the meeting started, Moshe shared with me that he had considered calling off the session. When I asked him why, he responded, "We were doing better the past few days. I thought that if we would come to see you, we would start dredging up all the dirt from the past and we'd be in the hole again."

I assured them that I have learned that the only communications that help a couple feel closer are positive ones. These are communications that gently stir the embers that enable the deeper self to emerge from its hiding place and feel safe enough to be touched by words and gestures of caring and understanding.

◇ The Art of Listening

Daniel and Leah had been married for about two years. Their marriage was on a rocky footing from the beginning. Leah had lost her mother while she was still in her early teens, to a long and painful bout with cancer. Daniel had struggled through school and was diagnosed with ADD. Throughout high school, he required special instruction and ongoing sessions with the school guidance counselor, as well as some personal therapy. Both were now competent professionals, with Leah working as a physical therapist and Daniel as a nursing home administrator.

Leah was the oldest in a family of six children. With the tragic death of her mother, the role of family caretaker was thrust upon her while she was still suffering from the trauma of her mother's prolonged illness and subsequent death. Suddenly her life as a teenager came to a halt. She spent all her non-school hours caring for her siblings and the family's needs. While her father attempted to free her up to "be a normal teenager," Leah's sense of responsibility precluded her from leading a life similar to that of her friends.

Daniel, on the other hand, was a young man who found that having people nearby to talk to and understand him was essential for his ongoing coping and adjustment, and eventual success in his field. He had learned the value of expressing the challenges of his life struggles and the need to talk to anyone who would listen. So when he and Leah dated, Daniel spoke and Leah listened. For Leah, marrying Daniel was a chance to finally have her own life. Daniel expressed his gratitude for her listening to and understanding him, and showered her with gifts, such as a large engagement ring and expensive jewelry.

However, after marriage, Leah grew tired of listening. She needed someone to listen to *her*. But trying to get Daniel to stop talking about "his needs" was an exercise in futility. The more she tried to get him to listen, the more insecure he felt and the more he needed to talk. This resulted in Daniel delivering long diatribes that lasted until 3 a.m. One day, Leah finally ran from the house and hid in a friend's home. No one knew where she was.

The couple was now separated and spent the next few months trying to reconcile. Their attempts were very erratic. I saw them after they had decided to try once again to be together.

It took me a while to grasp the dynamics between them. When I did, I asked to see Daniel alone. I explained to him how I appreciated his need to be understood, and then shared my own perspective about Leah.

"But I gave her everything she ever needed!" was his response.

"Tell me," I asked, "what have you always wanted most from her?"

"I wanted her to understand me and care about me," he replied.

"And if she would tell you that she couldn't listen to you but would prefer to give you a Piaget watch, would that make you feel better?"

"I guess I would take the watch and it would help for a while, but not for long. Because that's not what I really wanted."

"So why don't you give her what *she* really wants?" I asked him.

"What is that?"

"The same as what you want. She needs someone who knows how to be quiet and just listen."

I explained how I understood Leah—how she has always taken care of others, including Daniel. As I spoke, I wasn't sure whether he would understand or accept what I just said. But suddenly a big grin broke out on his face.

"All my life, I knew I had this need to talk. Sometimes I asked myself what it would be like to just learn to be quiet and listen to others the way I wanted them to listen to me. But I never really had the chance."

"Well, Daniel, now's your opportunity," I told him.

A couple of days later, Leah left me a voice mail. "I don't really know what happened in your office," she said, "but he's been very different since he got back from the meeting. I can't figure it out, but for some reason I feel like he really wants to know what's going on inside me."

I spoke to Daniel a few days after that. He was elated to experiment with his new gift—the gift of listening and understanding. In a few moments, he had grasped a concept that created a sea change in his behavior and had an immediate effect on his marriage. Many more changes are required before this couple truly feels secure and safe with each other. But when a couple struggles for so long without a clue as to what can help them as a couple, then one concept that transforms thoughts, behavior and communication can prove to be a very significant development in their lives.

◇ Take Responsibility for Your Communications

Your expressions are a function of your state of mind. If you're in a state of *pizur hanefesh*, you will express yourself accordingly, and if you are in a state of *menuchas hanefesh*, it will be expressed and felt. We know this concept from *Mishlei* (27:19) when Shlomo *HaMelech* says, "As in water, face answers face, so the heart of man to man."

Therefore, your communication has the potential to either evoke a positive response that will strengthen bonds, or provoke a negative reaction that will cause conflict and hurt.

I came across the following concept in Dr. Pransky's excellent book on marital relationships, *The Relationship Handbook*.

If you are critical, you will cause hurt.

If you are angry, you will damage others.

If you are hostile, others will fight you.

If you are indifferent, others will be hurt by you.

If you are annoyed, others will drag their feet.

However …

If you are patient, others will join you.

If you are appreciative, others will put themselves out for you.

If you are caring, others will pull out all the stops to help.

It's time to realize that it all depends on you.

◇ ### *Pizur Hanefesh* Expressions

Being in a state of *pizur hanefesh* causes you to focus on yourself, particularly when you are feeling insecure, needy, upset and disconnected. Falling into a state of *pizur hanefesh* will cause you to use expressions that divide and hurt.

Pizur hanefesh expressions are frequently heard in the following way:

Criticism
> "I can't stand when you wear that ugly tie. I'm just telling you the truth."

Loudness
> "I realize that I'm raising my voice. I'm just trying to make my point."

Anger
> "You're darn right I'm angry—and I have every reason to be!"

Vulgarity and *Inappropriate Language*
> "There's nothing wrong with a few choice words. That's the way people speak today. If it makes you feel embarrassed, you're just too squeamish about these things."

Impatience
> "I realize I'm impatient. It's my nature."

Coldness, Silence and Not Caring
> "You may feel hurt, but I don't have to buy into your hurt."

Tension
> "If my tension is getting you nervous, that's your problem."

Abuse (Physical or Verbal)
> "It's not my fault. There's nothing I did to you that was harmful. You're just too sensitive."

◇ **Expressions that Flow from *Menuchas Hanefesh***

Menuchas hanefesh expressions reflect a quieter, healthier state of mind, enabling you to express yourself in a way that rekindles the embers of trust and closeness. Elevating yourself to a state of *menuchas hanefesh* activates the inner wisdom of your *neshamah* to discover creative and positive expressions of self, which include:

Affirmations: Sharing thoughts and feelings that recognize each other's striving for greatness:

> "I really admire the way you devote so much effort to me and the kids."

Gratitude: Learning to say "thank you" is a loving act:

> "I deeply appreciate how you helped me out this morning when I was in a rush. I realize it was an imposition. It showed me how much you care."

Sharing Expressions of Affection: Learning to share your human need for warmth:

> "It really makes me feel special when you're there to hug me."

Caring: Demonstrating your interest and sincerity:

> "I know what you've been going through, and I want you to know that I care about what's been happening."

Vulnerability: Learning to share your humanness:

> "I guess there are times like this when I realize how fragile I can be. Thanks for being there for me."

Interest: Demonstrating you care enough to be genuinely interested:

> "I was thinking about you and called to see how you are doing."

Acceptance: *Learning to accept and value differences:*

> "I've come to understand that we don't have to be the same. I've come to appreciate you for your differences and uniqueness."

Judging Favorably (Dan L'chaf Z'chus): *Being able to see the positive side:*

> "I've learned to trust that whatever you are doing, your intentions are correct; and if I'm patient, I'll find you've made the right decision."

Compassion and Warmth: *Understanding that your partner needs you to be caring through challenging times:*

> "I really feel what you are going through. I just want you to know that I'll be there for you."

Expressing Commitment: *Learning to share that you are in this forever:*

> "I understand that things are difficult right now. I want you to know that I am in this marriage forever."

◇ Some Additional Guidance on Expressions

Be Aware of Your Tone: *When you are communicating something important, speak softly and gently:.*

> "I've learned that when I speak softly and gently to you, you feel that I understand you and it helps you listen as well."

Maintain a Positive Way of Communicating: *Speak in positive and gentle terms. Using profanities always horrifies and creates emotional distance.*

Always Give Feedback: *Learn to provide clear and coherent feedback so your spouse feels heard and understood:*

> "I believe I understand what you are saying. I think you are saying that ..."

Communicate Clearly and Directly: *If you have something complex and difficult to say, perhaps you should write it down first to clarify it in your mind. You can then share it verbally or in a letter.*

Listen Thoughtfully: *You don't always have to speak. However, you do have to listen carefully and avoid all distractions, such as cell phones, other people, newspapers, looking at a TV, and anything else that will prevent you from giving your spouse your full attention. Your spouse will feel heard.*

2. MOODS

The EMBERS Principle: *In a state of menuchas hanefesh, we experience moods that are secure, trusting, and loving, and each of these positive moods contributes to shalom bayis. However, in a state of pizur hanefesh, we experience moods that are emotionally insecure, isolating and hurtful. Our goal is to learn that we always have the ability to transform our moods and regain our shalom bayis.*

A young wife who felt belittled by her husband shortly after their marriage asked me in all earnestness, "But you understand what I have been going through ever since that happened. Who can blame me for feeling resentful? Actually, I have a responsibility to feel it and even show it, so it never happens again."

In another situation, a husband found out after their wedding that his *kallah* had suffered from anorexia during her adolescent years. When he learned of her history, he was upset for not having been informed. He was especially upset at his in-laws for suggesting to their daughter that it wasn't important to share this information. He informed me that he cared for his wife very much and didn't blame her. However, he could not permit himself to forgive her parents for telling her to withhold the information. The problem was that his anger toward them was very obvious to his *kallah* even though he tried to mask it. She told him, "Every time we go there or they come to us, I can just see you knot up into a ball. It gets me so depressed to see you do that."

I have no way of determining whether the husband who embarrassed his wife was completely at fault, or whether the wife's parents in the second scenario were acting *"l'shaim Shamayim"* or in their own narrow interests. However, in both situations, these young people were unable to overcome their long-standing moods. And in my experience, being unable to overcome our moods will always undermine a relationship and bring out the worst in both partners.

I have already cited the well-known concept that a face is similar to a *reshus harabim* — a public domain. Our moods and state of mind affect us and those around us. A negative mood, or, as Dr. Pransky calls it, a low mood, is actually contagious. No one can escape its influence. We pass it around like a flu virus.

Karen and Sol were driving to their vacation destination, and they were lost. Karen was trying to get the GPS to recalculate their position. Sol was on the phone, and Karen couldn't hear the instructions. Karen blurted out, "Can you please stop talking? I'm trying to get us out of this mess!"

Sol was clearly hurt. He simmered silently until they got to their destination. All that night, he didn't talk to her. In the morning, the mood finally lifted and they continued on in a fairly peaceful manner.

When we got together, Sol told me, "At that time, I just wanted to go home. I felt upset and disgusted. I really didn't care about her or the vacation. It was only after the fog lifted that I realized how easy it was to blow things out of proportion."

Our *shalom bayis* is enhanced or endangered by our moods. And while we can usually ascribe a reason for them, I have found them to be a dimension of our emotional functioning over which we have little control. When a husband or wife claims that "you may disagree with my anger, but I have every reason to feel this way," it is also a way of saying, "I'm stuck in this feeling and helpless to escape from it. Therefore, I have no choice but to accept it as real and true." This is how we come to see our negative moods as reality.

Some people will be aware of their frustrations throughout the day. Others may feel hopeless and depressed, while others will harbor anger. Most will defend their state of mind. Yet in all my years of working with couples, and in my own marriage of over four decades, I have never witnessed a negative mood, either in a couple or in myself, that I came to appreciate as ultimately legitimate. It's the same as someone telling me that they have a body temperature of 103°, and that's where it should be — while I know that our bodies were not created to accommodate such a high temperature. It's all part of our *pizur hanefesh*. The fundamental principle is that regardless of our trials and challenges that Hashem gives us, we are always expected to cultivate the inner strength to overcome our negative moods.

This is why moods are so essential to our ability to kindle EMBERS. I consistently tell couples that regardless of the past, even if you have become accustomed to expect disappointment, resentment or frustration, or feel you can't forgive, your marriage depends on not permitting your negative moods to be a significant driving force in your life and marriage. Love, trust and closeness can only emerge when you learn to take the first step and begin creating an environment free of these moods.

We create *shalom bayis* through these EMBERS. We learn to take responsibility for our *pizur hanefesh* moods by being aware of their presence, and then take measures to transform them.

◇ The Rules to Remember about Moods

1. There is no negative experience that can define your experience of self.

2. Never trust your negative or low moods. They are never your friend. These moods will follow three characteristic patterns:

    a. They will always distort your perception about yourself and those closest to you.

    b. They will always cause you to make the wrong decision.

    c. They will never apologize for having misled you when you realize how tragically you have acted as a result of your negative mood.

3. Know that you can change your moods. Appreciation and trust are just a thought away.

4. You are never your *pizur hanefesh* thoughts or moods. There are always "healthier ones" waiting inside you to be discovered.

5. Be aware that you are not that bird mesmerized by the snake. Hashem always gives you the keys to freedom.

6. Appreciate that your negative moods have consequences:

    + A chip on the shoulder creates animosity.
    + Frustration and anger create fear.
    + Depression creates distance.
    + A positive mood creates closeness.

7. Your turning point for discovering your freedom from your negative moods is to remember the three principles of *Chiddush, Tzomet and Mishkan.*

◇ A Story about Being a Master over Your Moods

There are many moods that can undermine *shalom bayis.* Some can emerge from our past experiences, while others can be part of the ongoing challenges of our lives.

Yaakov and Naomi were married in 1970 and had raised a family of seven children. In 1990, Naomi was diagnosed with cancer and began radiation treatment. Her prognosis was poor.

The couple and their children managed to see themselves through the initial stages of Naomi's treatment, and the illness was brought under control. However, Naomi's condition was never quite stable. Hospital stays and an ongoing fear for her life had become part of their marriage and family experience.

About seven years after the initial diagnosis, Yaakov, a computer analyst, filled in one day to teach a *daf yomi shiur*. It took him many hours to prepare, but the experience was very meaningful. He decided to continue. Meanwhile, Naomi's condition slowly deteriorated. But somehow she, Yaakov and the children found the strength to always continue on to the next round of radiation, the next hospitalization and the next crisis. In 2009, Naomi finally passed away. By that time, they had seen all their children married, and Yaakov had completed teaching the *daf yomi* cycle, uninterrupted from the day he began.

Just before her passing, when all the treatments that had succeeded in keeping her alive for almost twenty years could no longer extend her life, it was time to finally say good-bye. Yaakov gathered all the children and their families together around their mother's bed. As a family, they sang the *Shir Hamaalos*, Psalm 128, that we say each night before we go to sleep and on Shabbos before it draws to a close.

A Song of Ascents

Fulfilled is each person who fears
Hashem, who walks in His ways.

*In the labor of your hands
when you eat.
You are worthy of praise and
all is good with you.
Your wife will be like a vine,
fruitful in the inner chambers of
your home; your children will be
like shoots of the olive tree around
your table.
So is the blessing of the man
who fears Hashem.
May Hashem bless you from
Tzion and may you gaze at
the beauty of Yerushalayim all
the days of your life. And may
you see children born to your
children.
May peace be on Israel.*

Following her death, at the funeral, Yaakov gave her eulogy. His message was moving and inspiring. But one thought rang out beyond every other when he cried, "Naomi, we won!"

The victory was over every moment of torturous pain, despair and hopelessness. They emerged the winners over every battle of the body and mind and defeated every conceivable mood and thought to keep the family growing and loving. At the end, with their children around her bedside, and the *tehillah* of Dovid *HaMelech* on the lips of each child and grandchild, they understood the meaning of their victory.

For most of our lives, our challenges are, *baruch Hashem,* far less painful. But like Naomi and Yaakov, we are all tested to win the moment-to-moment victory over our *pizur hanefesh* moods and emerge with marriages solidly embedded in *shalom bayis* and the delicate emotions of love and closeness.

3. BEHAVIOR

The EMBERS Principle: *In a state of menuchas hanefesh we appreciate the value of behaving toward each other in ways that engender closeness, inclusion, caring and sensitivity. In a state of pizur hanefesh, we behave in ways that are self-serving, exclusionary and uncaring.*

> On a warm and balmy summer evening, Malkie and Yussie were having a barbecue dinner with their children and her parents. To the casual observer the scene was idyllic. However, Yussie was feeling a bit itchy and bored. He wanted Malkie's parents to leave and the evening to end. Being wise enough, he was silent. At about 8:00 P.M., Yussie received a text message from a friend. "Going to Atlantic City, leaving at 9. Room for one more." Yussie's heart raced. The thought of piling into a car with the "guys" seemed like just what he needed! He started to watch the clock, uncertain of how long his in-laws planned to stay. He finally asked Malkie when she thought her parents would be leaving.
>
> "What's the rush?" she asked.
>
> "No rush," he answered. "I'm just trying to get an idea of how to plan the rest of the evening."
>
> A few minutes later, Malkie's parents began to gather their things. Yussie was relieved and texted his buddy, "I'm in!"
>
> As soon as her parents left, Yussie informed his wife that "Duvie asked me if I wanted to go with them to Atlantic City. I didn't think you would mind." But Malkie did mind; she wasn't a great fan of Duvie. She certainly didn't like the idea of Yussie driving off at 9:00 p.m. to a gambling casino.

"Is that why you wanted my parents to leave?" she asked.

"You know I wouldn't throw them out. I just wanted to get an idea," Yussie answered.

Malkie was exasperated, but didn't want to fight. And at 9:00 p.m., Duvie drove up with a full car. Yussie jumped in, threw a kiss and shouted, "We'll be back in a few hours." Malkie went off to her room to cry.

At 4:00 a.m., Yussie returned. He punched in the code on the combination lock, but soon realized that Malkie had used the deadbolt to lock the door. They hadn't used the deadbolt in years. Her message was clear: She was locking him out. He called her on the phone. No answer. He knocked, rang the bell and finally banged on the windows. Malkie came to the door, opened it and blurted out, "Who asked you to come home?"

The next morning, I received a call from their rabbi asking me to see them. Malkie refused to let Yussie back home unless he agreed to meet with someone who could help them with their marriage.

This scenario occurs more frequently than we would like to acknowledge. While there are many aspects to this episode, I want to address one narrow yet crucial dimension. Yussie's actions — from his "itchiness," his boredom, the texting between him and Duvie, his impulsiveness, his leaving the house while being totally impervious to Malkie's personal distress and pain, and finally returning at 4:00 a.m. — are all one elongated behavioral symptom of *pizur hanefesh*.

This scenario is right out of the playbook for *pizur hanefesh* behavior. It is impulse-driven, uncaring and insensitive. Yussie's behavior is fueled by the "right now" of texting, his obsession with the excitement of being with the "guys" in the car and his irrepressible urge to gamble and be a part of the empty fizz of

Atlantic City. Mostly, under the influence of his *pizur hanefesh* behavior, his greatest urge is to temporarily get away from his wife and kids and, for those precious hours with the guys, act like an adolescent with no restrictions, responsibilities or concern for his family.

As I came to know Yussie, I appreciated him for his personal strengths, and for having much love for his wife and children. However, under the influence of his *pizur hanefesh*, he was thoroughly estranged from all that is meaningful and precious in his life.

The essential difference between behavior that emerges from *menuchas hanefesh* and that which springs from *pizur hanefesh* is that in our *menuchah* state we are acting in the fullness of our beings. We are related to our deepest yearnings, fully aware of the feelings of those we love and very much connected to our own deeper *ruchnius* that is our connection to Hashem. *Pizur hanefesh* behavior is always centered on our own interests; it is never sensitive to the deeper needs of others and has no inherent connection to Hashem. It is behaving in the vacuum of life.

Pizur hanefesh behavior comes in many shapes and colors. But all carry this thoughtless and impulsive quality.

> Ahuva and Tzvi were married for over a year. They spent their *"shanah rishonah"* (the first year of marriage) in *Eretz Yisrael*, and were now back in the States and living in a yeshivish community. Ahuva's mother called me as she noticed that her daughter was increasingly sad, and at times crying. Ahuva never revealed what she was crying about, but it seemed evident to her mother that the marriage was not going well. With her mother as the initial go-between, Ahuva agreed to meet with me to discuss the causes of her unhappiness.
>
> Ahuva was a strikingly beautiful girl, tastefully dressed with a *shaitel* that seemed to have cost more than the large

diamond she was wearing. On the surface, they seemed to be the "perfect" yeshivish couple." However, her sadness was also evident, and within moments of beginning our meeting, she tearfully began to describe the "nightmare" of her marriage.

At first, everything seemed like a beautiful dream. Their wedding, she told me, was "everything I ever wanted it to be."

"However," Ahuva continued, "right after the wedding everything I did was wrong. Starting from *sheva berachos,* Tzvi began to pick me apart. I was never pretty enough, thin enough or anything enough for him. I did everything I could to look great, cook delicious meals and clean the house, but he always found something that wasn't right. I went from feeling like a princess to a complete failure. My self-esteem was destroyed. No one had ever prepared me for this. On the outside, everything looked like a fairy tale. My friends told me how wonderful Tzvi and I looked together and how they wished they could be me. On the inside, I was the saddest *kallah* in the world."

After listening to Ahuv,a I asked if it would be possible for me to speak to Tzvi. At first, she was reluctant and even frightened to ask him to see me. In the end, she agreed and we met.

Tzvi was tall, handsome, well groomed and tastefully yeshivish. Like Ahuva, he appeared to have benefited from a very comfortable upbringing. Yet, he too was sad. Marriage was not what he had hoped for. He was disappointed in Ahuva. "I realize that I have high expectations. But I believe a man has a right to expect that his wife know how to take care of herself. That's just the kind of person I am."

As he expressed his values, I saw this beautiful young woman's face redden, as her eyes moistened and tears began rolling down her cheek.

"I do everything I can to be noticed by you, but you appreciate nothing. All you do is make demands that I can never meet. Before we were married, you told me how special and beautiful I was. Since then, I never heard it again. All you want is perfection, and you are making me feel lower than I ever have before in my life."

After hearing what she had to say, I asked to speak to Ahuva alone.

"What do you think is the reason you have made such an effort to look so flawless to Tzvi? Do you think that unless you win his compliments you are worthless? Where did you ever get the notion that your physical appearance was the essence of who you are? Why have you permitted this to happen to yourself? Inside, you are a *tzelem Elokim*. You have a value that is deeper than the image of perfection you are trying to create. Do you truly believe that without the expensive *shaitel*, designer clothing and jewelry, you are really not worth being loved and cared for?"

Ahuva was silent, and then finally spoke. "All my life, I was told I was a beautiful girl who could get the best boy. Ever since I met Tzvi, I have been feeling so scared that I would be rejected because I wasn't pretty or smart enough. That's the real nightmare of my marriage."

After speaking to Ahuva, I spent some time with Tzvi. "I find it very difficult to accept how a *ben Torah* could be so focused on superficialities and completely blind to the pain you are causing your wife and even yourself. You insist that it is a *mitzvah* to have a beautiful wife. However, what you really have done is give yourself the right to say that a human being should be treated as a personal toy devoid of humanity, self worth and feelings."

Tzvi was unprepared for my directness. His eyes began to moisten and tear. "I don't want to be this way. I get sucked into wanting to have everything about myself and around me perfectly in order. I know Ahuva is being hurt. I want to stop. If you can help me, I'd feel much better and so would she."

From that initial session, I began teaching them how their behavior was rooted in *pizur hanefesh*. After a few sessions, they were able to feel greater control over their relationship and learned that they had real choices. For Ahuva, it was learning that there was a deeper person beneath her need to be seen and praised as "perfect." For Tzvi, it was learning that his need to see his wife as a doll was an expression of his *pizur hanefesh*.

This young couple was experiencing a crisis that was threatening their marriage. Both were disillusioned and in a painful spiral of hurt. Much of it was being driven through clinging to superficial ideas of perfection similar to children with their Ken and Barbie dolls. They believed it was possible for a husband and wife to appear as perfect and flawless people. This was the ultimate expression of behavior rooted in *pizur hanefesh* — the state of mind that covers up our ability to be deeply caring and human. It is a feeling of emptiness that defies description, which revolves around the emphasis on a *gashmius* lifestyle that has engulfed our world.

In this marriage, *pizur hanefesh* meant that their "selves" were defined by their clothing, body weight, car, home and everything else that contributes to empty superficialities of life. To the world they created an impression of being the "dream *shidduch*," while underneath there was a continuous sense of insecurity driven by our community's empty infatuation with superficialities and the couple's own inability to gain mastery over their *pizur hanefesh* behavior.

This newly acquired pursuit of meaningless superficialities is as harmful to marriage as any website, or any other form of addiction in our society. It leaves a couple feeling empty, vacuous and isolated from each other. It deprives us of our *tzelem Elokim*, sets up dreams that are impossible to achieve and ultimately leaves us feeling hollow and alone.

I am aware of the reasons. We live in a country that has enabled us to grow financially, numerically and spiritually. However, the price of our revival is that so many have bought into its excesses and superficialities. The result is an emptiness that hurts deeply while it ensnares and destroys lives.

When we are in a *menuchas hanefesh* experience of self, our behavior is the result of our *bechirah chafshis*. It is focused, meaningful, productive, inclusive and relationship-building. When we are in a *pizur hanefesh* experience of self, our behavior tends to be self-centered, need-gratifying, unaware and uncaring of consequences, insensitive to others and compelled by forces we can't control.

◇ **You are expressing *pizur hanefesh* behavior when:**

- You have a need to draw attention from the opposite sex.
- Your use of the Internet keeps you away from your spouse's and family's needs.
- You spend long hours at work at the expense of your spouse's and children's needs.
- You have a need to watch inappropriate movies or television shows.
- You are addicted to any of the following:
  ○ Cigarettes
  ○ Alcohol
  ○ Gambling
  ○ Compulsive sexuality
  ○ Working unnecessarily long hours
- You use sexually charged language.
- You use profane language.
- You find yourself shouting and threatening.
- You find yourself compulsively complaining about your marriage to yourself or to others who are unequipped to be helpful.

- You maintain "friends" of the opposite sex on your Facebook or any other social network account.
- You drive too fast or without a seat belt, and need to be first out of the intersection when the light changes.
- You purchase a car, house or anything else that you hope will impress others.
- You read racy novels, listen to rap or other sexually charged music, or go to movies for their sexual or violent appeal.
- You have a habit of biting your nails or pulling your hair, skin, etc.
- You get bored easily and need excitement.

◇ **You are expressing *menuchas hanefesh* behavior when:**

- You show patience and understanding.
- You understand that no marriage is without its challenges and struggles, regardless of your spouse.
- You do not see your possessions as your self.
- You realize that one day you will stand face to face with Hashem and give a *cheshbon hanefesh*.
- You put your marriage and family above your job, profession and personal interests.

◇ **Strategies to Transform Your *Pizur Hanefesh* Behavior**

- The most important first step is to understand and appreciate the impact of your *pizur hanefesh* behavior on your marriage, family and relationship to Hashem. Nothing you will ever gain from this behavior will be of ultimate benefit. And if it is severe enough, it will undermine all that is truly precious in your life.
- Know what love means to your spouse and start to act in these ways, even before you overcome your behavioral problems. An excellent book to use to help you determine

your spouse's needs is *The Five Love Languages* by Gary Chapman.

+ When you find yourself ready to engage in one of your *pizur hanefesh* behaviors, use the three principles I have discussed as a way of reducing your urge and compulsion to act in a destructive manner.

+ Whenever you succeed, even by small victories, congratulate yourself for the courage and strength you are showing.

+ If your behavior is an addiction to substances or sexual acting out, you will require a rehabilitation program and support group. Anything short of this will not work.

+ If you are demonstrating intense anger, you will require an anger-management program.

+ If you smoke, you can attempt to use an over-the-counter program. If that fails, you will need to be part of a support group.

Before we finish this segment, I want to share one moment in a couple's life that made a significant difference.

> It was about 7:00 p.m., and Josh had just left his last client. Before he had gone to work that morning, he had told Leah that he would try to be home before eight to have dinner together and even get in a bedtime story with the kids.
>
> The couple had been married for seven years and was trying to hold the marriage together. Recently, Leah had told Josh that she didn't feel as if she was married. "You just happen to sleep here at night when you're not working," she stated. Josh insisted that he was hardly managing to stay afloat. "It's very tough out there selling insurance. I can't help it if people need to see me at night when they're home. There are a lot of other guys ready to pounce and

take the accounts away from me. Then what will we do about the mortgage and camps and school?"

Part of my work with the couple was attempting to teach Josh how to contain his urges instead of deluding himself that his urge to work was answering to a "higher calling" that would benefit his family and mankind.

That morning, before he left for work, Leah was firm in her insistence that she was feeling more and more like a single parent, and that when she complained, she would take the brunt of Josh's impatience and anger. "As far as I'm concerned," she told him, "you have no control over yourself. Your work has become an addiction you can't control. For you, work is your life, even more important than me and the kids."

Leah was in deep pain and was threatening to end the marriage. Josh began to understand how fragile the marriage had become.

That evening, as Josh was getting into the car to get home on time, he received a call from a wealthy potential client to whom he was trying to sell insurance. "Josh, this is Ben. I'm home now and I have a few minutes. If you're in the area, come over so we can talk." Josh's heart was racing. He had been trying to nail down this meeting for months. "I'll make it quick," he promised himself. "I'll be in and out in half an hour." He told Ben he was on his way.

Fueled by adrenalin, Josh began pulling out of the spot instinctively drawn like a magnet to Ben's house. Suddenly he stopped himself. He was aware of the rush and the excitement of the deal that awaited him—and realized that Leah was right. It wasn't the money. He was out of control. He wasn't driving his life; he was being driven.

Josh composed himself, remembered how to use the principles he had learned about *menuchas hanefesh* and began to feel more in control of the urge. He realized what was at stake and was able to pull back. He called back the potential client. "Listen, I didn't realize what time it was; my wife and kids are waiting for me. Can we make it tomorrow?" He then took a deep breath and called Leah. "I hope you're waiting for me because I'm on the way home."

When I saw Josh and Leah a few days later, he told me the story. He shared with me that it was one of the most important decisions he ever made. "I decided that being a husband and father comes first," he stated. I never asked him about the follow-up meeting with the client. But that was over a year ago, and Josh and Leah are closer than ever before.

4. ENJOYMENT

The EMBERS Principle: *In a state of menuchas hanefesh, we share enjoyable moments that deepen the foundations of our marital bond and bring our families closer together. In a state of pizur hanefesh, enjoyment is self-centered, narcissistic and progressively destructive to our marriage and family life.*

"*Samayach tesamach rayim ha'ahuvim …*" This is the fifth of the *sheva berachos*, which are the seven blessings we recite at the wedding ceremony and at meals held during the week following the wedding. Its meaning is that the new couple should share a life dedicated to bringing joy and happiness into each other's lives in the same manner that the blessings of joy were experienced in *Gan Aden* between Adam and Chavah. Marriage is a celebration of sharing love and *simchah* with this one special person. One rabbi performing a wedding ceremony said, "You are now husband and wife — *to the exclusion of everyone else.*"

The treasures of marriage are only available to the couple that shares the enjoyment and intimacy of emotional and physical pleasure exclusive of everyone else. Only this kind of very private pleasure enables a couple to experience love and *shalom bayis*.

◇ Our Contemporary Concept of Enjoyment and Pleasure

True enjoyment and pleasure that is shared between a husband and wife enables a couple to feel just what this rabbi said, "to the exclusion of everyone else." Within this exclusive relationship, we experience a bond that brings our lives closer together. It creates the love, trust and security that tells us there is no other relationship in the entire world that is more important and central to the core of our beings than the one we share. It is this relationship that gives us the stability, self-esteem, meaning and depth to be better parents, *ovdei* Hashem and members of our communities, and more secure and caring individuals. With this level of shared enjoyment, there is no danger of being distracted by others or believing the fantasy that our lives can be improved with another partner.

However, as we follow the drumbeat of contemporary life, we are frequently distracted and are pulled in other directions to seek enjoyment. While we all need to experience pleasurable times away from our spouses, there is an increasing tendency to seek these pleasures outside of marriage. The reason is that much of the economy of the society we live in is fueled by its own definition of enjoyment. It's a definition that drives our need to be excited and entertained, and suffuses every aspect of our lives including our food, vacations and leisure hobbies, and extends to destructive habits and addictions. One couple insisted that I "get real" and learn to accept the enjoyment and countless benefits of smoking marijuana with their friends. I have come to appreciate that these forms of "enjoyment" are actually empty expressions of *pizur hanefesh* designed to fill the vacuum of our deepest feelings of emptiness, unhappiness and loneliness. In the end, they only result in intensifying these painful feelings and are almost always detrimental to the stability of the marriage.

I recently received a call from a local rabbi about a couple in distress. While the couple had been experiencing conflict during the three years of their marriage, the rabbi informed me that they were now in a particularly difficult crisis.

It was Shulamis's thirtieth birthday, and she decided to celebrate it with her girlfriends at a New York nightclub. Her female friends, both married and single, all felt this was a legitimate opportunity to get away and "really enjoy themselves." Mark, her husband, was not very keen about the idea of Shulamis's "clubbing," and he tried to convince her that this was not an appropriate place for her to be, even with all female friends. Tension rose when Shulamis accused Mark of "trying to control everything I do, even how I enjoy myself on my birthday." She added, "All I ever get from you is what I can and can't do. Every time I try to do something that I can enjoy, you're there to tell me how to act. I feel like I'm in a prison. I should have known better than to marry someone so controlling."

Mark had his own difficulties with control. He frequently demonstrated these tendencies with Shulamis and was told by more than one therapist that he needed to learn how to loosen up. Not wanting to precipitate a full-blown crisis, he decided to back down.

However, his decision to loosen up seemed to backfire when he received a call from Shulamis. He thought she was calling to tell him what a great time she was having. He would have accepted this. He answered the call only to realize that she had inadvertently dialed his number from her cell phone. For the next ten minutes, unknown to Shulamis, Mark listened as she and her girlfriends sang wildly to the beat of the music, laughed, told jokes and revealed a looser side of themselves than Mark had ever heard before. While nothing was said or done that could be viewed as morally questionable, Mark just listened in silence and seethed.

> When Shulamis came home at about 1:00 a.m., Mark was already in bed, pretending to be asleep. But his ability to hold in his anger was short-lived. A fight erupted over the nightclub, and while he never planned to tell her, in his anger he revealed that he had listened in on Shulamis's accidental call. She became irate and moved her bedding into the other room. The next day she called the rabbi, telling him, "I'm through. I want a divorce."

While a few details of this event have been altered, I have remained true to the essential drama that was threatening to end their three-year marriage. I realize that there are many other aspects to this tragic episode. However, my focus is on how our concept of enjoyment can either contribute to our sense of *menuchas hanefesh* and *shalom bayis* or how it can be a reflection of our *pizur hanefesh*, which then undermines our marital life.

This concept is not limited to when one spouse attempts to achieve this enjoyment outside the marriage. It can occur when a couple attempts to share moments of enjoyment together.

> Baruch and Shoshana decided to take in a movie at a local theater on *motza'ei* Shabbos. They deliberated between a comedy, a drama or a "family" movie. Selecting a drama with a "safe" rating, they were surprised to find that the language, sensual scenes and innuendos were far more explicit than expected. Upon arriving home, Baruch was aroused and wanted to be intimate. Shulamis was tired and discouraged him. However, Baruch was more insistent than usual. An argument ensued that became a shouting and crying match. Baruch walked out, exasperated. He finally came back a few hours later. Both were devastated by what began as an attempt to share an enjoyable evening and ended in a very painful and dangerous conflict.

Many would characterize such a conflict as part of maturing in marriage, but this is the kind of empty rhetoric that is common in a society that helplessly watches as over fifty percent of its married couples divorce. The reality is that under these conditions of arousing stimuli, such an experience is almost predictable. What society now defines as enjoyment turns out to be quite self-centered and narcissistic. The success of these forms of entertainment is that they profit by feeding on fantasy and self-centered needs that undermine a couple's ability to build closeness and intimacy into their shared lives. Whether it's a licentious movie scene, a glamorous ski vacation, a fast or luxury car, an expensive meal at a trendy "fusion steak house" where everyone is seen, or any other form of enjoyment that sells image and fantasy, these experiences serve to evoke feelings of profound personal hunger and emptiness.

All these environments increase *pizur hanefesh* by evoking distractedness and exaggerating our sense of entitlement and need. When a couple passively sits in a theater or in front of a TV screen and observes another couple in a loving embrace, whether it is scripted as "legitimate" or not, the unrestricted access we give these fantasy figures to our deepest human yearnings creates expectations that are impossible to ever fulfill. No shared romantic or emotional experience can ever fulfill the unrealistic fantasies evoked by these fictions of the silver or HD-TV screen. If anything, these manufactured images of "love and happiness" trigger our "love and happiness buttons" that create deeper and more indelibly embedded impressions of the screen characters than their true life partners.

I recently saw a young man who had been to a movie with his wife. He shared that he "just wanted to feel as loved as that woman made her partner feel." Notwithstanding his naïveté over scripted love scenes, his internalized images of love were directly influenced by actors paid to implant their illusion into his sense of entitlement. And when his wife cannot "deliver," he experiences a sense of deprivation, leading to frustration, anger and even exploration of other possibilities.

There are also couples who feel the need to sit in trendy restaurants, where the ambience is edgy and electric. These hot spots are filled with other couples, both married and single, out to enjoy themselves in a public environment that generates an excitement and the feeling of "me" and "now." The nervous tension that fills these places is actually its draw, where the uniqueness of self is subsumed by the superficiality of décor, noise, movement and attention-seeking patrons. Everyone has a need to "be seen." It gives them a sense of self that has not been cultivated in their lives. This is what occurs: When spouses grab the visual attention of other spouses, the illusion of possibilities is so powerful because other spouses just seem so much more "put together" than their own spouse. The reason is very simple. They know the flaws of the person with whom they are sharing their life. They know nothing of the man or woman at the other table, so filling in the blanks with fantasy is almost instinctive in such an environment.

In our society, which is so focused on enjoyment and pleasure, there are countless ways that individuals and couples participate in the "good life." Pursuing this illusion destroys any chance they have of sharing deep and true moments of mutual pleasure. The reason is simple. Superficial pleasure and enjoyment is a function of *pizur hanefesh*. It is never gratified. It always leaves us hungry for more because it emerges from the feeling that "I need to fill my needs." It's what *Chazal* teach: "When we have a hundred, we want two hundred." There is little meaning or deep emotional bonding in our society's concept of enjoyment, because it is driven by narcissism and economics. Enjoyment is reduced to the titillation of needs. The more a couple participates in the excitement of pleasure, the more frightened they become over being alone, and the more alienated they become from each other.

◇ **Your experience of enjoyment reflects *pizur hanefesh* when:**

+ You tend to feel bored easily and search for exciting experiences.
+ Your sense of enjoyment is hurtful or demeaning to your spouse.
+ Your need for pleasure is self-centered and causes your spouse to feel insecure, alone and uncared for.
+ You need crowds and others to experience your enjoyment.
+ Your sense of enjoyment requires you to masquerade as someone you are not.
+ You engage in fantasies about being with others instead of your spouse.

True and shared enjoyment that enhances a marriage always promotes the emergence of the authentic and deeper self that strengthens your affection and the stability of your family life.

◇ **Your experience of enjoyment reflects *menuchas hanefesh* when:**

+ Your shared experience of enjoyment enhances the unique and special qualities of your relationship.
+ You are able to be focused on sensitively caring for the enjoyment and pleasure of each other.
+ The bond between you and your spouse is deepened and strengthened.
+ Your enjoyment enables you to be more available to your family and important life tasks.

+ Your mutual enjoyment creates a clear demarcation between yourself as a couple, and others.

◇ **Activities that Create Enhanced Mutual Enjoyment**

+ Daily or scheduled walks that enable you to think through and share events of your lives
+ Trips to gardens, museums, parks or coastlines
+ Vacations where you can share moments alone
+ Sharing hugs, kisses and the enjoyment of physical intimacy
+ Engaging in discussion about Torah thoughts, ideas and books
+ Learning a *sefer* together that is appropriate for both husband and wife
+ Giving personal gifts that bring a sense of pleasure
+ *Simchos* with appropriate budgets and minimal financial strain

5. *RUCHNIUS* (SPIRITUALITY)

The EMBERS Principle: *Ruchnius is the development of our internal sense of spirituality. Through it, we grow in ways that enable a marriage and family to thrive with deeply meaningful religious and shared experiences of traditions and mitzvos. The absence of ruchnius creates a spiritual vacuum that is filled by many expressions of pizur hanefesh that undermine shalom bayis.*

◇ **Introduction**

This past year, the *rebbetzin* of Harav Avigdor Miller, *zt"l*, passed away. I went to comfort the *aveil*, Rav Shmuel Miller, *shlit"a*, who was sitting *shivah* in the house on Ocean Parkway in Flatbush (Brooklyn, New York) that his parents had lived in since their move from Canarsie in the 1960s. Rav Shmuel Miller was sharing the significance of the family's move to set up a new home and *kehillah* in Flatbush. In his telling, he revealed a fascinating and compelling piece of information. "In the thirty-four years since establishing the *shul* here on Ocean Parkway, there was not a single divorce in our *kehillah*."

I was not surprised. The fact that there was not a single divorce in a community for a third of a century is testimony to the strength of leadership of a man of deep vision and commitment to Torah life. Hearing Rav Miller's lectures on *shalom bayis* provided clear and indelible guidelines for how Hashem desires a husband and wife to create their lives within the ever-fulfilling environment of Torah life.

Rav Miller's achievement was clearly based on his ability to enable couples to integrate the *ruchnius* of Torah into their lives. In the same way that our *neshamah* breathes life into our physical beings, *ruchnius* brings depth, meaning and fulfillment into our home and marriage. On the other hand, the absence of this *ruchnius* creates a hollowness and a vacuum that drains marriage and home life of its life-giving powers.

Sometimes we can observe the vacuum through a couple's cultural and social values.

> Pearl and Steve were in their mid-twenties and had been married for three years. Pearl was a teacher and Steve an accountant. Their main problem was that they found themselves in constant conflict, particularly when it came to deciding on leisure activities. Both described themselves as "movie and TV addicts." Yet, their taste in entertainment was very different. Pearl preferred comedies and romantic movies and TV shows, while Steve enjoyed adventure sagas and sports broadcasts. And given their subscription to the cable networks, there was always a sporting event to watch.
>
> Each viewed the other's disinterest in their movie and

TV preferences as a sign of disloyalty. Frequently their conflicting interests would result in an argument. And while
they disagreed on the content, they steadfastly insisted on
the legitimacy of their behavior. "Maybe everyone who is
frum doesn't agree, but we think it's normal for us to have
an outlet from our work and pressures."

Hearing them talk reminded me of a magazine ad I saw for
TV headphones. In the ad, there was a picture of a couple, both
wearing headphones and watching their own shows. Underneath the picture was the caption: "These headphones saved
our marriage." Clearly there is no marriage, and probably never
was one.

Steve and Pearl's values and behavior posed a great challenge
for me. The content of these movies was only serving to further
divide them as a couple. Yet their investment in these forms
of entertainment reflected a profound emptiness in their own
sense of *ruchnius*. With each movie and TV show, they continued to numb their sensitivities toward each other, themselves
and Hashem. They had both grown up in spiritual deserts,
which were *frum* in behavior yet lacked any understanding or
appreciation of *ruchnius*. As a result, on one level they truly were
"normal," and on another, they lacked an appreciation for *ruchnius* as the very essence of human experience. On the surface
they were "*frum*." They kept *taharas hamishpachah* (the laws of
family purity), observed Shabbos and kept kosher, and Steve
attended his regular *shiurim*. Yet on a level beneath their practice, they were the equivalent of being "spiritually challenged."

There are also situations in which there is a lack of *ruchnius*
even where Torah observance is intense. The absence of this
spirituality creates a void of human feelings and sensitivity.

I sat with a *kollel* couple while they were still in their
first year of marriage. On the surface, all appeared to be

ideal. However, beneath this idyllic image they conveyed to the outside, the young *kallah*, Miri, was experiencing a deep sense of suffering. Her husband, Moshe, came from a family that was very demanding in their precise practice of *mitzvos*, and in regard to cleanliness. Miri's family was more relaxed and easygoing, and more emotionally expressive and gentle with each other. From the beginning of their marriage, Moshe openly expressed his disappointment over the many areas in which Miri fell short of his expectations.

During our first few sessions, she was close to tears. "I feel like I'm always on probation, where everything I do is evaluated and scrutinized," she admitted.

When I questioned Moshe about his criticism of Miri, he was insistent and unyielding in his standards. "A *frum* home needs to be clean and orderly," he said. "And if you're going to do a *mitzvah*, make sure you do it well."

After understanding the source of the conflict, I asked Moshe, "What do you believe the *Shechinah* requires before it can safely dwell in your home: a spotless floor or a wife who feels loved and cared for?" It took a while before he began to get the message.

In both situations, which seem to be quite different, the dynamics are really the same. *Ruchnius* enables us to experience our deeper need for each other and for Hashem. It is based on an understanding of the love that Hashem feels for each of us and our ability to create this love in our lives with our spouses. In this way, we learn to feel whole and complete.

When we are passively watching a movie or a baseball game, we have cut off our relationship to our self. When we are obsessing over cleanliness, here, too, we have lost our awareness of our deeper and more human self.

Ruchnius is our ability to experience the delicate internal awareness of this warm and deeply human self as we perform

Hashem's *mitzvos,* learn His Torah, *daven* and cultivate close-ness and human feelings within our married and family lives. Living within *ruchnius* creates a bridge between our own *neshamos* and those closest to us. Without this sensitivity that is so much a part of *ruchnius, shalom bayis* will always elude us.

With true *talmidei chachamim,* we are continuously inspired by the level to which they have refined their *ruchnius* in a way that is reflected in their own lives and experienced by others.

Rebbetzin Basha Scheinberg, *a"h,* was the wife of the *gadol* Rabbi Chaim Pinchus Scheinberg, *shlit"a.* Their relationship was legendary. They had been married for almost eighty years without ever arguing. To many this seems absurd, almost as if they were missing out on something special. But to anyone who cultivates *ruchnius* in his or her life, this is very understand-able. *Ruchnius* is the ability to have all of our thoughts, feel-ings, language and values carefully guided by a deeper sense of Hashem's love for us that is inherently experienced in each rela-tionship and *mitzvah.*

Rav Reuven Feinstein, *shlit"a,* tells of his father's (Reb Moshe's) love for him that he experienced each morning. He shared that when he was growing up, his father would awaken at 4 a.m. On cold winter mornings, his father would place his son's pants on the warm radiator, so that when he woke up later he would feel the warmth against the bitter New York winter cold. Surely he meant the warmth of his father's love as much as the warmth of his clothing. *Ruchnius* is not isolation or asceti-cism; it's living a life that continuously experiences the warmth of Hashem's love, and sharing the beauty of this love with oth-ers. This is why it is one of the EMBERS and why it plays such a central role in *shalom bayis.*

How do we gain this sense of *ruchnius?* While it's certainly a quality of our *neshamah,* given the secular and self-absorbed environment in which we live, we cannot use our intuition to cultivate this sensitivity. *Ruchnius* is a direct result of three central elements.

First, it is acquired through emulating and internalizing the gentleness and caring of individuals and couples whose lives thrive in the beauty of Torah life. We cultivate our own sense of *ruchnius* by making these individuals part of our inner circle and emulating their language, behavior and acts of greatness, both overt and covert.

Second, we acquire *ruchnius* by opening our homes to the wisdom of the *bais medrash* and the world of Torah. *Ruchnius* means filling our homes and lives with Torah knowledge, *shiurim*, attending learning groups and creating a Torah atmosphere that permeates our lives.

Third, we develop *ruchnius* through learning that we have the power to limit ourselves. We limit our exposure to the influences of the secular world in our homes and lives. And we can control ourselves by carefully observing that we can express our thoughts, feelings and needs in harmony with the *ratzon* Hashem.

Therefore, when we consider that Rav Miller's *kehillah* went for thirty-four years without a divorce, it was clear that under his guidance, *ruchnius* became an intrinsic and stabilizing dimension of their lives. In contrast, the challenge faced by so many couples today is that their lives are filled with so many empty personal pursuits and rarely by shared experiences of *ruchnius*.

> I attended a wedding one June evening, and noticed a young married couple that stood out among the others in their attention-getting mode. I recognized the wife, who had come to see me about two years earlier when she was still single. She was now thinner, wearing a tight skirt and blouse, and her *shaitel* was long and natural looking. Her look was attention-grabbing, even seductive. She was not at all the way I remembered her when she was single. Her husband was also dressed smartly. As he

passed by, I smelled his cologne, mixed with the odor of cigarettes. He was clearly a smoker. He kept looking at his Blackberry, sending and receiving messages. I couldn't help but notice that he was wearing a Rolex watch worth at least $5,000.

The couple had a conspicuously prosperous look. Even more obvious was that while they were together, their focus was on how others saw them. They measured their own value as individuals by the mask of affluence and success they wore.

Later that evening, the *chassan* and *kallah* finally returned from their prolonged photography session. The band began their dramatic countdown, culminating with an ear-splitting blast: "Ladies and gentlemen, for the very first time as husband and wife ..." As I heard the brashness of the bandleader and remembered the couple I had observed before, I felt saddened over the loss of *ruchnius* in our lives. We seem unable to comprehend that in this *"goldenah medinah"* ("golden country") of America, something very precious has been lost, and we are just too busy celebrating the emptiness to be distressed.

The story doesn't end there. About a month later, I received a call from Judy, the same young woman I saw at the wedding. Judy did not realize that I had seen her there. She and Shmuel had been married for about a year and she was fearful that their relationship was not going to last. As we spoke, she shared her initial excitement about finally finding a guy who was *frum* and successful in business. As a *kallah*, she looked forward to enjoying the "good life." But all the illusions were now gone.

In their marriage, she felt constant pressure to be someone she was not. "Shmuel wants me to dress like a model, and likes when other men look at me." She seemed embarrassed to share this with me. She also revealed that Shmuel had become friendly with girls in the office, and had a group of guys who would impulsively "fly to Vegas for a night." She proceeded to describe their life as a *"frum"* couple that was not only profoundly superficial and empty, but also filled with endless anxiety, hurt and insecurity. For this couple, the *frum* version of Camelot really turned out to be a life of endless hurt and suffering. And now, just a year after their "dream marriage," the persona was falling apart at the seams. It was a marriage of all show and no *ruchnius*.

I have come to understand that Judy's description of her failing marriage is the tip of a giant iceberg that threatens the core of our families' stability. There are countless expressions of this emptiness when we believe that we are truly fulfilled with our watches, cars, clothing and the attention we crave. When *shtick* and loud music, fast cars, expensive clothing and break-the-bank Pesach vacations are viewed as signs of success and happiness, we have lost all sense of our inner lives. When young yeshivah men are in search of girls with that "look," and so many others are chasing that empty persona of success, we have lost our bearings. We can no longer understand, experience or protect all that is special and unique about marriage within Torah life.

◇ **Balaam's Vision**

When Balaam, the Gentile prophet, gazed down from his mountaintop view, he saw the tents of Israel laid out in front of him in the desert sands. Startled by the unspeakable beauty of *Am Yisrael's* families living in close yet distinct proximity to each other, he expresses the words that we repeat each morning, even before we *daven*, "*Mah tovu ohalecha, Yaakov, mishkenose-cha, Yisrael* — How beautiful are your tents, Yaakov, your tents, Israel." *Chazal* say that he was expressing his awe over how families can be so close yet so respectful of each other's uniqueness and privacy. Each family was careful to look inward into its own home and away from the homes of others. Personal, marital and family fulfillment emerges within the very private boundaries of marital and family bonds. This is the essence of the *ruchnius* that Rav Miller taught his *kehillah* and which has accompanied every intact Torah family since Avraham and Sarah laid the foundation for all our families.

Here are a few guidelines for cultivating *ruchnius* in your home and marriage:

Guidance in Life

+ Develop a relationship with a *rav* and a *posek* you both trust.

Praying from the Inside

+ Learn to *daven* more slowly, thoughtfully and with feeling. If possible, use a *sefer* such as *Pathways to Prayer* (Feldheim) or *Praying with Fire* (ArtScroll) to enhance your focus and feelings.
+ Learn to be quiet and reflective in *shul*.
+ Shut off your cell phone and never check your Blackberry while davening. This is your time to spend with Hashem.

Growth through Torah

+ Join a *mussar* or *hashkafah vaad*.
+ Get a *chavrusa* or join a morning or evening *kollel*.
+ Use travel time to listen to Torah material.

Language and Expressions

+ Never use an angry tone, a vulgar phrase or profanity of any kind.

The Home as an Ark

+ Decorate your home with portraits of individuals who personify the essence of *ruchnius*.
+ If you have an Internet connection, use a filter to ensure

your safety from the immorality that pervades our society.

* Don't bring newspapers, magazines, videos and music into your home that in any way promote the destruction of your *ruchnius* and *shalom bayis*.

Choose your Interests and Relationships Wisely

* Never expose yourself to any sensuality outside of marital intimacy.

* Never try to attract attention from the opposite gender through your dress or lifestyle.

* Stay away from social network websites that leave you exposed to contact with the opposite gender.

Be Proactive about Chessed

* Develop a *chessed* project that can be run from your home, so caring for others becomes an integral aspect of your home environment.

◇ The Centrality of Shabbos

There are countless areas of our lives where we can internalize this sense of *ruchnius* that enhances *menuchas hanefesh* and *shalom bayis*. However, I believe Shabbos may be one of the most important.

Shabbos is central to our *ruchnius* and *menuchas hanefesh* because through it Hashem provides us with the opportunity to be free of the incessant compulsions of our work and stress. It has a power to elevate us beyond the pull of our own primitive needs and habits. In my earlier years of smoking, I can vividly remember grabbing that last cigarette before Shabbos. I felt like a prisoner desperately stuffing down his last meal before being taken away, as if I just couldn't get enough of the smoke. Yet once Shabbos set in, for a reason that I could never explain, I experienced no need for a smoke for the next twenty-five hours nor any nicotine withdrawal. This actually defied everything we know about nicotine dependency. I can still remember feeling the itch for that column of black tar seeping into my lungs once again when Shabbos drew to a close.

Since then, I have come to discover that Shabbos serves our lives in many more beautiful ways, because it is the primary source of our *menuchah, shalom bayis* and *ruchnius*. Not only did it free a confused adolescent from a noxious addiction, it frees an entire People to learn how to acquire the *menuchah* that serves as the foundation of our inner freedom from all life's compulsions. On Shabbos, we are free to have a relationship with Hashem, ourselves and all those around us. Perhaps this is why the *berachah* in *Shemoneh Esrei* says, "and through the *menuchah* of Shabbos we sanctify Hashem's name." Just by experiencing this *menuchah*, we elevate our existence.

Shabbos is not just cessation from work. We can stop working with our bodies, yet our minds can still be spinning with all the worries and pressures we need to leave behind. It's only through the *menuchah* of Shabbos that, for this period of time, the veil is lifted on the illusion that it is our efforts and the blind forces of nature that drive our existence and the universe around us. The reality is that it is always Hashem Who creates our success and brings life to the world. On Shabbos, our focus is on cultivating our experience of inner quiet and *menuchas hanefesh*.

In the *Sifsei Chaim*, Rabbi Friedlander describes how we can enhance our sense of *menuchas hanefesh* on Shabbos. The Torah says that we should finish "*kol melachtecha,*" which means all our work. Yet we all know that "all our work" is not finished. We all anticipate returning to our work after Shabbos. Rabbi Friedlander tells us to actually believe that all our work is finished, and there is nothing more to be done, now and forever. With such an approach, our minds can let go of all the compelling influences that continuously create a sense of *pizur hanefesh*. With this, we can train and control our minds to achieve a level of inner calm and belief, which is the essence of *ruchnius* and *menuchas hanefesh*.

Through the *menuchah* of Shabbos, we learn to quiet our minds and feel "as if" all our work is done and there is nothing left to do. The illusion that we are the "doer" gives way to the deeper awareness of the reality that every moment of our existence the entire universe is brought into being by Hashem. All our achievement and every stirring in our world is lovingly empowered by Him. While throughout the week this is no less true, when we achieve *menuchah* on Shabbos, we can actually experience it. With *menuchah*, the veil is lifted on the deepest and quietest secret of the universe.

Why are we compelled to work hard throughout the week? We work hard and are driven to make the effort because this is the *mitzvah* Hashem gave to Adam *Harishon* in *Gan Aden*: "You will eat bread by the sweat of your brow." In the words of the *Alter* of Kelm, we must never lose sight that our *hishtadlus* — our effort — is merely our motions, and it's Hashem Who creates the achievement. The *Alter* continues by explaining that when we achieve this awareness of the true secret of the universe, it is similar to breaking the barrel and discovering that it wasn't the barrel that was keeping the wine within its walls. It was always Hashem. The retaining powers of the walls were just an illusion. It is the same illusion that causes us to believe it is our efforts that create our achievements.

Therefore, when Shabbos enters, we have the ability to quiet our minds, which are so busy with completing our work, and accept the reality that our work is truly finished. In this way, Shabbos becomes our portal to *ruchnius*. When we achieve this, we can access the strength to experience *menuchas hanefesh*, which has the power to remain within us all week. This is why *Chazal* refer to a *tzaddik* as Shabbos. When we learn to cultivate this essence of *ruchnius* on Shabbos, we can integrate its count-less lessons into the way we live as individuals, as couples and as families.

◇ Bringing *Ruchnius* into your Shabbos

Shabbos is the ideal time for enhancing *shalom bayis* because it is so embedded in *menuchas hanefesh*. *Chazal* inform us that after the Creation of the world, Hashem understood what was missing. It was *menuchah*, spiritual rest, and with the introduc-tion of Shabbos as the seventh day of Creation, *menuchah* was introduced into our world. Following are some suggestions for maximizing the *shalom bayis* potential of Shabbos.

Begin Each Shabbos the Right Way

As Shabbos approaches, attempt to bring it in a few minutes earlier so you are not harried. Then tell yourself, "I am begin-ning Shabbos by feeling and believing that all my work is done. Hashem does everything and there is nothing left for me to do. I will cultivate this feeling throughout the day."

Create a Shabbos Table Filled with Wonderful Thoughts and Inspiring Ideas

I very much like the idea of having a designated *sefer* for the Shabbos table. Rav Shimshon Pincus's thoughts on Shabbos are contained in *Nefesh Shimshon* (Feldheim), from which I try to read each Shabbos at the table.

Learn to Sing Inspiring Zemiros at the Shabbos Table

There is a well-known *gadol* in *Eretz Yisrael* whose son, while still *frum*, had clearly left the path of his father. When the *gadol* had been asked what could have caused this, his response was, "Per-haps because we never sang together at the Shabbos meals."

Bring Guests into Your Shabbos Environment

Chazal tell us that guests at the Shabbos table do more for the hosts than the hosts for the guests. You will find this is true as guests frequently inspire talk, song and a greater appreciation of the meaning of Shabbos.

Spend Time Together as a Couple
Shabbos is a time for closeness and intimacy, whether you are together in an intimate way or you share a quiet walk or discussion to appreciate each other's company.

Avoid Anything that Can Lead to an Argument or Anger
Chazal were very sensitive to maintaining the *shalom* of Shabbos. The *Gemara* asks: If there is only enough money to purchase either Chanukah lights or lights for the Shabbos candles, which is more of an obligation? The answer is that Shabbos candles are more important, because without the light of the Shabbos candles, families would have to sit in the dark and this would lead to frayed nerves and arguments.

Cutting the Challah
Chazal suggest that when preparing to slice the challah, the husband should make an initial indentation before cutting so that the slicing procedure would be smoother and quicker. This may seem insignificant. However, if people are hungry and impatient, even a short delay in the slicing of the challah could undermine *shalom bayis*.

Be Gentle and Thoughtful about Teaching the Halachos of Shabbos
A husband told me of his impatience over his wife's habit of preparing for Shabbos at the last moment and not being careful about her preparation of food on Shabbos. This had been going on for more than a decade. However, when he learned how to focus on his own *menuchas hanefesh*, he was able to speak to her in a gentle and patient manner.

6. SENSITIVITY

The EMBERS Principle: *In a state of menuchas hanefesh, we develop a sensitivity and understanding of how Hashem has guided our precious individual and shared life journeys. We use this understanding to continuously balance each other through marriage. In a state of pizur hanefesh, we lose our understanding of the meaning of our individual life journey and can no longer be sensitive to each other's unique needs that enable us to feel secure and cared for.*

◇ **Introduction**

When Jake and Ruthy came to see me, they had been married for just three months. Both were young and had dated for five weeks before deciding to get engaged. However, in the three months since their wedding, their marriage had been a series of ongoing crises, which now threatened to tear them apart.

During our first meeting, Ruthy shared, "For me, dating and engagement had been like a dream. Our relationship was all that I had hoped it would be. I dated a lot of guys, but I was very careful because my parents had a difficult life together. There were many times I felt they would divorce. My father had a terrible temper. I was always fearful that I would marry someone who would treat me like I saw my father treat my mother. So I always looked for someone who was gentle and sensitive. I thought Jake was everything I had dreamed of in a husband. I even told him how important it was that he was gentle with me. All through our dating and engagement, I never saw anything in him that made me worry he could be angry or hurtful."

"So when did the problem start?" I asked her.

"I know exactly when it began. It was the first night of *sheva berachos*. We were driving to Jake's family and he was listening to one of those talk-radio stations. It was close to election time, and everyone was very agitated.

The talk-show host was very loud and angry. I'm not used to hearing these things. And on top of everything else, I hadn't slept in two nights. I was very tired and had a headache. So I asked Jake to lower the volume or change the station. He kept on telling me another minute, another minute. My head was aching and I thought it was going to split. So I asked him again. Just then, a car came out of nowhere and almost hit us. Jake slammed on the brakes and shouted at me. He said things that I never heard him say before. I was shocked and very hurt. I couldn't believe that this was my *chassan*. I started to cry. He saw how upset I was. But instead of apologizing, he just started driving again and never said a word. I felt more and more hurt. I waited the whole night for him to apologize. It never happened.

"Then I started to notice other things about his behavior toward me. I began to feel more and more upset and depressed. All he ever told me was that I was just too sensitive and always making a big deal about things. Ever since that time, nothing ever really got better. I'm not sure I want to stay married to him, because there is no way I can go on living with someone who hurts me and doesn't care."

The scenario could have happened to anyone. It was a perfect storm of conditions. The political climate was tense with an upcoming election. Talk-radio hosts, particularly around election time, tend to be loud and abrasive. A young *kallah* feels tired and worn out on the way to *sheva berachos* after weeks of preparation for the wedding. A *chassan* is pulled in by the hype of the hot presidential election and is riveted to every word. Suddenly a car comes out of nowhere and an accident is just barely averted. Tension escalates, and the *chassan's* temper flares for just a moment. Yet, that moment is all it takes. In a second, his *kallah's* dreams are shattered. She's been deeply wounded — in a fight over a loud and abrasive talk-show host. Her *chassan's* behavior triggers her fears of earlier life experiences. Even if these experiences had never occurred, her husband's momentary loss of control creates a breach in her sense of trust and safety that she feels toward the person she committed her life to less than twenty-four hours earlier.

Ruthy's fears do not go away. Where she comes from, angry men continue to be very hurtful. She discovers that her new husband is also an angry man. Yet Jake is unaware of her fears about anger, and he has never developed the skills to address her hurt. So he hides his embarrassment and remains silent. Jake's attitude is, "I'll be quiet and it will go away." But as anyone who has ever been married will testify, these wounds never really go away. They may go into hiding, but they fester and ferment deep beneath the surface, always fearful of the same event or outburst recurring. Ruthy's wounds will only go away when Jake can truly understand her, when he feels her hurt and can deeply and truly ask her forgiveness and reassure her that it will never happen again.

Hashem creates us with a *neshamah* of silk that serves as the delicate and pure sense of our self. Without this sensitivity, Ruthy can never be a loving wife. She can never feel close to her *chassan* and he cannot feel close to her. Without this sensitivity, none of us can ever bring love and warmth into our lives and learn to be *ovdei Hashem*. We need these qualities to bring children into the world and to raise them to be caring people. We need these sensitivities to feel that our deepest self can feel safe and trusting with the person with whom we share our life.

The interface between the sensitivity of self and our *neshamah* is as interwoven and delicate as where the sky meets the horizon. When we do something that is hurtful, the wound to the self also touches the *neshamah* and therefore does not fade with time. Perhaps this is the reason *Chazal* tell us that when we embarrass someone, our punishment is eternal. This is because until we heal the person we have embarrassed, their pain never subsides. This is why couples need to learn to become each other's healers.

◇ Developing Sensitivity in Marriage

Because we are created with a soul of silk, there can be no *shalom bayis* without sensitivity. Even the slightest abrasion mars the gentleness of who we are deeply within.

There are two levels by which we understand this sensitivity. The first is a shared understanding that pertains to all marriages. We never use abrasive or foul language, raise our voice in anger, or communicate in any manner that a healthy individual would understand to be hurtful. This first level is common to us all. No one can tolerate hurtful or critical behavior from a trusted life partner. We can never defend against its damage.

The second level relates to how each of us struggles through our challenges in life. For example, the Torah tells us that reminding a *baal teshuvah* or a *ger* about the past is painful because it evokes memories that may be embarrassing. In the same way, we all carry our own memories of painful moments of our growing up and life experiences, which can be triggered by even a suggestion or a gesture. Married partners need to be aware of these vulnerabilities and be ever sensitive as to the triggers that can cause such penetrating pain.

◇ Guidelines for Sensitivity

I would like to present a number of guidelines that can be helpful toward integrating this level of sensitivity into the EMBERS of our marriage.

Gaining Insight into Our Childhood Years

Developing sensitivity requires us to be aware of how we carry the hurts, wounds and disappointments of our earlier years, particularly in childhood, and to understand how these experiences have contributed to our own growth in life.

Developing Insight into the Challenges of Our Spouse
In the same way that we need to understand how our growing-up experiences have impacted our lives, we also need to gain insight into how these experiences have affected the experiences of our spouse.

"Just As"
When we feel hurt by our spouse, our emerging sensitivity enables us to say "just as":

"Just as I am feeling hurt by the conflict we are experiencing, you, too, are feeling hurt."

"Just as I like to be remembered on my birthday, so do you like to be remembered."

Sharing Our Life Story
The more we share and learn about our growing-up experiences, the more sensitive we can be about each other's deeper selves.

Caring
Caring means learning to be empathic about what your spouse has been through and still goes through in life. This requires deep understanding and commitment.

Vulnerability
Each of us experiences vulnerabilities. Sensitivity requires that we become aware of these vulnerabilities. They may be related to losses we have suffered, to physical or emotional impairments, or to painful life experiences.

Creating a Secure and Safe Environment
Sensitivity means learning to create a safe and comfortable

environment for our marriage and family through our tone, gestures, expressions of caring and concern, and displays of affection.

Attraction
Know what helps you feel attracted to each other, while not attempting to create jealousy and insecurity by attracting others.

Entertainment
Entertainment should always bring a couple together and never compromise each other's values and sensibilities.

Love and Respect in the Home
Couples should encourage and enhance their mutual feelings of love and respect, while working together to teach their children this value toward them and others.

Significant Personal Events
Always be aware of significant personal events, including:
+ Birthdays
+ Anniversaries
+ *Yahrzeits*

Religious Preferences
Sensitivity means learning to respect and deal with religious differences. This will frequently require a couple to select a mutually acceptable religious authority or *posek* to settle all halachic questions.

Maintaining a Level of Caring Contact
Sensitivity means everyone needs to feel remembered. Achieve this by:
+ Calling each other during the day (and answering each other's calls when they come in).

+ Being generous with hugs and non-intrusive gestures of affection.
+ Providing small ways of showing you care through flowers, candy and other little gifts that are symbolic of your deeper feelings.

Be Sensitive to Your Changing Moods

Sensitivity means learning to be aware of the quality of your moods. Once you are aware, you can create transformations or share your positive state of mind.

Dr. Pransky provides a useful color chart to own the color of your moods.

+ Black Moods: Gloom
+ Gray Moods: Stress
+ White Moods: Feeling easy
+ Silver Moods: Feeling enjoyment and appreciation
+ Golden Moods: Experiencing fulfillment and gratitude

Daily Flow of Life

Sensitivity means learning to engage in the daily activities of your shared lives, including:

+ Eating at least one relaxing meal together every day
+ Taking frequent walks
+ Planning enjoyable vacations
+ Eating out once in a while
+ Filling your house with pleasant music
+ Visiting relatives and friends you enjoy being with

EMBERS Communication Exercises

◇ **EMBERS Preferences**

Communication represents a crucial area of marital life. Cultivating a meaningful marriage means learning to communicate your own EMBERS preferences and learning to understand your spouse's preferences as well. The following communication exercises will guide you to learning to define and share your EMBERS preferences with each other in a safe and coherent manner.

One way to enhance your marital relationship is through an interactive dialogue that is based on sharing the six areas of EMBERS.

To use this program, follow these guidelines for each of the EMBERS preferences you wish to communicate:

Define your Preferences: Select an area of EMBERS and fill out the personal worksheet. (5-10 minutes)

Share your Preferences: Give each other your worksheet and study your spouse's preferences. Write your comments and observations. (5-15 minutes)

Communicate your Preferences: Share your understanding by following these communications guidelines. (20-30 minutes)

- Study your spouse's preferences and select any preference you wish to comment on.
- Share your understanding of your spouse's preference by saying, "I think you are saying ...," and then share your comment.
- Your spouse can either say you are correct and thank you, or can add an additional thought. You will then incorporate this additional thought into your understanding.
- Switch and give your spouse a chance.

◇ Some Guiding Principles

+ Always listen from your spouse's perspective.
+ Don't try to resolve or answer; just listen quietly and understand.
+ Your goal is to help your spouse feel understood.
+ Once you feel your spouse has understood you, always express gratitude.

EXPRESSIONS

These are your verbal and non-verbal expressions that enable me to experience a sense of comfort and trust:

Example: *When you speak to me in a quiet and unhurried tone*

_____

_____

_____

_____

_____

_____

These are the verbal and non-verbal expressions that cause me to feel discomfort:

_____

_____

_____

_____

_____

_____

_____

Comments, Insights and Awareness

_____

_____

_____

_____

_____

_____

_____

_____

_____

MOODS

Your moods that enable me to experience a sense of trust and security are:

_____

_____

_____

_____

_____

_____

_____

_____

_____

Your moods that have an effect on my sense of insecurity are:

_____

_____

_____

_____

_____

_____

_____

Comments, Insights and Awareness

_____

_____

_____

_____

_____

_____

BEHAVIOR

Ways you behave that enable me to experience a sense of trust and security:

_____

_____

_____

_____

_____

_____

_____

_____

Ways you behave that have a negative effect on my sense of insecurity:

_____

_____

_____

_____

_____

_____

_____

_____

_____

Comments, Insights and Awareness

_____

_____

_____

_____

_____

_____

_____

_____

_____

ENJOYMENT

Things we enjoy doing together that enable me to feel closer and more fulfilled:

_____

_____

_____

_____

_____

_____

_____

Comments, Insights and Awareness

_____

_____

_____

_____

_____

_____

_____

_____

RUCHNIUS

Aspects of our religious life that enable me to experience a deeper sense of fulfillment and meaning:

_____

_____

_____

_____

_____

_____

_____

_____

_____

_____

I feel our lives would be enhanced if we undertook these com-
mitments toward *ruchnius*:

_____

_____

_____

_____

_____

_____

_____

_____

_____

Comments, Insights and Awareness

_____

_____

_____

_____

_____

_____

_____

_____

_____

SENSITIVITY

These are the areas of my personal and married life that I feel are important for you to be sensitive to:

_____

_____

_____

_____

_____

_____

_____

Comments, Insights and Awareness

_____

_____

_____

_____

_____

_____

_____

_____

CHAPTER IX

Bringing *Menuchas Hanefesh* into our Homes and Communities

This book has focused on the centrality of *menuchas hanefesh* in marital life. However, this work is only the first step of our vision to promote the integration of this principle into every area of our Torah lives. With this goal in mind, we have established the Menuchah V'Simchah Foundation. The Foundation will concentrate its efforts on educating our Torah community about incorporating this precious gift of *menuchas hanefesh* into the fabric of our individual and communal lives. The Foundation will focus on seven areas of individual, marital, family and communal life:

1. **Center for Marital Enhancement**
   Couples in all stages of their marriage will be provided with services that strengthen existing bonds and teach them skills to heal conflicts and dysfunctional patterns of married life.

2. **Curriculum Development for Boys' and Girls' *Yeshivos***
   Programs will be developed for teaching young men and women from high school through *bais medrash* and seminary.

3. Center for Dating and Relationship-Building Skills
Singles will be taught skills to enhance their ability to successfully date and marry.

4. Center for Divorce Intervention
Couples in the midst of divorce proceedings will be provided with the means to consider healthier and more productive options based on their growth in *menuchas hanefesh*.

5. Parent and Child Programs
- Guiding children to achieve emotional and relational maturity
- Developing pathways for healthy parent and child communications
- Teaching children to navigate the challenges of contemporary society from a Torah perspective

6. Professional Training Center for:
- Mental Health Practitioners
- Rabbis
- Teachers
- Yeshivah *rebbeim*
- Social workers
- Volunteers
- *Shadchanim*

7. Center for Healthy Living
Services will be provided for:
- Emotional well-being
- Stress and anxiety in the home and workplace
- Contemporary addictions

Glossary

Adam Harishon — the first man

Adam gadol — a great Torah personage

Aharon HaKohen — Aaron the High Priest, brother of Moshe

Ahavah — love

Am Yisrael — the Jewish nation

Aron HaKodesh — the Holy Ark

Askanim — community activists

Av — the tenth month of the Jewish year

Aveil — a mourner

Avodah Zarah — tractate of the Talmud that focuses primarily on sins of idolatry

Avodas Hashem — service of Hashem

Avos — our forefathers, Abraham, Isaac and Jacob

Avraham Avinu — Abraham our forefather

Baal teshuvah — a Jew who has returned to religious observance

Baalei emunah — people who possess faith

Bachur, bachurim — young, unmarried yeshiva student(s)

Bais din — a Jewish court

Bais Hamikdash — the Holy Temple in Jerusalem

Bais medrash — house of Torah study

Bar mitzvah — thirteen, the age at which a Jewish male becomes obligated to observe the Torah commandments

Baruch Hashem — thank Hashem

Bas kol — a form of Divine

communication that is on a level lower than actual prophecy

Bas mitzvah — twelve, the age at which a Jewish female becomes obligated to observe the Torah commandments

Basherte — one's Divinely chosen mate

Bechirah, Bechirah chafshis — choice, free choice

Ben Torah — a Torah-educated person

Berachah, berachos — blessing(s)

Berachos — tractate of the Talmud that primarily focuses on the laws of blessings

Beraishis — the Book of Genesis

B'tzelem Elokim — in the Divine image

Bitachon — trust in Hashem

B'nei Yisrael — the Children of Israel, the Jewish people

Bris — circumcision

Chag — holiday

Challah — traditional bread (usually braided) used at Sabbath and holiday meals

Chanukah — festival that commemorates the victory of the Jews over the Syrian Greeks and the restoration of the Holy Temple

Chas v'shalom — Heaven forbid

Chassan — groom

Chassidic — pertaining to Chassidus, a branch of Orthodox Judaism promoting spirituality and joy, which arose in eastern Europe and Russia in the latter half of the eighteenth century

Chasunah — wedding

Chavah — Eve, the first woman

Chavrusa — Torah study partner

Chazal — acronym for "the Sages, may their memory be blessed"

Chessed — kindness

Cheshbon hanefesh — spiritual accounting

Chiddush — novel Torah insight

Chinuch — education

Chol Hamoed Pesach — intermediate days of Passover

Chovos Halevavos — Duties of the Heart, a classic Jewish work by Rabbeinu Bachya ibn Pakuda

Chumash — the Five Books of Moses

Chutzpah — audacity

Da'as Torah — the insights and opinions of a true Torah personality, which are assumed to be in consonance with Torah ideals

Daf yomi — the daily study of a page of Talmud

Daven (Yidd.) — pray

Dayan — judge

Dovid HaMelech — David the King, founder of the Davidic dynasty and forebear of the future Messiah

Eisav — Esau, brother of Jacob

Eliyahu HaNavi — Elijah the Prophet

Eretz Yisrael — the Land of Israel

Erev Shabbos — Friday

Esrog — the citron fruit, taken as one of the Four Species, which are a Torah commandment on the holiday of Sukkos

Frum — religiously observant

Frumkeit — religious observance

Gadol hador — Torah leader of a generation

Gan Aden — the Garden of Eden

Gaon — Torah genius

Gashmius — materialism, physicality

Gedolim — Torah giants

Gemara — Talmud

Hakaras hatov — gratitude

Halachah, halachos — Torah law(s)

Har Sinai — Mount Sinai

Harav — the Rabbi

Hashem — the Almighty

Hashkafah, hashkafos — Torah-based outlook(s)

Hashra'as haShechinah beineichem — the Divine presence resting among you

Kallah — bride

Kavanah — intention, focus

Kedushah — holiness

Kehillah — congregation

Keruvim — the angelic statues on top of the Holy Ark

Ki Sisa — one of the weekly Torah portions in the Book of Deuteronomy

Kiddush Levanah — blessing over the New Moon

Klal Yisrael — the Jewish people as a whole

Kohen Gadol — the High Priest

Kosel — the Western Wall

Krias Shema — recitation of the Shema, the traditional Jewish prayer that proclaims the absolute unity of Hashem

L'chaim — lit., "to life!"; a traditional Jewish toast

Leviim — Levites

Maariv — the evening prayer

Mashgiach — spiritual supervisor or guide, responsible for the non-academic areas of yeshiva students' lives

Matzos — unleavened bread eaten on Passover

Mazal tov — good luck

Menorah — the Candelabra in the Tabernacle, and later in the Holy Temple

Menuchah — tranquility

Menuchas hanefesh — tranquility of spirit

Middos — characteristics

Minchah — the afternoon prayer

Mishkan — the Tabernacle

Mishloach manos — gifts of food to fellow Jews, one of the commandments on the holiday of Purim

Mitzrayim — Egypt

Mitzvah, mitzvos — Torah commandment(s)

Moshe Rabbeinu — Moses our Teacher

Motza'ei Shabbos — Saturday night

Mussar vaadim — a group of people focused on character improvement

Nachas — satisfaction

Neshamah, neshamos — soul(s)

Niggun — Jewish melody

Nisan — the seventh month of the Jewish year

Ovdei Hashem — servants of Hashem

Parashah, parashas — the weekly Torah portion (of)

Pasuk — verse

Pesach — Passover

Pizur hanefesh — lit., "scattering of spirit," the feeling of being fragmented, troubled, hurt and alone

Posek — halachic decisor

Purim — holiday that commemorates the salvation of the Jews from destruction at the hands of the wicked Haman in the days of the Persian-Medean empire

Ratzon — will

Ratzon Hashem — Divine will

Rav — rabbi

Re'eh — one of the weekly Torah portions in the Book of Deuteronomy

Rebbe — leader of a Chassidic group

Rebbetzin — rabbi's wife

Rebbi, rebbeim — Torah teacher(s)

Rosh Hashanah — the Jewish New Year

Rosh Yeshivah — head of a yeshiva

Ruach — spirit

Ruchnius — spirituality

Satan — the angelic force that tempts a person to sin and acts as the accuser in divine judgment

Sefer, sefarim — Torah book(s)

Seudah — festive meal

Shadchanim — matchmakers

Shaitel — wig

Shalom bayis — domestic peace

Shanah rishonah — the first year of marriage

Shanah tovah — Good Year

Shechinah — the Divine presence

Shema Yisrael — traditional Jewish prayer that proclaims the absolute unity of Hashem

Shemoneh Esrei — the Silent Devotion, the central prayer recited every morning, afternoon and evening

Sheva berachos — meals of celebration during the seven days following a Jewish wedding

Shidduch, shidduchim —
marital match(es)

Shiur, shiurim — Torah class(es)

Shivah — seven-day period
of mourning following the
death and burial of an immediate family member

Shlit"a — acronym for *"sheyiz-
keh l'chayim tovim v'aruchim,"*
he should merit a good, long
life

Shtick — gimmick

Simchah, smachos —
celebration(s)

**Simchas chassan
v'kallah** — gladdening a
groom and bride

Sukkah — temporary dwell-
ing occupied by Jews on the
hioliday of Sukkos

Tallis — prayer shawl

**Talmid chacham, talmi-
dei chachamim** — Torah
scolar(s)

Talmid, talmidim — Torah
student(s)

Tanach — Scriptures

Tanna — Torah sage of the
Mishnaic era

Tefillah, tefillos — prayer(s)

Tefillin — phylacteries, small
black boxes containing
scrolls with specific Torah
portions, worn by adult Jewish males during morning
prayers

Tehillim — Psalms

Tishah b'Av — the ninth of
the month of Av, the national day of mourning for the
destruction of the First and
Second Temples in Jerusa-
lem, as well as for the numer-
ous national Jewish tragedies
throughout the millennia

Tzaddik — righteous man

Tzedakah — charity

Tzelem Elokim — the Divine
image

Vaad — group

Vayechi — one of the weekly
Torah portions, last in the
Book of Genesis

**V'ahavta es Hashem Eloke-
cha** — and you shall love
Hashem your G-d

Yaakov Avinu — Jacob our
forefather

Yahrzeit — anniversary of
someone's death

Yamim tovim — holidays

Yarmulke — skullcap

Yerushalayim — Jerusalem

Yeshivah — Torah school

Yiddishkeit — Judaism

Yitzchak Avinu — Isaac our forefather

Yom Kippur — the Day of Atonement

Yosef HaTzaddik — Joseph the Righteous

Zemiros — traditional Jewish songs sung on the Sabbath

Zt"l — acronym for *"zecher tzaddik livrachah,"* may the memory of the righteous be for a blessing